THE IMAGE OF JEWS IN CONTEMPORARY CHINA

JEWISH IDENTITIES IN POST-MODERN SOCIETY

SERIES EDITOR: Roberta Rosenberg Farber
(Yeshiva University, New York)

EDITORIAL BOARD
Sara Abosch *(University of Memphis, Memphis, Tennessee)*
Geoffrey Alderman *(University of Buckingham, Buckingham)*
Yoram Bilu *(Hebrew University, Jerusalem)*
Steven M. Cohen *(Hebrew Union College, New York)*
Deborah Dash Moore *(University of Michigan, Ann Arbor)*
Bryan Daves *(Yeshiva University, New York)*
Sergio Della Pergola *(Hebrew University, Jerusalem)*
Simcha Fishbane *(Touro College, New York)*
Uzi Rebhun *(Hebrew University, Jerusalem)*
Reeva Simon *(Yeshiva University, New York)*

ACADEMIC
STUDIES
PRESS

THE IMAGE OF JEWS IN CONTEMPORARY CHINA

Edited by
JAMES ROSS
AND
SONG LIHONG

BOSTON
2016

Library of Congress Cataloging-in-Publication Data:
A bibliographic record for this title is available
from the Library of Congress.

Copyright © 2016 Academic Studies Press
All rights reserved.

ISBN 978-1-61811-768-7

ISBN 978-1-61811-421-1 (electronic)

Book design by Kryon Publishing
www.kryonpublishing.com

On the cover:

'Next Year in Jerusalem'
Paper-cut style illustration,
Passover Haggadah of China,
© Dvir Bar-Gal
haggadahchina@gmail.com

Published by Academic Studies Press in 2016
28 Montfern Avenue
Brighton, MA 02135, USA
press@academicstudiespress.com
www.academicstudiespress.com

Contents

Contributors.. vii

Introduction 1
James R. Ross

Perceiving Jews in Modern China.................................... 5
Zhou Xun

Images of Jews in Contemporary Books,
Blogs and Films 24
James R. Ross

Distinctiveness: A Major Jewish Characteristic 37
Fu Youde

Chinese Policy toward Kaifeng Jews 54
Xu Xin

Sukkot and Mid-Autumn Festivals in Kaifeng:
Conundrums at the Crossroads of Sino-Judaic
Cultural Identity 72
Moshe Y. Bernstein

Understanding of the Bible among the
General Public in Mainland China: A Survey on the
"Bullet Curtain" of *The Bible* 99
Meng Zhenhua

The Changing Image of the State of Israel in
People's Daily during the Cold War 125
She Gangzheng

The Reception of Contemporary Israeli
Literature in China 145
Zhong Zhiqing

China's Relationship with Israel, Opportunities and
Challenges: Perspectives from China 161
Chen Yiyi

Holocaust Studies and Holocaust
Education in China 185
Glenn Timmermans

Reflections on Chinese Jewish Studies:
A Comparative Perspective 206
Song Lihong

Index 235

Contributors

Moshe Yehuda BERNSTEIN is a native of Quincy, Massachusetts. In 1989, he received a diploma in Rabbinic Studies from the Eeyun ha-Talmud Institute. He has served as Director of Jewish Studies for secondary schools in both Sydney and Perth, and lectured extensively at venues throughout Australia, China, and the US. In 2010, he completed a BA in Mandarin Chinese at Curtin University followed by an Honours degree in Asian Studies at the University of Western Australia. His current doctoral thesis explores the effects of globalization and translation in the contemporary transmission of Sino-Judaic cultural identity in Kaifeng.

CHEN Yiyi was trained in Biblical and Near Eastern Studies and received his PhD from Cornell University in 2000. He taught at Peking University and is currently Professor of Middle East Peace Studies at Shanghai Jiao Tong University. He serves as a peer-review college member of UK's Arts and Humanities Research Council and the editor of the *Journal of Sino-Western Communications*. Chen heads several Chinese government commissioned projects related to the Hebrew Bible, Israel studies, and the Middle East. He is the author of several books, including the recent Chinese college textbook *Introduction to the Hebrew Bible* (in Chinese, 2011).

FU Youde received his PhD from Peking University. He studied at the Oxford Center for Hebrew and Jewish Studies and Leo Baeck College, and he was a visiting scholar at a number of universities and research institutes in England, America, Canada, Australia, Israel, Italy, and Germany. He is currently Yangtze River Chair Professor at Shandong

University, where he founded the Center for Judaic and Inter-Religious Studies. He is the vice-president of China Society of Religion, and the editor of the *Jewish Studies* (in Chinese). His recent publications include *A History of Jewish Philosophy* (in Chinese, 2010) and *Essays on Jewish Philosophy and Religion* (in Chinese, 2007). He is the editor of the translation series *Translation Series of Classics of the Jewish Culture* including „The Guide of the Perplexed" by Moses Maimonides.

MENG Zhenhua is an Associate Professor at the Glazer Institute for Jewish and Israel Studies and Department of Philosophy and Religious Studies and is a resident research scholar of the Institute for Advanced Studies in Humanities and Social Sciences at Nanjing University. His recent publications include *The Society of Yehud and the Redaction of the Bible in the Persian Period* (in Chinese, 2013), *Understanding God in the 21st Century* (editor, 2013), and *The Basic Concepts of Judaism* (coeditor, in Chinese, 2013).

James ROSS received his BA in American Studies from Yale University in 1972 and MA in Journalism from American University in 1982. He is an associate professor at Northeastern University in Boston and is the author of three books including *Fragile Branches: Travels Through the Jewish Diaspora* (2000), and he is one of the editors of *From the Protocols of the Elders of Zion to Holocaust Denial Trials: Challenging the Media, Law and the Academy* (2007). He also is the author of *Escape to Shanghai: A Jewish Community in China* (1994) and *Caught in a Tornado: A Chinese-American Woman Survives the Cultural Revolution* (1994). He served as a Fulbright lecturer at Nanjing University in 2008–2009.

SHE Gangzheng is a doctoral student in the Department of Near Eastern and Judaic Studies at Brandeis University and a fellow of the Schusterman Center for Israel Studies. His research explores China-Middle East Relations in general and China's involvement in the Arab-Israeli Conflict during the Cold War in particular. Prior to coming to Brandeis, Gangzheng worked as a research associate at China

Development Research Foundation and the Foreign Affairs Office of Guangzhou Municipal Government.

SONG Lihong is Professor in the Department of Religious Studies and Deputy Director of the Glazer Institute of Jewish and Israel Studies at Nanjing University, China. He has served as Fellow or Research Scholar at Tel Aviv University, the Reconstructionist Rabbinical College, the United States Holocaust Memorial Museum, the University of Pennsylvania, and the Summer Institute of Israel Studies at Brandeis University. He is the author of *Rome and Jerusalem* (in Chinese, 2014), the editor of *From Sinai to China* (in Chinese, 2012), and a coeditor of *The Basic Concepts of Judaism* (in Chinese, 2013).

Glenn TIMMERMANS is associate professor of Literature at the University of Macau, Macao SAR, China. A graduate of Oxford University (Magdalen College), where he wrote his doctoral thesis on religious violence in Irish drama, he has taught at universities in the UK, the Czech Republic, and Poland. Since 2008, he has been active in the London Jewish Cultural Center's annual China summer school on Jewish history and the Holocaust; in 2010, he initiated, and now organizes, the annual Yad Vashem Seminar for Chinese Educators; and since 2011, he has been a founding director of the Hong Kong Holocaust and Tolerance Center. He is an active fellow of the Salzburg Global Seminar on Holocaust Education and Genocide Prevention. He teaches courses on the Holocaust and genocide and also on Holocaust literature and film.

XU Xin is a professor in the Department of Religious Studies and the director of the Center for Jewish Studies at Nanjing University, China. His research field is Jewish culture and the Jews in China. His publications include *Legends of the Chinese Jews of Kaifeng* (1995), *The Jews of Kaifeng, China: History, Culture, and Religion* (2003), and *A History of Jewish Culture* (in Chinese, 2006). His article "Practice of Judaism in China" appears in the *Encyclopedia of Judaism* (Brill, 2002). In 2003, Bar-Ilan University of Israel awarded him the degree of Doctor of

Philosophy, honoris causa, in recognition of his accomplishment in studying the Jewish people in China.

ZHONG Zhiqing is Research Professor at the Chinese Academy of Social Sciences, Beijing. She received a PhD from Ben-Gurion University, where she completed a dissertation on a comparative study of Hebrew and Chinese literature in response to World War II. She was a visiting scholar at Tel Aviv University, the British Academy, and Harvard Yenching Institute. She is the author of *20th Century Hebrew Literature in Transition* (in Chinese, 2012), *"To Put a Finger on the Wound": Reading Hebrew Literature and Culture* (in Chinese, 2010), and *A Study of Contemporary Israeli Authors* (in Chinese, 2006). She also translated into Chinese numerous works by Israeli writers, including *A Tale of Love and Darkness* by Amos Oz.

ZHOU Xun was born in Sichuan province, China and received her PhD from the University of London in 1998. In the past 20 years, she has lived in London, Jerusalem, Beijing, and Hong Kong. Between January 2001 and December 2007, she was a research fellow at the Department of History at the School of Oriental and African Studies, University of London. From December 2007 to December 2012, she was Research Assistant Professor at the School of Humanities, University of Hong Kong. Dr. Zhou has also a long track record of media activities. Her most recent media appearances include the new French documentary film *Mao's Great Famine* (2012) and BBC Radio 4 program *As History is My Witness* (October 2012). She also writes a regular op-ed column for *South China Morning Post*.

Introduction

JAMES R. ROSS
Northeastern University

The relationship between China and the Jews has been explored in several studies in recent years. The works range from Xiao Xian's textual analysis of Chinese newspaper reports about Jews before 1949 to M. Avrum Ehrlich's edited volume exploring the influence of Jewish thought on Chinese culture. Irene Eber also has written on this topic in Hebrew and English. Yet few scholars have examined the relationship from the contemporary perspective of ordinary Chinese citizens and the images they share about Jews and Judaism. This volume explores those images with innovative studies by both Chinese and Western scholars.

Zhou Xun, who has written widely about Chinese perceptions of Jews, frames this volume by reviewing the history of Chinese stereotypes of the Jews and offering her analysis of contemporary images. As the Chinese economy surges under economic reforms, Jews represent money, power, and success, goals to which most Chinese aspire. She also examines the growth of the expatriate Jewish community in Beijing and how communal functions, like a state-of-the-art mikvah, and businesses, including kosher restaurants and a bagel shop, have thrived. The definition of Jews and Judaism, she concludes, is complex and ever evolving.

James Ross examines the images of Jews in popular culture, including best-selling books, blogs, and films. He finds that popular authors such as He Xiongfei perpetuate stereotypes and misunderstandings about Jews. Many best sellers focus on how Jews make money and raise their children. But Ross suggests these stereotypes are evidence of philo-Semitism rather than anti-Semitism.

Fu Youde has written previously on Jewish distinctiveness. He expands on his earlier work by showing that despite the wide admiration of Jews in Chinese society, Jewish ways of thinking (including advocating for freedom and equality) are sharply different from the traditional Chinese emphasis on uniformity. He finds Jewish distinctiveness in Jewish law, holidays, and customs.

But there is no Jewish distinctiveness to be found among what remains of the ancient Jewish community of Kaifeng, at least in the official view of the Chinese government. One of the foremost scholars on Kaifeng, Xu Xin, provides new evidence of how Chinese government policies toward that community evolved in the 1950s. The government set requirements for what constituted an ethnic group: a common language; area of inhabitation; a unique set of customs, attitudes, and beliefs; and traditional means of livelihood. The government's investigation found that the Kaifeng Jews had completely mingled with the Han population and had no distinctive traits. They did not qualify for government recognition as an ethnic group. This report, Xu Xin discovered, was approved at the highest levels of the Chinese leadership.

Moshe Bernstein examines the Kaifeng community from a different perspective. He visited the contemporary Jewish community during Sukkot, a holiday which coincides with the Chinese mid-Autumn festival. Bernstein reports that 11 Kaifeng Jews have formally converted and made aliyah with the help of Shavei Israel, an organization based in Israel that reaches out to lost Jewish descendants. There are 50 families that continue to remain involved in communal activities, Bernstein writes, but they are a fragmented and confused community. It remains to be seen how their Jewish identity will evolve.

There is no translation of the Hebrew Bible in China—all current translations of the entire Bible have been produced by Christians. But in his innovative study of how ordinary Chinese people understand the Bible, Jeremiah Meng looks at the responses of Chinese viewers to a television series on the Bible produced by pious American Christians. The viewers expressed their opinions about the shows on a "bullet curtain," rolling responses from audience members that is shown on the top of the television screen as the viewers comment and interact with each other. Previous studies, Meng notes, are usually limited to intellectuals with backgrounds in religion.

People's Daily is the official newspaper of the Chinese government and is also representative of mainstream Chinese media. Gangzheng She examines Chinese images of Israel in *People's Daily* from 1948 to 1991. The changing image of Israel in China, he notes, shows the shifting development of Sino-Israeli relations as well as Israel's position in China's foreign policy. He notes that the coverage changed based on domestic fluctuations in China. As China focused on economic reform in the late 1980s, for example, the coverage was predominantly about scientific developments in Israel.

Zhong Zhiqing's article on contemporary Israeli literature available in China looks at both intellectual and common readers. Interest in Israeli literature has grown dramatically since establishment of diplomatic relations between Israel and China in 1992. There are currently 114 books and anthologies that have been translated from Hebrew into Chinese: 74 books of prose, 5 books of poetry, 27 books for children, and 10 anthologies. Amos Oz's visit to the Institute of Foreign Literature at the Chinese Academy of Social Sciences in 2007 was a key development in the literary exchange between China and Israel. Oz participated in a series of events, which drew attention to contemporary Israeli literature from Chinese publishers, intellectuals, and common readers.

Chen Yiyi ("China's Relationship with Israel") notes that there has been extensive scholarly literature on this subject but that many questions remain to be answered. None of the existing work takes into consideration the implication of China's dramatic economic growth in the past decade. China now makes substantial purchases of Israeli agro-technology, water purification, and telecommunications systems, and Israel imports a variety of mechanical, electronic, chemical, and textile goods from China. There have been regular cultural exchanges between Israel and China as well as growth in tourism for both countries in recent years. Israeli and Chinese universities, research institutes, and scientific academies cooperate in almost every field of study.

But American objections have forced China and Israel to forgo any weapons exchanges.

The essay by Glenn Timmermans is one of the first studies of how the Holocaust is perceived and studied in China. He notes that this emerging field is shaped by China's role in offering refuge to German and Austrian Jews during World War II as well as by the Japanese atrocities on Chinese soil in the 1930s and 1940s. China's tumultuous contemporary relationship with Japan had shaped perceptions of World War II atrocities as well as perceptions of the Holocaust. The Nanjing Massacre Memorial, first opened in 1985, was redesigned in 2007 based on Yad Vashem. There are no institutions in China with Holocaust studies, he writes, but study of the Shoah is included in the major Jewish Studies programs. Mainland China, Hong Kong, and Macau offer seminars and symposia on the Holocaust.

One of the anomalies of Jewish studies in China, Lihong Song writes, is that there is no study of Jewish liturgy. The liturgy is essential to understanding the lived Jewish experience, he argues. After reviewing the unique aspects of Jewish studies in China, he concludes with a question that is central to this volume. "Should we face inward toward satisfying academic colleagues," he asks, "or should we face outward and endeavor to leaven an undistorted, meaningful, and accessible knowledge of the Jewish people to a broader Chinese audience?"

Perceiving Jews in Modern China

ZHOU XUN
University of Essex

In modern China, the definition of "Jew" and "Jewishness" is problematic and complex. It is a symbol for money, deviousness, and meanness; it can also represent poverty, trustworthiness, and warm heartedness. It has religious as well as secular meanings. While it represents individualism, it also stands for a collective spirit. On the one hand, it is the symbol for tradition; on the other hand it can equally invoke modernity. One day the Jew is a stateless slave, another day the Jew is the dominant power in the world. The Jew is nationalist and at the same time cosmopolitan. He can be a filthy capitalist or an ardent communist, a committed revolutionary or a spineless loser. In other words, anything which is not Chinese is Jewish, at the same time anything which is Chinese is also Jewish; anything which the Chinese need is Jewish, at the same time anything which the Chinese despise is Jewish.

Although these representations seem to correspond with images of the Jews in Europe, it would be superficial to reduce them to purely Western influence. Representations of the Jews have been endowed with indigenous meaning by modernizing elites in China since the late nineteenth century. To a great extent, these images of the Jews were, and still are, generated by the *difference* of the Jewish race, which is marked by its non-Chineseness.

By establishing the Jews as a homogeneous group that acts as a constitutive outsider and embodies all the negative as well as positive qualities that were feared or desired, various social groups in China could thus identify themselves as an integrated, homogeneous in-group, the "Chinese." They are, therefore, able to project their own anxieties onto outsiders like the Jews. In this respect, this dynamic corresponds with a widespread fear as well as the need for an "other," a dynamic that can be found in many cultures and societies.

The Emergence/Construction of the Image of the Jews

For the Chinese modernizing elites of the early twentieth century, the Jew was an integral part of the new racial taxonomies they had invented in order to represent the world as a collection of unequally endowed biological groups. Described as a "historical race," the "Jewish race" stood in symbolic contradistinction to the historical "yellow race," as the reformers now refer to the Chinese. As early as 1903, Jiang Guanyun, a modernizing journalist, depicted the "Jewish race" as a "historical Caucasian race" which had descended from the Semites. The physical appearance of the "Jewish race" was imagined by Jiang to be characterized by an oval face, big eyes, thin lips and a convex nose. In the following years, similar descriptions prevailed in representations of the Jew in China. In 1910, for instance, when Zhang Xiangwen, a historian and geographer, visited Kaifeng in central China, he perpetuated these stereotypes by claiming that the Jewish descendants there had big noses and deep-set eyes and that one could still distinguish them from genuine Chinese by their Caucasian physical features.[1]

Although representations of the "Jewish race" in China were actively constructed by Chinese intellectuals themselves, the language of anti-Semitism was appropriated from Western sources to reconfigure and legitimize indigenous racial discourse. It was the Christian missionaries who first introduced the image of the Jew as the "seed of Abraham."[2]

From the middle of the nineteenth century onward, travel to the West also provided opportunities for Chinese intellectuals to encounter and appropriate the arguments of anti-Semitic discourse. However, in contrast to the European anti-Semites, Chinese intellectuals' attitudes

---

1   Zhang Xiangwen, "Daliang fangbeiji" [A Report on the Visit to the Stone Tablets in Kaifeng], *Nanyuan conggao*, in *Contemporary Chinese Historical Documents* series 30, Wenhai chubanshe, vol. 1, n.d., 282.
2   For further readings see Zhou Xun (2001), *Chinese Perceptions* of the *Jews and Judaism*: A History of the Youtai, chapter 2.

toward Jews were often mixed with curiosity and envy. Why should the Jewish, not the Chinese, be the dominant culture of the world? Why should Judaism, not Confucianism, have been widely accepted as the guiding moral principle of human society? Why should a Jew, not a Chinese, be the richest man? While they asked these questions, many modernizing elites in China also attempted to prove that Chinese culture was superior to the Jewish one. For instance, Wang Tao, one of the very first Chinese scholars who travelled to Europe in the nineteenth century, the father of the modern newspaper in China, as well as James Legge's collaborator (Legge introduced Confucian classics to a Western audience), found it was most thrilling that an Eastern culture—the Jewish culture or Judaism—should survive within Western culture. He used it to show the conservatives that they need not fear Western culture, because Judaism, which had survived and had an important role to play in the Christian West, had not managed very well at all in China. The sinification of the Jewish community in China was for him powerful proof that Chinese culture was far superior to Jewish culture; therefore, it was still more superior to Western culture. Hence, according to Wang Tao, opening the door to the West would not destroy the superior Chinese culture.[3]

The Jew and Money

In order to construct the Jews as a "race with biologically specific features," Jiang Guanyun even traced the Western anti-Semitic image of the "Jew as financier" back to its Semitic ancestry. However, representations of the "Jew as a financier" were not always perceived to be entirely negative. Xue Fucheng (1838–1894), a famous diplomat who regarded the development of commercial industry to be essential for China, saw rich "Jewish financiers" as a positive illustration for his theory. According to Xue, if Chinese were as rich as Jews, then China would be the most powerful nation in the world.[4]

---

3 Wang Tao, *Manyou suilu* [Travel Diaries], (Hunan: Yuelu shushe, 1985), 82.
4 Xue Fucheng, *Chushi Ying Fa Yi Bi siguo Rinji* [Diaries of Diplomatic Missions to England, France, Italy, and Belgium, 1890–1894], (republished by Hunan renminchubanshe, 1985), 792–793.

The translation of Charles Lamb's *Tales of Shakespeare* in 1904 was used to further consolidate the image of the Jew as a money grabber. Shylock, the money lender, soon became a household caricature of the Jew amongst the reading public in China. Furthermore, a number of historians even identified as Jews some commercial groups who had been engaged in money lending in the past in the western regions of China. And the eagle-nose became the quintessential symbol for the "money-loving Jews."

The Jew in the Racial Struggle

The dichotomy of Europeans into Aryan and Semitic "races" also inspired some Chinese abroad to manipulate the Jews as a useful weapon in their "racial war" against the "whites." When Hong Jun, also a diplomat to Europe, was insulted by some white people of a Western church, he fought back by arguing that Jesus was a Jew with black hair and eyes like himself, therefore the white Europeans had no right to insult an Asian fellow-man of Jesus. Shan Shili, one of the earliest Chinese female intellectuals who went to Europe, in her travel diary of 1910, passionately compared the anguish of the Jewish people under the white domination in Europe with their freedom under the rule of the "yellows" in Kaifeng. The division between Aryan and Semitic races was thus projected onto a more fundamental opposition between the "white" and "yellow" races. Shan even warned the Chinese that if they did not learn from the lesson of the "Jewish race" they would not be able to win the racial war against the "whites."[5]

The Jew as a "New People"

The myth of "Jewish power" in the West was of great attraction for Liang Qichao. Liang was one of the first reformers in the 1890s to propose a racialized world view. During his tour of the New World, he pondered over the survival of the Chinese people. He saw the "powerful and wealthy Jews" as an anti-image of the backwardness of the Chinese. The Jews became a perfect example for his call for a

---

5   Shan Sili, *Guijianji* [Dairy of Italy], (Hunan renminchubanshe, 1981).

"new people" (*xinmin*), or a collective nationalistic spirit, which he believed to be essential to the progress and social well-being of China. In his famous *Travel Diary to the New World,* Liang was convinced that if the Chinese race was going to survive, the Chinese must learn from the Jews, and eventually to become like the Jews to control the world economy and global politics. Hence, the future of China was projected onto the myth of "Jewish power."[6]

The Stateless Jew

With the rise of nationalism in China in the early twentieth century, some of China's revolutionary thinkers represented the stateless Jew as the imaginary prospect awaiting China. Articles on the pogroms in Russia began to appear in Chinese newspapers and journals after the Russo-Japanese War extended to the northeast of China in 1903. The Jewish problem, which was once unknown and uninteresting, now became of great relevance to the Chinese nationalists. The lamentation of the stateless Jew became a warning to the Chinese. The "Jewish race" was portrayed as an "ugly race" because they did not have a country. They were thought to have deserved their inhuman treatment. While stirring up the fear of becoming stateless like the Jews, many of the Chinese nationalists reasoned, "We are not like the Jews!" According to them, the superior Chinese still had a country of their own. The argument went further with a very strong anti-Jewish tone: the Jews deserved the awful situation they were in because they had neither a nationalistic spirit nor any collective responsibility. The Jews were portrayed as victims of materialism and individualism. It was suggested that their love for money and personal happiness finally drove the Jews into this terrible state. Schiff's huge loan to the Japanese in 1904 was seen by some Chinese as a bribe the Jews used to save themselves from the yoke of the Russians. The author of an article entitled "The Stateless Jews" thus commented, "Stateless, though [they] have money, money cannot save them [the Jews]." His solution for the Chinese was to avoid emulating the Jews: not to love money more than one's country,

---

6   Liang Qichao, "Xindalu youji" [Travel Dairy of the United States], (first published in *Xinmin congbao's* special supplement, 1903), section 12, 51.

otherwise the Chinese would end up stateless like the Jews. In order to avoid being like the Jews and to preserve the "Chinese race," China had to promote nationalism first.[7]

The Jews as a Nation

With the fall of the Qing dynasty and the establishment of the Republic of China in 1911, racial nationalism was further promoted by Sun Yatsen, the father of Chinese nation. Nationalism, in the eyes of Sun and his followers, was the sole generator of the rise and fall of any race. Sun perceived Zionism as the nationalistic movement of the Jewish people, and he believed that it was the Jewish nationalistic spirit, or Zionism, which held the Jewish race together. As the Jewish nationalistic spirit became an inspiration for these Chinese nationalists, the image of "ugly" and "stateless" Jews shifted to that of the "wonderful and historical nation." In the same way in which they portrayed the so-called "Han Chinese" as a pure biological entity, Sun and many of his contemporaries perceived the Jewish nation/race as a homogeneous racial group characterized by common blood, language, and culture. Since the Jews were perceived as a nation, with a common ancestor and a territory, Palestine was accepted by many Chinese nationalists as "the national home of the Jewish people."[8]

The Jews as Imperialists

Together with nationalism, the newly founded Republic of China also provided the ground for an increasingly growing anti-imperialism. The Jews were sometimes portrayed as imperialists. As in Europe, Chinese nationalists needed a scapegoat. Many of the articles on Jewish imperialism were drawn from Japanese or Western sources. They followed the age-old anti-Semitic pattern by listing Jewish dominance in the world of finance, politics, and the media. In some cases, they conflated Freemasonry with Zionism, the Jewish plot to control the world. The Jews were often portrayed as the epitome of imperialism and the driving

---

7 "Eren luesha youtianren" [The Slaughtering of Jews by the Russians], *Jiangsu* 4 (1903).
8 For further readings, see Zhou (2000) chapter 6.

force of evil in the capitalist world. In one article entitled "The Jewish Empire", the author declared, "If one does not know the truth about the Jews, how could one say that he understands the truth about the Western imperialism?"

The Jews as a Superior Race

As mentioned earlier, having classified the "Jewish race" as a branch of the "white race," some Chinese intellectuals also regarded it as a biologically "superior race" alongside the "yellow race," in contrast with the inferior "red, black, and brown races." The image of the Jews as a "wonderful and historical nation" was further defined as a "superior race." It was claimed that such superiority was manifested in the intellectual ability of the Jews. Hu Shi, a celebrated scholar and philosopher of modern China, stereotyped the Jews as an "intellectual race" with impressive academic ability and adventurous spirit. The need to create such a representation was obviously rooted in the anxiety over the backwardness of China and the belief, shared by many Chinese intellectuals of the New Cultural Movement, that the intellectuals bore the responsibility for the reconstruction of their chaotic country. The New Cultural Movement first emerged in 1915 as a result of the demand for a new urban culture by the growing urban population in China.

According to You Xiong, an outstanding writer of the Movement, the reason the Jews were able to control world politics, world finance, and the world in general was that the "Jewish race" had intellectual gifts of quick understanding, rational thinking, good judgment, good organization, and fast action, and that it produced more superior lawyers, philosophers, thinkers, politicians, doctors, scientists, musicians, and even chess players than any other race in the world.[9] It may be argued that in the same way that Liang Qichao had used the Jews as an example in his call for a "new people," many intellectuals of the New Cultural movement also found in the Jews a model for the restoration of the "Chinese race." The present backwardness of the "Chinese race," or more correctly the anxiety within these intellectuals

---

9   You Xong, "Youtaiminzu zhi xiagzhuang jiqi qianli" [The Present Situation of the Jewish Race and Its Potential], *Dongfang zazhi*, (18:12 1921), 23.

themselves, was often explained as the result of a lack of talent in China. This did not, however, indicate that the "Chinese race" was less superior to the "Jewish race" since China also had produced world-class geniuses in the past. Furthermore, Qian Zhixiu was able to prove that although the "Jewish race" and the "Chinese race" had very different characteristics, the latter shared all the advantages of the former, including intellectual ability. In conclusion, Qian proclaimed, "the Chinese will be the Jews of the future" and "China is the giant yet to be awakened."[10]

The Jews as a Product of Racial Discrimination

It would, however, be an oversimplification to presume that all intellectuals in modern China articulated racial discourse in the same way. While many Chinese intellectuals viewed the Jews as one homogenous race, a few divergent voices, such as He Ziheng and Wu Qinyou, challenged such a view. In an article entitled "The So-called Jewish People," He Ziheng used scientific methods to undermine the idea of a "Jewish race." By using various statistics, he showed that a large percentage of Jews in different countries did not have the so-called "Semitic nose," shape of head, deep dark eyes, or black hair, and "no one can tell a Jew from an American or a European unless the Jews write the word 'Jew' on their forehead." He also dismissed the idea that all Jews shared "common blood," pointing out instead that intermarriage between Jews and other races was commonly practiced throughout history. He concluded that the Jews were not a race but merely a product and victim of racial discrimination.[11]

For many left-wing intellectuals of the 1930s, this representation of the Jews as an oppressed people had a much more profound and symbolic implication in their own struggle against the immediate enemy—the Japanese—and their own imagined enemy, the "white" imperialists of the West. As Wu Qinyou put it, "The significance of the

---

10 Qian Zhixiu, "Youtairen yu Zhongguoren" [The Jews and the Chinese], *Dongfang zazhi*, (8:12, 1912), 40–46.

11 He Ziheng, "Shijieshang you chuncui de minzhu ma?" [Is There Any Pure Race in the World?], *Xueshujie* (Academic Circle, 1:2, 1943), 12–16.

Jewish people is not in whether they can be seen as a race or not, but in their common goal to unite together with all the oppressed people and to liberate the human race." The old dichotomy between the "white" and "yellow" races was reconstructed by merging the social notion of class with the biological myth of race. As the problem of race was reconfigured into a question of class, the symbolic role of the Jews was remodeled, "the tears, blood and death of the Jewish people have awakened the oppressed Chinese."[12] The "oppressed Jews" had become the comrades of the Chinese in their struggle against all oppressors.

The Old Myth and New Phenomena (1949–1995)

With the official banishment of racial discourse by the communist government after 1949, the myth of the "Jews as a race" seemed no longer to be current in the "New China." The notion of race, however, did not disappear completely. Mao Zedong, for instance, defined nation as a distinct racial and cultural group. By the same token, Israel was perceived in China as the Jewish nation state: the *old* Jewish race with a *new* country and *new* language. Like the left-wing intellectuals of the 1930s and 40s, Mao also conflated the notions of class and race into a vision of the life and death struggle of the colored and oppressed people against white imperialists. China's political role in African-Asian solidarity since the 1960s meant that the Jews in Israel, as the enemy of the oppressed Palestinians, could no longer be defined as the oppressed people; instead, their image was reconfigured into the image of "the poisoned knife which the American imperialists pushed into the heart of Palestine." Closely associated with the PLO, "Mao Zedong thought," or Maoism, had been restyled as the "compass for the suffering Palestinians." Communist China terminated all official diplomatic contacts with the state of Israel. By then, the last group of Jewish residents together with the rest of the remaining foreign population had left China. Generally speaking, until late 1980s, the party propaganda portrayed the Jews as a distant enemy, associated with one of China's

---

12 Wu Qingyou, "Youtaiminzu wenti" [Problems of Jewish Race], *Xinzhonghua zazhi*, (4:4, 1936), 7.

biggest enemies—the Americans—as well as one of China's closest allies, the PLO.

However, among intellectuals, the image of the "superior Jewish race" continued to enthrall scholars, such as Pan Guangdan. Known as China's foremost eugenicist, Pan was at the time a professor of ethnology, focusing his research on the ethnic minorities. His eugenic theories played an important part in his approach to ethnicity studies. For instance, Pan put great emphasis on the assimilation between the Han and other "highly intellectual ethnic groups." He opposed the government proposal for an ethnic self-rule policy, which was carried out in the Soviet Union. To be politically correct and to stand in line with Mao's class struggle ideology, Pan claimed that the "self-rule" policy might result in class hatred between the Han and other ethnic minorities in China. In order to build a "great superior Chinese race," as commissioned by Chairman Mao, Pan pointed out that the Han Chinese must live in harmony with other minority groups in order to absorb their "goodness" and pass on to them the "superiority" of the Han, so that they would eventually form a "great superior Chinese race." As a result, Pan wrote his famous case study on the Jewish ethnic group in ancient China. The assimilation of the Jews into the Han Chinese became his example *par excellence* for his "ethnic harmony" theory. However, like many other intellectuals, Pan did not escape during the Anti-Rightist Campaign in the late 1950s. Being purged as one of the ten members of the "anti-party group" and "a poison seed planted by imperialism," Pan's academic career and research came to an end. The Soviet model of ethnic self-rule was implemented in China under the banner of ethnic harmony. Pan died in the beginning of the Cultural Revolution. His work and theories on eugenics and ethnic studies were officially banned until the end of the 1970s when the Cultural Revolution finally came to its end.

After the death of Mao and the collapse of the Cultural Revolution, the class hatred between Jewish Israel and the Chinese people also came to a close. However, the myth of the Jew in China did not stop there. Since the 1980s, interest in the present state of Israel and the Jews have reached unprecedented levels. In addition to the sprouting of numerous Jewish study centers in Shanghai, Harbin, Nanjing, Tianjin, Jinan, and many other Chinese cities, a huge number of publications on Jewish subjects, especially in relation to Chinese Jews, have been published and republished. Pan Guangdan's essay on "the ancient Chinese Jews" was re-edited several times and published as a monograph in 1983. One of China's most celebrated anthropologists, Wu Zelin, wrote a preface for the book. In it, Wu recalls that in his youth, he regarded the Jews as "laughable, despicable, pitiable, admirable, enviable, and hateful." While admitting such impressions were not objective and shallow, Wu's perceptions of the Jews continued to be overshadowed by the images of the Jews as money lenders, the Jews as the oppressed, the Jews as smart, the Jews as capitalists, and, most of all, the Jews as a race.

As of the early 1990s, when the Chinese government made a drastic decision to embrace a neo-liberal market and to emphasize economic development, the symbolic link between the Jews and money has reemerged, especially in cities such as Shanghai and Harbin. While Shanghai and Harbin opened their arms to welcome Jewish investments from all over the world, the medieval city of Kaifeng also declared itself to be a "Jewish economic zone" and eagerly joined the international project to reconstruct a Kaifeng Jewish history.[13] Even more striking is that in 1992, the same year when Chinese government embraced the neo-liberal market economy, China and the state of Israel formally reestablished the diplomatic relations. Soon after, Israel became the second most important trading partner of China. The sale of Israeli army and military know-how to China has played the major part in this ever growing trade.

However, China's interest in Jewish issues is not exclusively economic. In recent years, especially in the post-Tiananmen era, interest in Jewish studies, as shown by some intellectuals, such as Zhang Sui, is a response to efforts to reconfigure indigenous identities of race and

---

13 For further readings see Zhou Xun, "The 'Kaifeng Jew' Hoax: Constructing the 'Chinese Jew,'" in *Orientalism and the Jews*, eds. Ivan Davidson Kalmar and Derek Penslar (Waltham, MA: Brandeis University Press & University Press of New England, 2005), 68–80.

nation. As Zhang Sui puts it, "In order to have a real deep understanding of the vitality of Chinese culture, one must first study the interesting anthropological fact that the Hebrew race, well known for its immutability, was assimilated by the Han race and adopted a 'Chinese-Jewish identity' after entering China."[14] The superiority of the "Han race" and Chinese culture, it is claimed, seems to be manifest by the assimilation of the "Jewish race."

Such dubious studies also are encouraged in order to cover up discrimination against so-called minority groups. Thus, the assimilation of the Jewish community in China is portrayed by scholars like Wu Zelin as a demonstration of "the traditional magnanimity and the tolerant spirit of the Chinese race, not only toward the Jewish people, but also toward all other races."[15]

At the same time, the representation of the Jews as a superior race has been retranslated into the image of "the Jewish eternal nation/race." To redefine, or to reconstruct China's national identity and reinterpret the nation's future, the "eternal Jewish race," together with "the super American nation," "the strong German spirit," and "the long and mysterious Indian culture" again became inspirations for many intellectuals of a new generation.

Outside the academic communities, for millions of young Chinese who are desperately seeking success and money in a rapidly changing society, images of successful and rich Jews have become their inspirations. A popular series, edited by He Xiongfei, entitled *Revelations on the Jews' Superior Intelligence*, was launched in 1995. It claims to be not only the first popular literature on the subject of the Jews ever published in China, but also "a good book which will probably change your life."[16]

The Jews, according to the editor, have two characteristics: the first is that they are good at managing money, and the second is that

---

14 Zhang Sui, *Youtaijiao yu Zhongguo Kaifeng Youtairen* [Judaism and the Chinese Jews of Kaifeng], (Shanghai: Sanlian chubanshe, 1990), 1.

15 Wu Zelin, "Preface," for Pan Guangdan's *Zhongguojingnei Youtairen de ruogan lishi wenti* [The Jews of China: A Historical Survey], (Beijing: Beijingdaxue chubanshe, 1983), 11.

16 He Xiongfei, ed. *Youtairen chaofan zhihui jiemi* [Revelations on the Jews' Superior Intelligence], (Beijing: Hualing chubanshe, 1995), back page.

"the Jews are well educated." He then goes on to list some of the most famous Jewish politicians, businessmen, artists, scientists, and thinkers. Among them are "the Jew Karl Marx," "the Jew Freud," the "Jew Einstein," and others. He also, bizarrely, added Beethoven and Charlie Chaplin to the "smart Jew" list. Obviously, for the editor, the criterion of being Jewish is neither racial nor religious. For him, a Jew is but a hat for the rich, the famous, and the successful. Clearly, to the readership of such popular literature, their interest is beyond the Jews. To them, the term "Jew" represents money, power, and success; these are the things which many of them are dreaming of and seeking after. In other words, being rich, successful, or a Jew, is a new identity to which many young Chinese aspire. While one may claim that about fifty years ago, "the Jews" was still an unfamiliar term to the majority of Chinese, today, due to the efforts of He Xiongfei and others, even a taxi driver on the streets of Beijing will tell you that "Jewish people are very rich and clever."

The Jewish Presence in Contemporary Beijing

As result of rapid development since 1992, Beijing is now a world-class metropolis, and its Jewish population is growing fast. Unlike Shanghai and Harbin, Beijing has no claim to a Jewish legacy, yet it has become the religious and cultural center for Jews living in or travelling to China. This is largely because this political center of the PRC also has grown to become an economic as well as cultural center of the world in recent years. While religious freedom is enshrined in theory in the PRC constitution, the practice of religion has remained tightly controlled under the CCP leadership since the party took over China in 1949. Controlling religion is, however, not new in China. From the second century BCE, "cults" and "superstitions," as they were labeled at the time, have played an integral part in imperial politics. For the rulers of China, to control religious groups was seen as essential to ruling.[17] Beijing's recent

---

17 For further readings see T. H. Barrett, "Superstitions and its Others in Han China," in *Past and Present*, Supplement 3, *The Religion of Fools? Superstition Past and Present*, eds. S. A. Smith and Alan Knight, (Oxford University Press, 2008), 95–114.

modest toleration of a wider range of forms of worship by some recognized religious groups such as Buddhism, Taoism, Islam, Protestantism, and Catholicism has been paralleled by an anxiety about other religious groups such as Falun Gong. Judaism is seen as a religion practiced by foreigners and is thus tolerated rather than legally recognized. This toleration allowed Jewish groups to flourish in this former imperial city, and present political capital, of China. Since September 2003, the number of Rosh Hashanah celebrants in the Jewish communities of Beijing has swelled significantly; individual Jews flew in from remote cities in different parts of China to join with the Jewish residents in China's capital to welcome the Jewish New Year. In 2008, there were more than 1,500 Jews from all over the world who resided on a regular basis in Beijing. They had choices of three congregations—two Chabad-Lubavitch centers and Kehillat Beijing, a self led community serving the needs of liberal and reformed Jews or any Jews who are uncomfortable with Chabad.

Kehillat Beijing

Kehillat Beijing was the first Jewish congregation established after the Communists came to power in China in 1949. Its origins date back to 1979, the year when Deng Xiaoping launched the "Open Door" policy. It was founded by Elyse Silverberg and Roberta Lipson, two young American women from New York who had gone to China for adventure. Over the years, the two have built up a successful business, Chindex International Inc.—a leading supplier of cutting-edge Western medical technologies to the Chinese healthcare system. During this time, they also built up the first Jewish community in China's capital. In a country with restricted religious freedom and which does not recognize Judaism as an official religion, Kehillat Beijing had to acclimatize itself to various restrictions. In its early days, Kehillat Beijing focused on getting together for Passover and the High Holidays, which were usually celebrated at the homes of members. After the community held its first seder in 1980, Lipson and Silverberg tried to put an advertisement for their High Holiday service in China's new English-language newspaper, the *China Daily*, but their advertisement was cut. They were told it was for their safety: Beijing had a strong Palestinian presence and a PLO delegation, and the Jewish community mustn't publicly disclose the location of their services. Expatriate Christian groups, who do not have the same safety issues, also were banned from advertising their services, and until today, only foreign passport holders are allowed to attend any community events held by Jews and Christians. One may speculate that this is due to lack of religious freedom in China and not security issues.

Despite the Chinese government's concerted effort to control religious activities, Jewish life in Beijing has managed to thrive. Over the years, Kehillat Beijing has supplied for various needs of Jews from the United States, as well as Canada, Australia, England, France, Germany, Hungary, Israel, Luxemburg, Poland, and Russia. Most of them have lived or worked in Beijing.

The Chabad

In 2000, just as Kehillat Beijing was beginning to enjoy great success and growth, Chabad decided to open its branch in Beijing. In the beginning, the Chinese authorities were suspicious and questioned whether Chabad was fanatical. They were assured by existing Jewish community leaders in Beijing that the Chabad was kosher. A year later, the Chabad rabbi of Hong Kong, Shimon Freundlich, arrived at Beijing, and soon the only Hebrew day school in northern China was opened.

To cater to the Russian Jewish community in Beijing, most of whom are from Azerbaijan, Chabad went on to open another branch in the center of the city known as "Little Russia" and brought in an additional rabbi, Rabbi Mendy Raskin, "to cater to them and perform their customs and speak to them in their language."

In 2005, Beijing saw the opening of its first kosher restaurant, Dini, in the vibrant expatriate area not too far from where Freundlich lives. It is named in honor of the rabbi's wife, Dini Freundlich. While it serves the needs of the local Jewish community and Jewish travelers, it also has become a destination restaurant for both non-Jewish expatriates and aspiring young Chinese professionals in search of adventure or exotic global experiences. There is little doubt that the opening of Dini in Beijing has turned Jewish food, sometime also referred to as Israeli food, into a global commodity, adding another star to Beijing's international gastronomical map.

In the meantime, China has grown to become one of the major exporters of kosher food in the world. Each year, China exports $2.3 billion in food ingredients to the US, and half of that is kosher. In addition to kosher food and restaurants, Beijing also is well catered for bagel lovers. Mrs. Shanen's Bagels and Cream Cheese shop was opened by a Brooklyn-raised Taiwanese filmmaker named Lejen Chen in 1996. Her passion for bagels began when she was making a film on bagel bakeries in Brooklyn. When she moved to China to pursue her film business, she wanted to share her love for bagels with the Chinese but also satisfy her own craving for Brooklyn bagels. She then met a local Chinese businessman, with whom she got together to open the first bagel shop ever in the Chinese capital. The two not only became good business partners, they also fell in love and got married. They called their shop Mrs. Shanen's, after the name of the husband, Shan En. Silverberg and Lipson decided to Yiddishize it and called it Mrs. Shayna's, thus make it a "Jewish brand" in Beijing. Today, the shop supplies not only the Jewish community in Beijing, but also major Chinese supermarkets. While bagels may not be a novelty in China since bagels are in fact a common type of local bread throughout Xinjiang in China's northeast frontier, "Shayna bagel" or "pretty bagel," as it is also called, is not just any bagel. It is a famous international/Jewish brand in Beijing. From Brooklyn to Beijing, Mrs. Shanen's bagels are a product of globalization, and in a way, it helped to make Jewishness a global experience.

Side by side with the Chabad day school in the suburb of Beijing is the exotic-looking Mikvah Mei Tova. In Chinese, it is called Meiteshui, which means "beautiful special water." Situated in a bizarre looking American-style villa in the Grand Hill estate, not far from the rabbi's home, this is a five-star modern spa with a Chinese traditional theme and with luxury facilities. The water in the pool is gathered from natural rain water. When I asked Dini Freundlich, the rabbi's wife, why there was a need to have a mikvah in Beijing, she explains, "Every Jewish community needs a mikvah, it is an integral part of Jewish life.

Married women use it after the end of their menstrual cycle." But according to Dini Freundlich, Mei Tova in Beijing is not just any mikvah, "Mikvah is a beautiful tradition, and I wanted it to be an especially beautiful place. There are mikvahs all over the world and in every community, but I wanted ours to be unique to China, a meshing of China and Judaism." Mei Tova is beautifully constructed. The design takes on a Chinese theme with a modern twist and is in line with the global fashion one sees throughout Beijing, from Sanlitun to Houhai or to the Drum Tower area, where trendy bars, cafes, and boutique hotels cater to international communities and travelers.

In addition to the regular residents, each year there are 2000–3000 Jewish business people and tourists who travel through Beijing. Chabad is to serve for them as a "home away from home and help to take care of their Jewish needs." This can range from Shabbat services, Shabbat meals, hotel reservations, and general information. Throughout the year and especially during the spring/summer months, many Israeli backpackers travel through Asia. As they pass through Beijing, Chabad will not only provide them with food and a place to stay, but Chabad will also help them to reconnect with their "Jewish roots." It may be ironic, but it is in China's capital city of Beijing that many of them feel more "at home" with Judaism. For many Jewish tourists looking for an "Oriental experience" in China, they find Mei Tova's mixture of Chinese and modern design exotic and attractive, and Chabad's openness to accommodate the varied needs of Jews comfortable. Dini Freundlich told me that "Beijing is very unique as the community is made up of people from all over the world. We are usually just a short(ish) stop for them, and they then move on or return home. One needs to juggle everyone's perception of Jewish life and supply everyone with what they need. It's also hard as people come and go often. However, it has been so rewarding to be a part of something as new and as exciting as the growth of the Jewish community in Beijing as it to grows and develops."

Chabad Beijing's mission statement emphasizes that Chabad Beijing, as in the original vision of the Lubavitcher Rebbe, is not a center or institution, but "a home for any Jew no matter where they are standing in their Jewish observance," and a place for "every Jew to feel that no matter how far they may have traveled, they can always call it home." "Every Jew" here does not mean individual Jews, but rather implies a globalized Jewish experience.

For many Jews living in Beijing, "home" implies feeling more comfortable with Jewish religion and traditions. There is a sense of spiritual mystical familiarity, even if one has not experienced them before. After arriving in Beijing, quite a number of Jews begin to attend Jewish services on a regular basis even though they have not done so back home. Being with other Jews to perform Jewish rituals gives them a sense of identity and comfort in a strange, foreign land. Leo Lazar from France was in Beijing for six months working for General Electric. He said going to religious services in China was more appealing to him than in other places he has lived. Maybe it's the sense of community and the sense of adventure—as opposed to a painstaking diaspora. Beijing has become a global city for Jews from all over the world, and the Chabad Beijing is a global home for every Jew. It is here their sense of Jewishness is awakened, and they are introduced/reintroduced to Jewish spirituality. After I took a number of my friends with Jewish ancestry to Mei Tova, they were amazed by the experience. It is not only an adventure but also a journey into "Jewish life" in Beijing. Mei Tova also mirrors their own lives in Beijing: the mixture of Western and Chinese, cosmopolitan yet Jewish.

Furthermore, a number of them also told me that it's easier and nicer to be Jewish in Beijing because "'here everyone tells you Jews are so clever" and "no one tells you what you must do to be Jewish here." The latter echoes Kehillat Beijing's take on an egalitarian lay approach. Without a permanent location for worship, it prides itself on being nondenominational: a community that blends Reconstructionist, Reform and Conservative beliefs and traditions. "The beauty of this is that we get to pick and choose from the various traditions," its leader Elyse Silverberg said. "We have people who come from a fairly Reformist background, some are Conservative, and some are Orthodox, so we have a bit of a mix, which is nice for us."

Conclusion

Two hundred years after Protestant missionaries first introduced the concept of Jew and Judaism to the people in China, definitions of Jews and Jewishness remain complex and are ever evolving. Ironically, in today's global world, this complexity allows Jewish culture and Judaism to flourish in this country that is known for its lack of religious freedom. At the same time, China has become for many Jews a place where they feel more at ease with Judaism. While China has become a distant "home" for thousands of Jewish business people, professionals, immigrants, and travelers, the myth about the Jews carries on in contemporary China, and the Jews continue to serve as a distant mirror for millions of Chinese in urban cities. The Jews continue to play a role in the "strong Chinese dream" which has recently been revived by President Xi and the CCP leadership. More than a century ago, fearful for the survival of China and the "Chinese race," the "powerful and wealthy Jews" inspired modernizing Chinese to envision a strong and powerful China for the distant future. Today, the people in China have been told that they have become Liang Qichao's "new people"; in other words, the Chinese have become as "powerful and wealthy as the Jews." However, the reality is different as instability is felt in most corners of China. This strong sense of instability brings an even greater need to assure the people in China that they are the world's new "Jews": smart and rich.

Images of Jews in Contemporary Books, Blogs, and Films

JAMES R. ROSS
Northeastern University

During my first trip to China in the summer of 1985, I visited English Corner in People's Park in Shanghai one Sunday afternoon. It's one of the places where young Chinese people go to practice their English with visiting foreigners. Officials from the university where I was teaching in Shanghai escorted me there, and a big crowd quickly gathered to talk with me—a tall, curly-haired foreigner—and pushed closer to shower me with questions.

Some of the questions seemed strange to me ("Do all Americans have AIDS?") but most were routine, such as, "Where are you from? How do you like China? Are you married? Do you like Chinese girls?" After two months in China, none of this was surprising to me except for one additional question, "What is your religion?"

I was taken aback at first—it's not a question I often hear when I travel abroad—but after a brief pause I answered, "I am Jewish." The young questioner gave me a thumbs up and said, "Jews are the best."

I got a similar question—and similar response—everywhere I traveled in China later that summer: Kunming, Chengdu, Nanjing, Suzhou, and Guangzhou. My unscientific survey suggested that the Chinese liked and admired Jews, although they didn't seem to know much about them. I knew that there had been Jewish communities in Shanghai and other Chinese cities until shortly after World War II but that there was little evidence of their presence after the Communist takeover in 1949. There were a handful of Jewish tourists and visiting faculty at the time of my first visit. But I was curious about how average Chinese people had developed an image, seemingly a positive one, of Jews.

I visited China several times after that summer, but it wasn't until 2008–2009, when I was selected as a Fulbright lecturer at Nanjing University, that I had a chance to explore the popular Chinese image of Jews. By then, there were many Jewish visitors and business people from the United States and Israel. And economic reforms were transforming the country. Making and spending money seemed at least as important as Communist ideology.

When I first arrived in Nanjing, I was joined by Yan Li, a history graduate student from my home university who had been staying with her family in Beijing. Yan and I visited bookstores throughout the city. We started at a small bookstore that featured books about evangelical Christianity. Yan asked the young woman who worked there if they had books about Jews, but the clerk had trouble answering the question. She didn't know what Yan meant by "Jew."

Judaism is not officially recognized as a true religion by the Chinese government—only Taoism, Buddhism, Islam, Catholicism, and Protestantism have official recognition and receive state funding for their leaders and religious buildings. But despite attempts at government control, "[r]eligion is growing rapidly, and has overwhelmed the CCP [Chinese Communist Party] regime's systems of surveillance and control."[1]

> [G]enerally recognized world religions such as Russian Orthodoxy, Judaism, Mormonism, and the Bahá'í Faith can all be found in China. Rural China, moreover, is home to millions of temples—many of them built in just the last decade—that serve as centers for local folk religions and their associated festivals...Traditional rituals, myths, and practices are being enacted with modern technology such as video cameras and websites, and reconfigured to fit the

---

1 Richard Madsen, "The Upsurge of Religion in China," *Journal of Democracy*, Vol. 21, No. 4 (October 2010), 60.

sensibilities of villagers who are no longer farmers, but factory workers, entrepreneurs, and even professionals.

Even within the five officially recognized religions...most of the growth is taking place outside the state-supervised patriotic associations...[T]here is an extensive 'underground' Catholic Church that is about three times larger than the officially recognized Chinese Patriotic Catholic Association...[and] an extremely wide array of rapidly growing unregistered Protestant 'house churches.'

Finally, there is the growth of new religious movements with flexible organizations that combine traditional social networks with sophisticated multimedia technologies. The best-known of these is the Falun Gong...[2]

Yet even though Judaism isn't officially recognized and most Chinese don't know much about Jews, there was an established Jewish community in Kaifeng as early as the eighth century. There are still a handful of Chinese who claim to descend from that community. In more recent times, there were small communities of Sephardic Jews from India (known as Baghdadi Jews since they originated in Iraq), Russian Jews who fled before and after the 1917 revolution, and Jewish refugees from the Holocaust who settled primarily in Shanghai and lived through the war under Japanese rule.

Chinese scholarly interest in the Jews and Judaism dates back to Protestant missionaries who translated the Christian Bible into Chinese in the early nineteenth century. They used the term "youtai" for Jews, with a character often used for a person considered devious or suspicious. The missionaries suggested the Jews had been punished for their hatred of Jesus. Later in the nineteenth century, the missionaries wrote about Jewish stereotypes, portraying them as arrogant, rich, and unreliable. The Chinese came to see Judaism as part of Christian history and civilization.

At larger bookstores, we found entire sections devoted to books about Jews. Most of the books focused on finance, such as *16 Reasons for Jews*

---

2   Ibid., 61–63.

Images of Jews in Contemporary Books, Blogs, and Films   27

Getting Wealthy by Chu Ke; *The Secret of Talmud: The Jewish Code of Wealth* by Jiao Yiyang; and *Secret of Jewish Success: Ten Commandments of Jewish Success* by Li Huizhen. Yan helped me translate the books and we found they were filled with misunderstandings and stereotypes. And books purporting to be based on the Talmud were mostly pithy sayings about wealth with little or no connection to actual Talmudic passages.

Some of the misunderstandings are almost comical. One of the best-selling books is *What's Behind Jewish Success*[3] by Tian Zaiwei and Sha Wen. "It is said that Jews are distinguished by their noses," the authors write. "All Jews have hooknoses. This is not accurate. Despite hook-nosed Jews in cartoons, only Jews in Russia and the Near East have hooknoses in real life." They also write that "to save time, Jews never beat about the bush in negotiations as Chinese often do."[4] Jews control the diamond market, the authors also write, since diamonds are "valuable and easy to carry which is ideal for Jews who are always drifting."

The most prominent author and editor of books about Jews is He Xiongfei, who identifies himself as a literary critic, orator, Jewish studies expert, and visiting professor at Nankai University. He is director of Xiongfei Limited in Hainan and has edited a number of book series on intellectual, literary, and cultural studies. His most popular series is titled "Revelations on the Jews Superior Intelligence," launched in 1995. His books include *Jewish Wisdom of Family Education: The Cultural Code of the Most Intelligent and Wealthy Nation in the World* (2005); *Secrets of Jewish Success: The Golden Rule of a Miraculous Nation* (2004); and *Uncovering the Enigma of Jewish Success in the World* (2002). He also has edited *Collection of Jewish Strategies* (1995); *Jewish Life of Money* (2002); *Jewish Magnates of Ideas* (1995); *Legend of World Famous Jewish Celebrities* (1996): *Riddle of Jews* (1997); and *Jewish Bigwigs' Skills of Making Money* (1996). His most recent publications are cartoon books for children about Jewish wisdom and the Talmud.

---

3   Tian Zaiwei and Sha Wen, *What's Behind Jewish Success* (Beijing: Central Compilation and Translation Press, 2006).
4   Ibid.

In the best-seller *The Spirit of Jewish Culture*[5] (the English title on the cover is *Whats [sic] behind Jewish cleverness*) by Sai Ni Ya, one of He Xiongfei's pseudonyms, he writes that Jews "are the most intelligent, mysterious, and the wealthiest people in the world. In a sense, not knowing about Jews equals not knowing the world! When Jews sneeze at home, all the banks in the world would catch a cold one by one. Five Jews together can control the gold market of the humankind; the antagonism between the East and the West, in a sense, can be said to be that between two Jews—Jesus and Marx." The book continues with a series of lessons. Lesson 1 tries to define "who is a Jew." It starts by discussing maternal descent then states:

> Yet the chief criterion is whether one's religion is Judaism. In the Jewish perspective, Judaism and Jews are integrated—Jews are the materialization of Judaism and Judaism is the spiritual kernel of Jews. Thus Jews have identified themselves with Judaism: those who believe in Judaism are Jewish, and Jews all believe in Judaism. This outlook that unifies religion and ethnicity is closely related to their unique history and experiences. It is not because of religious radicalism.[6]

These oversimplifications are typical of He Xiongfei's work. Other lessons focus on Jewish rituals, such as circumcision, and great Jewish figures in philosophy, finance, science, art, and politics. (He mistakenly identifies a number of people as Jews, such as the Rockefellers.) Another lesson discusses anti-Semitism.

> [T]his hatred towards Jews has gone deep into most non-Jewish people's consciousness with no sensible reason and has been passed down from generation to generation. Jews have become the object of persistent and conventional worldwide hatred and genocide. Orthodox Jews are charged with ethnic chauvinism; Jews being assimilated are accused of being the Fifth Column of contaminating non-Jewish people by way of assimilation; rich Jews are regarded as

---

5 Sai Ni Ya (He Xiongfei), *The Spirit of Jewish Culture* (Lanzhou: Gansu People's Press, 2006).
6 Ibid.

the vampire of the nation; poor Jews are looked down upon as the burden of society...[7]

The main reason for this hatred is their "Jewishness," Sai Ni Ya writes. Their belief in one god is "so conceited as to be disrespectful of gods of other religions. Their 'Jewishness' is also embodied in their strict adherence to the 613 doctrines, which has made them an eccentric community that is hard to coexist with and merge into other cultures." There is also a brief lesson on the Torah and chapter on Jewish humor.[8]

He Xiongfei was a Buddhist who eventually turned to Christianity through his study of Jewish culture. In an interview with Christian Times, he discussed his feelings towards Judaism:

> Though I have long since studied the Jewish culture, I always have a feeling that I am a spectator rather than a practitioner. Through my study I know the progenitor of Jewish culture is God. If you do not believe in Him, all of the study are in vain, so I think it is imperative to accept God if I want to study the Jewish culture, otherwise I will remain a spectator for good.[9]

He also developed new ideas and patterns for his "Project of Jewish Education." With projects like "Bar Mitzvah: Training Camp of Jewish Wisdom," he hopes to help more and more Chinese children get an opportunity not merely to learn Jewish wisdom but also to know God. The interviewer referred to He Xiongfei as "the doyen of Jewish education in China"[10]

Another popular book is *The 101 Business Secrets in Jews Notebook* by Zhu Xin Yue. It suggests that the Jews' systematic experience and knowledge are part of their secret for creating wealth. In addition, Jews are born with the ability to make money.

> There is a classic saying that 'the world's money is in the pocket of Americans while the Americans' money is in the pocket of Jews.'...

---

7 Ibid.
8 Ibid.
9 http://www.christiantimes.cn/news/11418. Interview with Lee Hannah, June 26, 2013, accessed October 11, 2013.
10 Ibid.

For smart Jews, everything has its own value, and everything can be regained except priceless wisdom...The most important point is Jews' attitude toward money. In their view, money is the gift for God rather than something shameful. You can get respect, high social status with enough money.[11]

Other popular book titles include: *The Secret of Talmud: The Jewish Code of Wealth* by Jiao Yiyang; *Secret of Jewish Success: Ten Commandments of Jewish Success* by Li Huizhen; *Stranger from Mars: Nobel Prize and Jews* by Yang Jianye; *Voice of Wisdom: Speeches of Jewish Celebrities* by Yu Xin; and *Jewish Conspiracy of Destroying the World* by Zhang Daquan.

Most of the Chinese authors who write about Jews really don't know much about them. They use the success of Jews, especially in business and education, to promote values the Chinese traditionally cherish, such as hard work and knowledge or, in China's burgeoning market economy, getting rich. Perhaps the Chinese are fascinated by the characteristics they see in Jews that correspond to their own concepts and outlooks.[12]

Some of the books available in China have been translated from English, including Jack Rosen's *Jews: The Secrets to their Success*. Many other books about Jews that are popular in China have been translated from Japanese. Japan, like China, has had a long fascination with the Jews and also has virtually no Jewish population. Best-selling books blame international Jewish cartels and conspiracies for Japan's economic problems. Masami Uno, a leading anti-Semite, has sold more than one million copies of two books, *If You Understand the Jews, You Will Understand the World* and *If You Understand Jews, You Will Understand Japan*.

In the preface of the second edition of *Jews in the Japanese Mind: The History and Uses of a Cultural Stereotype*, David Goodman and Masanori Miyazawa write that the fantasies of a Jewish plot to destroy Japan culminated in the 1995 gas attack in a Japanese subway by

---

11 Zhu Xinyue, *101 Money Earning Secrets from Jews' Notebooks* (Beijing: Beijing Life and Flying Trading Ltd., 2011).
12 I am indebted to Yan Li, now an assistant professor of history at Oakland University in Rochester, Mich., for this insight.

members of a Japanese cult incited by anti-Semitic propaganda. A dozen people were killed during the morning rush hour attack.[13]

Belief in this worldwide Jewish conspiracy is widespread in Japan, Goodman and Miyazawa write. Yet Jews who visit Japan, much like Jews who visit China, are often treated with admiration and respect. The 20,000 European Jewish refugees who fled to Japanese-controlled Shanghai during World War II were protected from the Nazi's demands that they be exterminated. Goodman and Miyazawa embrace the theory that Japanese racism has more to do with defining and elevating Japan's perception of itself than with demeaning Jews. They suggest that "anti-Semitism has nothing to do with Jews and everything to do with anti-Semites."[14]

The coexistence of anti- and philo-Semitism is not unique to Japan. In the "Introduction" to *Philosemitism in History*, Jonathan Karp and Adam Sutcliffe reject the claim that "philosemitism can be or should be neatly separated from antisemitism."[15] They continue:

> Indeed, an intricate ambivalence combining elements of admiration and disdain has arguably been by far the most common feature of non-Jewish constructs of Jews and Judaism, while the philosemitism of many Christians has been motivated by a conversionist desire ultimately to erase Jewish distinctiveness altogether.[16]

In recent years, much of the popular discussion on Jews and Judaism appears on Chinese blogs. In a July 2012 blog titled "Jewish Education,"[17] Wang War writes that the "Jewish nation is the world's smartest, richest and most mysterious nation." He cites Marx, Darwin, Freud, Einstein, and Mendelssohn as "Jewish gurus," notes the high number of Jewish Nobel Prize winners, and praises Jewish success at

---

13 David G. Goodman and Masanori Miyazawa, *Jews in the Japanese Mind: The History and Uses of a Cultural Stereotype* (Lanham, Md: Lexington Books, 2000), xiii.
14 Ibid, 12.
15 Jonathan Karp and Adam Sutcliffe, eds., *Philosemitism in History* (London: Cambridge University Press, 2011), 3.
16 Ibid, 3.
17 Wang War, "Jewish Education," http://blog.sina.com.cn/s/blog__603d862d0102ee3n.html, accessed October 10, 2013.

business. "Seventy percent of world trade is controlled by the Jews," he writes, and Jews account for 25 percent of the 400 richest Americans. "It is said that most of the world's wealth is in the pockets of the Jews," writes Wang.

One of the main sources of their success, according to Wang, is education. Learning and education are "spiritual beliefs," he writes, and part of the "national spirit." In Israel, Wang writes, pregnant women are always singing, playing the piano, and reading from mathematics textbooks. He also writes about the myth that Jewish mothers place a drop of honey on the Bible and have their young children lick it off so they learn the Bible is sweet.[18] In "How to Train Children to Study Jewish," another blogger writes that "in every Jewish family, shortly after birth, the mother would read 'the Bible' (Hebrew Bible) to him. And after reading each paragraph, let the child lick honey. When a child is slightly bigger, the mother will present the 'Bible' with little drops of honey on top, then have the child lick honey off."[19] (A similar myth is repeated in evangelical Christian websites).

> Most Jewish children know three languages: Hebrew, Arabic and English. From first grade to sixth grade, kids should learn mathematics and economics, but also dabble in competitive sports, such as bows and shooting...Beginning from early childhood, parents train the child to play the piano and violin...Jews believe that such training will improve a child's IQ, and help them become a genius.[20]

Wang also writes about the respect Jews have for teachers. "In the Jewish community, teachers are even more important than the father. If both father and teacher are sent to jail and only one person can be rescued, then the child will decide to rescue the teacher, because teachers impart knowledge in the Jewish community."[21]

A similar blog, "How to Train Children to Study Jewish,"[22] repeats these myths. The author, who is not identified, writes that "in ancient

---

18 Ibid.
19 http://blog.sina.com.cn/s/blog_603d862d0102ee3n.html, December 21, 2013.
20 Ibid.
21 Ibid.
22 http://blog.sina.com.cn/s/blog_603d862d0102ee3n.html

Images of Jews in Contemporary Books, Blogs, and Films 33

times, many Jewish cemeteries were often stocked with a variety of books, because the Jews believe that in the dead of night, dead people will come out reading, which of course is impossible. But it has a certain symbolic significance: even at the end of life there is a never-ending quest for knowledge." (This is apparently based on a misunderstanding of the Jewish custom of burying damaged prayer books and sacred documents.)

The blog also comments on the success of Jews:

> The Jews are indeed a great race and account for America's 200 most influential celebrities, Jews account more than half of the 100 Nobel laureates; one-third of the professors at prestigious universities in the United States; one quarter of the nation's lawyers; 60 percent of the nation's leading writers of literature, drama, and music; and one half of the world's richest entrepreneurs and one-third of the millionaires in the United States.[23]

Although many of the blogs are exaggerated or false in their praise of the Jews, some seem openly anti-Semitic. On the "History Forum" at www.mitbbs.com on November 1, 2008, the forum moderator wrote:

> Jews are an inferior people, non-European, non-Arabian. Nothing glorious but self-claimed 'chosen people of God.' Painstakingly they set up a pseudo-Jewish country backed by capitalism, but at the same time they never cease battling with Arabs, their brothers by blood and language. Typical perverts, who were nearly exterminated by the Europeans but found pleasure of revenge in the Arabs. However, Jews and Arabs are brothers in genes and language.
> It seems that Chinese are very much into adulating Jews blindly. What is worth praising in this inferior people? It is necessary to investigate how this trend was started from the very beginning. Blind worship of the Koreans started from the fad for Korean soap operas, but what was the origin of worshiping Jews?[24]

Some blogs also discuss the Holocaust and Hitler. One, written by Jianmang Li in June 2010, suggests that Germans traditionally

---

23 Ibid.
24 This is an American website, which is blocked in China. Its author, most likely a Chinese Muslim, must have been living in the United States. The view expressed in these paragraphs is not unusual among Chinese Muslims.

hated Jews for religious reasons (the belief that Jews killed Jesus). But modern Germans hated Jews, the blogger wrote, because of their prosperity.

"We people are always jealous of others' achievements and, if someone exceeds us, we will feel very uncomfortable. This uncomfortable feel will let us look for reasons to rob others," he wrote.

The blogger also wrote that Germans blamed the Jews for their defeat in World War I and believed the Treaty of Versailles was supported by Jewish bankers. The Germans also believed, he wrote, that Communism was the beginning of a Jewish conspiracy to conquer Germany and the rest of the world. As for Hitler, he writes:

> Hitler wants to set up a powerful army to launch a world war and he also needs to flatter people to work for him [who] all need money. While money is in the hands of the Jews, so only robbing them can get a lot of money. It is said that Jews like revenge. The best way to avoid revenge is to slaughter all of them.

Stereotypes about Jewish wisdom are common topics in Chinese blogs. Blogger Zhou Biao speculated in October 2009 as to why so many Jews have won Nobel Prizes in science and literature. (The Jewish Virtual Library notes that 193 of the 855 Nobel Prize honorees have been Jewish [about 22 percent] since the prize was first awarded in 1901. Jews make up less than 0.2 percent of the world's population.) Zhou Biao suggested that "misfortune" is probably the reason. He notes that Jews [actually, ancient Hebrews] were slaves in Assyria and Babylon and that their cities were destroyed by the Roman Empire and they were driven out.

> Later in the Middle Ages, they had to survive in the Islamic world and Europe ruled by Christianity where their legal and political status were very low, many rights were deprived of, even sometimes they might suffer expulsion and genocide. Faced with the difficult situation which lasted for at least two thousand years, they were forced to develop a unique lifestyle.

The blogger then discussed Medieval Europe and how Jews did not have the right to own land and that "forced them to turn to more knowledgeable and skillful industries, such as the handicraft industry, financial industry and so on..." Jews used their savings, he wrote, to develop the lending industry and, "because of their instability and high risk, the decent middle class despised them."

In the capitalist era, Zhou Biao wrote, "the inferior position of the Jews can quickly turn into a huge advantage." He compared this with unemployed and educated youths in China who succeeded under Chinese economic reforms in the late twentieth century. "The Jews are the pioneers of business and they have done business for two thousand years," Zhou Biao wrote.

> Although the tide of anti-Semitism fell and rose, the Jews could always find shelter. The attitude toward the Jews became a touchstone which can test tolerance and freedom of the regime. Therefore, where there were Jewish communities, there was a golden age. The Jews moved from Baghdad, Maghreb to Umayad, from Spain to Holland, from Venice, Florence to Genoa, from Krakow, Prague to Budapest, Vienna and Berlin which were all prosperous in history.

Zhou Biao argues that Jews did not have financial support from states or other organizations but succeeded because they were "far from power, casting off the control and keeping tolerance and independence."

Another blogger, Liu Kai, discussed the "unique family education" of the Jews in his posting. For the Jews, he writes, "their property is not money but books since books are carriers of knowledge…[E]very Jewish child likes reading. When they grow up, parents put books everywhere to make sure that their children could reach them anytime."

In his blog post "Why are Jews so clever?" Gao Feng suggests that diet and "fetal education" are keys to Jewish success.

> In Israel, many pregnant women still keep singing, playing the piano, in addition, they solve math problems together with their husband. I was so confused that I asked one pregnant woman, "Why do you want to learn math, for your fetus or just for fun?" She answered, "Of course the purpose is to train my fetus." Another thing I notice is the food. It seems that the pregnant women show special preference

to almond, milk, and fish. They believe milk and fish are good for their baby to become a genius.

Gao Feng notes later that "all Jews firmly believe when meat and fish are mixed together, it will do harm to their body."

There also are discussions about Jews in popular culture. Zhang Xiaoxian, one of the most popular female writers of love stories, wrote in her blog, "I believe I was a Jewish woman in my before life, with bewildered and horror-struck eyes and a man who loved me. Escape for life and struggle with war."

In 2010, the Shanghai Animation Film Studio released "A Jewish Girl in Shanghai," written by Wu Lin, a former history teacher, based on his English-language graphic novel. The 85-minute Chinese-language film is set in World War II Shanghai, when 20,000 European Jewish refugees settled there. It tells the story of a Chinese boy who befriends a Jewish brother and sister who have been separated from their parents. The Chinese boy helps them survive as they fend off the Japanese forces that occupy Shanghai. It has been promoted as China's first homegrown Jewish film. It also was the first Chinese film to be included in the Jerusalem Film Festival and was nominated for an Avner Shalev Yad Vashem Chairman's Award for Artistic Achievement in Holocaust-related Film.

China's national television network, CCTV, aired a twelve-part documentary about Israel titled "Walk into Israel—The Land of Milk and Honey" beginning in August 2010. It covers 4000 years of Jewish history as well as the modern development of the State of Israel. Ties between Israel and China were virtually nonexistent prior to the 1980s because of China's support for the Palestinian Liberation Organization (PLO). The two nations developed military ties in the 1980s and formally established diplomatic ties in the early 1990s. Trade between Israel and China now exceeds $4 billion per year.

At the launch event for the television series, the Israeli ambassador to China said he hoped the series would bring better understanding of Israel and promote further cooperation between the two countries.

Distinctiveness: A Major Jewish Characteristic

FU YOUDE
Center for Judaic and Inter-Religious Studies, Shandong University, China

Every man has characteristics to distinguish him from other persons, and every nation, from other ones. So do the Jews and Jewish people. Although there is more than one Jewish characteristic, only one will be discussed in this paper—the quality of distinctiveness.

Distinctiveness is the pursuit, promotion, and admiration of distinctions and differences. There are dozens of phrases in Chinese that refer to it, namely *"yu zhong bu tong"* [out of the ordinary], *"yi hu xun chang"* [unusual], *"zhuo er bu fan"* [remarkable], and *"bu tong fan xiang"* [be not of the common sort]. Putting the words of *"zhui qiu"* [pursue], *"ti chang"* [promote], and *"chong shang"* [admire] before them is synonymous with the notion of "making distinction" here.

Distinctiveness and uniformity are two opposite inclinations in every nation and culture. The Jews and the Jewish culture are no exceptions. However, distinctiveness is extremely significant among Jewish characteristics and can be regarded as a major character trait of the Jews. This trait is inherent in the religion and belief, reflected in the Jewish way of living and thinking, both historically and contemporarily. It has become part of the Jewish subconscious, its inner spirit and orientation. It is essential to understanding Jewish identity on both an individual and group level.

This quality of uniqueness is not a doctrine, or a law, in Judaism. However, it is inherent in the Jewish faith, teaching, and laws as a basic spirit and pursuit of Judaism.

According to the Hebrew Bible, Abraham, the ancestor of the Jews, left his homeland Uhr in Babylon under God's "orders" and sojourned to a distant land, Canaan (Genesis 12:1-9). There, Abraham accepted God as the only god, and God gave him all the land of Canaan and promised that he "will greatly increase his numbers" and "be the father of many nations." (Genesis 17:1-8) After that, the ancient Hebrews began their unique worship of monotheism. In the age of Abraham, the Babylonians worshiped the sun, the moon, the stars, and other nature deities. In the land of Canaan, the native Canaanites believed in El, Asherah, and its offspring. Egyptians worshiped Amon, Anubies, Anuket, Aton and other deities. Abraham initiated the practice of monotheism, and his descendant Moses developed a systematic religion 500 years later. After generations of cruel struggles against polytheism and idolatry, the belief in monotheism was consolidated and gradually became the religion of the Israelites. The evolution from polytheism to monotheism was a great leap in the history of human civilization, and realization of this leap was the consequence of Abraham's and their descendants' advocacy of distinctiveness rather than uniformity. At this point, "uniformity" referred to the prevalent polytheism and idolatry in neighboring countries and the indigenous Canaanites; "distinctiveness" represented the monotheistic worship of one God. Jewish ancestors gave up the worship of polytheism and tenaciously sought a belief in monotheism in order to distinguish themselves from gentiles and their polytheism. From the analysis above, it is obvious that the Jewish trait of particularity had been contained in the process of its early inauguration of monotheism.

The concept of "the chosen people" in the Hebrew Bible is another reflection of the characteristic of distinctiveness. The basic meaning of this belief is that God chose Israelites from among all the people and made them a holy nation. In Exodus 19, God promises the Hebrews that "if you obey me fully and keep my covenant, then out of all nations you will be my treasured possession. Although the whole earth is mine, you will be for me a kingdom of priests and a holy nation." (Exod. 19:5-6) God rewarded the Israelites with the Ten Commandments and the Israelites agreed to accept and obey them.

This conviction highlighted the uniqueness of the Israelites, which meant they were the only nation—not others—which had been given the divine *Torah* (the law). Thus, they enjoyed a special status of priests and a glory as a holy nation. In other words, the Israelites were different from the gentiles in essence because of the covenant with God and the divine law. Obviously, the conviction of "the chosen people" in Judaism highlighted the expression of the nation's uniqueness. That is the characteristic of distinctiveness. Since biblical times, the Israelites and later the Jews have seen themselves as the chosen people of God and kept the sacred mission and unique sacred feeling. In the time of Diaspora and suffering, it was this unique awareness of being the chosen people that sustained the Jewish people. After the Nazi Holocaust in World War II, the conviction was diluted, or even abandoned, by some liberal and secular Jews. However, the more orthodox and relatively traditional Jews still insisted on this belief.

There are 613 laws in the Hebrew Bible; 365 of them are negative bans and 248 are affirmative teachings, and these are the "written laws." In the *Talmud*, the rabbis classified and made comprehensive interpretations of most of the laws. These interpretations are called the "oral law." The "written law" and the "oral law" cover all aspects of Jewish religious life, family life, social life, economic life, and political life. It could be considered a complete guide to Jewish life. In other words, Jewish law is the Jewish way of life. The distinction between Jews and other nations is closely related to their distinctive way of life.

Speaking of the law as a principle of life, it is natural to think of the Jewish holy days and festivals. There are three major holy days in Judaism, the Sabbath, New Year (Rosh Hashana), and the Day of Atonement. The Sabbath holds the strongest religious character among the three holy days. The fourth commandment of Moses' Ten Commandments says, "remember the Sabbath day by keeping it holy… for in six days, the LORD made the heavens and the earth, the sea, and all that is in them, but he rested on the seventh day. Therefore the LORD blessed the Sabbath day and made it holy."(Exod. 20:8, 11) Because God created the heavens and the earth in six days, the Israelites, who imitated God, worked for six days and rested on the seventh day to keep the Sabbath. For the Jews, the seventh day of a week is from Friday at sunset to Saturday evening. Every Friday evening, a family sits around the table in a joyful and peaceful atmosphere to enjoy delicious food. The next morning, adult Jews go to the synagogue for services, including the Torah readings and prayers. Children often go to Hebrew School to learn Hebrew and study Judaism. On the Sabbath day, everything defined as "work" is forbidden. In the chapter on the *Sabbath* in the *Mishna,* 300 kinds of work in 39 categories are prohibited. Devout Jews do not light fires or do other things forbidden. Even nowadays, they do not use electronic facilities, make phone calls, or drive on the Sabbath. In modern Israel, public facilities including buses are suspended as well. It is a unique way for Jews to keep a religious holy day. The tradition has about 2000 years of history, although there is no evidence to examine exactly when it started. The Jews keep the Sabbath once a week, 4 times a month, 48 times a year, 480 times every decade, 4,800 times every 10 decades, and 48,000 times every 1,000 years. The Sabbath has accompanied generations of Jews. The modern Jewish thinker Ahad Ha-am once said that it was the Sabbath which kept the Jews, rather than the Jews who kept the Sabbath.

The Jews have many unique festivals, such as Passover, Simchat Torah, Succot (Tabernacles), Chanukah, Tisha B'av (a mourning festival), and Shavuot (festival of weeks). These festivals are mostly related to biblical stories, with divine and agricultural origins and significances. Undoubtedly, these festivals also play an important role in shaping the Jewish character and spirit.

It is worth noting that there are many Jewish customs, such as dietary laws, which are closely related to daily life. According to Jewish dietary law, they may eat plants, poultry, and animals with cloven hooves which chew their cud. They should not eat fish without scales and fins, animals that die from disease or other abnormal causes, blood, or meat with milk, etc. Animals must be slaughtered by a professional butcher in accordance with the law. Otherwise, it would be considered impure and forbidden for consumption. There is no clear record about the origin of dietary laws in the Bible and other sources. According to Moses Ben Maimonides' interpretation, Jewish laws were intended to preclude idol worship in order to maintain and strengthen Jewish monotheism.

From the previous discussion on the worship of one God, the conception of the chosen people, holy days and festivals, and complex customs, it is obvious that Judaism, in essence, is a different religion from the gentile religions; the Israelites or Jews upholding Judaism are a unique people. In fact, the relationship between Judaism and the Jews is reciprocal causation. On one hand, Jewish ancestors created the extraordinary system of Judaism; on the other hand, Judaism shaped and distinguished Jews in turn. Therefore, it could be concluded that the characteristic of distinctiveness of the Jews and Judaism are derivative of each other.

II

Distinctiveness, especially as an antithesis to uniformity, is embedded in the Jewish way of thinking as well.

The Jewish way of thinking is diverse. From the biblical verses, varied modes of thinking could be generalized, including perception, intuition, belief, and imagination. Making distinction is the most prominent way of thinking in the Talmud but is not fettered by old conventions and does not drift with other opinions when pursuing novel ideas and disparate views. Let me take *Mishnah* as an example to illustrate this point.

In the very beginning of *Mishnah*, a question was put forward: when is the proper time to recite the prayer of *Shema*? Rabbi Eliezer said from when the priests enter rooms for food offerings. However, other sages said: till midnight. Laban Gamaliel said: till dawn appears. In the discussion of "when to read Shema in the morning," a rabbi said: begin from the time when blue and white can be told. Rabbi Eliezer said: from the time when one can tell the sky is blue and leek is green to sunrise. Rabbi Joshua said: till the third hour, because the princes got up at the third hour. On the issue of the position for reading Shema, the schools of Shammai and Hillel differed widely. The school of Shammai said: everyone should read by reclining at night and standing in morning, because Deuteronomy 6:7 said: when you lie down and when you get up.

Hillel's school also quoted from the Bible, when (you) walk along the road (Deuteronomy 6:7), to say man should read in his own way.

From the description above, we can see diverse opinions and arguments in the discussion about when and how to recite Shema. The dissidents' views are listed together. Discussions like this are not unusual. They can be found all through the Talmud, which has millions of words. The great book is composed of similar questions, discussions, and debates. For the same question, rabbis always put forward different opinions which all seemed to be well founded (generally based on the text of Bible). In the course of a discussion, there is no absolute, authoritative, established, unchangeable opinion. Every rabbi's words are respected, but not without a doubt or dispute. Each rabbi does not compromise with popular interest and does not agree with others blindly. Every rabbi has equal and free right to express his own views without the interruption from any authorities. In the Talmud, there is no one answer or opinion to one question. Different answers to the same question could be true at the same time, and all could be valid. This kind of thinking could be qualified as distinct in its encouragement of diversity and negation of uniformity.

This way of thinking, which emphasizes distinctiveness, is not only embodied in the texts of Talmud. It has a great impact on general Jewish thinking. Since the biblical era and into modern times, the Talmud has been viewed as the law book and the guide to appropriate Jewish life. There were many schools and academies to study and research the Talmud. Hence the tradition of talmudic thought is inherited and promoted. Within the family, Jewish children study the Talmud under the guidance of their fathers; on the Sabbath, Jewish adults and children study the Talmud in synagogues or schools; people, regardless of gender and age, perform laws from the Talmud in daily life. In the long history, after endless indoctrination and imperceptible edification, the way of thinking with the emphasis of uniqueness contained in the Talmud and other sources has been gradually translated into Jewish people's mode of thinking and into the way of thinking performed in their learning, working, and daily life. As the Jewish saying goes: "two Jews, three opinions."

In May 2008, I was invited by Israeli President Simon Peres to participate in the "Presidential Conference" held to commemorate the sixtieth anniversary of the founding of Israel. At the meeting, Prime Minister Ehud Olmert said half in jest: there are 7 million Jews in Israel, and 7 million prime ministers as well. Also at the conference, Israeli ministers argued fiercely around issues including the Palestinian-Israeli peace talks, national defense, and education, which impressed me deeply. People often say: "the habit is a second nature." To be good at expressing different opinions, arguing, and debating is the second nature of Jews acquired over thousands of years of life.

III

There are two aspects in the consequences of distinctiveness: one is remarkable achievements, and the other is the misery and suffering associated with it.

The outstanding achievements of Jews are known to all. A book named *Six Who Changed the World* wrote by Henry Enoch Kagan, an American psychologist, listed Moses, Jesus, Paul, Marx, Freud, and Einstein with biographies and psychological personality analyses. It is claimed that Moses' greatness lies in his creation of Judaism and the greatness of Jesus and Paul is that they developed from Judaism Christianity, which later became the mainstream of Western culture. They were the three religious leaders who changed billions of people's beliefs and convictions. Marx's greatness lies in that he put forward political economics and scientific socialism theory on the basis of surplus value. The communist movement he created has greatly changed the political setup of the world in the nineteenth and twentieth centuries. Freud was the first psychologist and philosopher who started to analyze personality from the angle of the subconscious. His psychoanalysis opened up a new field of psychological research and provided a new perspective and a new method. Einstein's special and general relativity was the greatest achievement of physics since Newton's. His theory and its applicative value in both macro and micro fields are beyond estimate. Certainly, people who changed the world are not restricted to the six above. Yet, they are among the greatest figures in the history of the world. As a matter of fact, in addition to the six Jews mentioned, there are a large number of prominent Jews excelling in almost every field.

I once wrote "Why the Jews Are Wise," a short essay analyzing outstanding Jews and the dialectical relationship between their anti-traditional spirit and the benefits of following tradition, the religious education accepted in their childhood, their learning habits, and the harsh environment in the Diaspora. Distinctiveness means questioning; criticizing the established, timeworn traditions; and creating new ideas, new values, new theories, new technologies, new industries, new subjects.... Moreover, the Jews' outstanding achievements are undoubtedly related to the environment in which they grow up, which, directly or indirectly, is associated with their distinctive religion and their unique way of life.

If the outstanding achievement of Jews is an affirmative explanation for their quality of uniqueness, the Jews' misfortune in history would be another interpretation of the same feature. Without delving into the Babylonian Siege of the biblical era, Alexander's conquest and rule of Rome, the following paragraph will focus on the persecution and massacre of Jews after AD 70 in Diaspora. "Anti-Semitism" is usually translated as "反犹主义" (fanyou zhuyi) in Chinese. As a matter of fact, anti-Semitism refers not only to the doctrines or theories against Judaism but also to any and all acts against Jews. In medieval European countries, the Jews lived in dark, crowded "ghettoes" filled with low and shabby shelters. Without civil rights, they had to make a living by trading or lending money, which was disdained by Christians, and were in danger of having their property confiscated at any time. They were framed and slaughtered during the Crusades, the Black Death, and time and time again. In 1290, Britain's King Edward I deported the Jews and seized their property. In 1392, King Philip II of France expelled them after they were exploited and persecuted. Since the beginning of the fourteenth century, the Spanish Jews suffered many mishaps in their lives, including the massacres of the crusades, forced conversions to Christianity, heavy taxes, and mandatory wearing of humiliating badges. In 1492, King

Ferdinand required Spanish Jews to dispose of their property and depart within four months. The Holocaust, the slaughter of 6 million Jews in World War II, was the peak of anti-Semitism. These are the world-shaking anti-Semitic incidents.

Admittedly, the root of anti-Semitism first of all lies in religion, especially the widespread crime of "deicide." As the Gospel noted, Judas Iscariot betrayed Jesus, which resulted in the execution of Jesus by the Roman governor after the Jewish high priest sentenced him to death. That is to say, because the Jews were accused of murdering Jesus Christ, they all became the enemies of Christians. Apart from this, the characteristic of distinctiveness should also be regarded as one of the factors which intensified anti-Semitism. As mentioned before, in Christian-dominated Europe, the Jews not only denied that Jesus was the Messiah but also dared to have three great debates with the Christian Church. Furthermore, the Jews living abroad as a minority still kept their own customs and way of life, i.e., keeping the Sabbath, reading the Hebrew Bible in synagogue, growing beards and side locks, wearing discrete clothing, observing dietary laws, etc. These unique differences in customs, religions, and lifestyle were tantamount to drawing a line between Christians and Jews, and this made them unwelcome in many Christians' eyes. Moreover, the Jews were good at management, business, lending, and generating wealth, which inevitably incurred jealousy. The image was that a few "alien households" lived in a village, kept no contact with others, but in time they became wealthy. What would the majority of the villagers think, and what kind of consequences would occur? There is no intention here to blame the Jews for anti-Semitism, or plead for Christians, or accuse the Jews for following their own religion and unique life style. The discussion here is only to objectively point out the consequences of distinctive Jewish conduct.

In brief, distinctiveness is a double-edged sword for the Jews. On the one hand, it created a large number of excellent Jews and their outstanding achievements in various fields; on the other hand, it became the direct or indirect cause of anti-Semitism. As the old saying goes, "A man's character is his destiny." If distinctiveness is essential to the Jews' character, the brilliant achievements and the suffering associated with it is their inevitable fate.

IV

The purpose of Jewish distinctiveness, in this final analysis, is to highlight Jewish identity in order to maintain their independent existence as a nation. Ernst Cassirer, the German philosopher, claims that the human being is the product of culture. It refers to both a person and a nation. Therefore, to maintain the existence of a nation is to maintain its ethnic culture. As for the Jews, it is the maintenance of Judaism.

In the beginning, monotheism was established by the ancient Israelites to distinguish themselves from gentile polytheism and to exist as an independent nation. In the Bible, God is often addressed as "the God of our ancestors Abraham, Isaac, and Jacob" and "the God of Israel." However, the God of Israel is believed to be greater than the gentile gods. In fact, in biblical times, people who believed in YHWH were Israelites, those who believed in other gods or idols were gentiles. Israel sternly rejected foreign gods and therefore drew a line between themselves and gentiles. Meanwhile, they strained every nerve to maintain their belief in monotheism and punished any violators with due severity. As recorded in Exodus: the people of Israel made a golden calf under Aaron's allowance and danced with joy around it, while Moses was on Mont Sinai. Moses was furious. He broke the tablets of the Decalogue, burned the golden calf and ground it into a powder, and commanded the Levites to ruthlessly kill 3,000 worshipers of the golden calf. It is obvious that the ancient Israelites were extremely serious, even cruel, in the preservation of monotheism. The primary purpose of that was to maintain the purity of monotheism, making Judaism a distinctive religion and the Jews a distinctive nation.

The Jews in the Diaspora settled in sovereign countries as a minor ethnic group. They had a stronger consciousness of crisis because they faced more direct assimilation than ever. Hence, Jews, scattered in many locations, tried making themselves distinctive by showing their independence and cultural uniqueness, by adhering to their beliefs, and by persisting in their way of life and daily rituals. In this way, they attempted to protect their people from the dangers of assimilation and the loss of their Jewish character and identity.

After the French Revolution in 1789, the Jews obtained civil rights in France and later in Germany and most European countries. It was called the "Emancipation" in Jewish history. Although Jewish citizenship was not fully implemented after the Emancipation, their living situation was improved significantly for a while. Therefore, an internal differentiation started. The "complete Westernizationists," represented by the poet Heinrich Heine, the children of Moses Mendelssohn, and a considerable number of Jewish millionaires and their wives, abandoned Judaism and converted to Christianity. People who persisted on keeping the Jewish tradition with the application of Western systems, such as Samson Raphael Hersch in Germany and Samuel David Luzzatto in Italy, believed that Judaism as a revealed religion was the root and soul of the Jews and could not be changed. It was the times that should be changed. They paid limited attention to secular culture and science and constituted a new Orthodox school of Judaism. The majority of Jews at that time were radical reformists. Abraham Geiger and Samuel Holdheim from Germany (and Isaac Wise in the United States), were typical representatives. They believed that Jews must be integrated into mainstream society, and an important way of

Westernization was the reform of Judaism. Therefore, they drastically carried out a reform and reconstruction of the Jewish faith, especially the rites and customs. In addition to the previous groups, there were the conservatives. They participated in the reform of Judaism at the beginning, then blamed the reformists for being too radical and stepped back, then formed an intermediate school between Orthodox and Reform. Their representatives included Solomon Schechter, Louis Ginsberg, and Isaac Lesser. The reform movement of Judaism started in the nineteenth century, and it indicated that a tolerant and free external environment could lead to an internal differentiation and external assimilation of Jews if they gave up their Jewish identity and unique lifestyle. Ultimately, it might contain the danger of disintegration of the Jewish nation.

Since the end of World War II, the Protestant and Catholic churches of Christianity have reexamined the Holocaust profoundly and sought reconciliation with the Jews. Decades later, anti-Semitism from Christians has been greatly reduced, and a harmonious atmosphere has been established. It could be claimed that the period from the 1950s up to now is the most harmonious era of the relationship between Jews and Christians in the past 2,000 years. Currently, the population of the Jews in the United States has reached 5,200,000, which is close to half of the world Jewish population. Statistics show that 56% of Jewish families in America belong to a synagogue and participate in religious services regularly. For the others, some are irregular in Jewish activities, while some only agree to Judaism culturally: thousands of people claim to be Jews culturally but without any belief in God. In conclusion, it is believed that the majority of Jews in America belong to a Jewish denomination and keep the Jewish faith and the unique lifestyle. Therefore, they can identify as Jews not only in ancestry but also in religion or culture. Nevertheless, according to the Orthodox view, most American Jews have lost their unique character by not strictly adhering to traditional Judaism. They are anxious and afraid that Jews will be completely assimilated in the future. Not long ago, I attended an international conference themed as a dialogue of Confucianism and Judaism held at Tel Aviv University. The famous Rabbi Adin Steinsaltz said in his keynote speech that many Israelis in modern Israel have not been Jewish but have only been the descendants of Jews. Through the words of the representative of Orthodox Judaism, we realize that the unique Jewish religion and way of life have been weakened due to the influence of Westernization, secularization, and non-religious immigrants. The Jewish character derived from Judaism is fading away in consequence. These examples indicate, from a negative perspective, that the religion of distinctiveness, with its unique way of life, is the proper course to preserve Jewish character and maintain cultural identity both individually and collectively.

V

Emphasizing the distinctive character of Jews does not mean that they only value differences without a common basis or a bottom line. There are theoretical foundations for this character, for both the individual and the community, one of which is the view on freedom in Judaism. There is a famous story in Genesis known by every Jewish man, that is: God created Adam and let him live in the Garden of Eden. God told him, "you are free to eat from any tree in the garden; but you must not eat from the tree of the knowledge of good and evil, for when you eat of it you will surely die" (Genesis 2:15-17). God took one of Adam's ribs and made Adam's wife, Eve. They did not obey God's command and, instead, were drawn to the serpent's allurement, eating the forbidden fruit from the tree of knowledge of good and evil. Hence, they were banished from the Garden of Eden, lived on labor, fed their offspring, and experienced the process of aging, illness, and death. Jews explicated human free choice in the interpretation of this story. Some theologians explain it as follows: man is born to be free to choose to comply with, or violate against, God's commands. Due to this freedom, they should take the responsibility of their own behaviors accordingly. Adam and Eve could "be capable of" choosing to obey God's commands, not to eat the fruit of wisdom, and vice versa. They chose the latter one, and they paid the price. According to Exodus, Jewish ancestors used to be slaves in Egypt for more than 400 years. With the help of the mighty God, Moses led them to escape the Pharaoh's rule successfully, and they gained independence and freedom of life.

In the 1950s, Isaiah Berlin, the British Jewish philosopher, divided freedom into the positive and the negative. The former refers to an active sense of freedom, namely, man as a decision maker acting on his own will; the latter refers to a freedom without others' coercion or interference on both will and behavior, namely, a free status without coercion or interference. Regardless of Berlin's political position, from a general philosophical standpoint, the two stories above happen to contain both the meanings of positive and negative freedom. Because of their advocating for freedom, the Jewish people, from rabbis to common people, have the courage to propose creative and distinctive views and to stick to their own views without the fear of authorities. That is why there are the sayings such as "two Jews, three opinions" and "the seven million prime ministers in a country"; and that is also the reason why there are a great number of outstanding Jewish elites in all walks of life. Due to advocating for freedom, the Jews dare to say "no" in the face of the forceful Christian religion and the majority of Christians, to push aside all obstacles and difficulties, while keeping their own religious beliefs and way of life. Hence, they have developed into an independent and self-reliant ethnic group. If distinctiveness is considered a major characteristic of the Jews and a reason for their success, then the view on freedom inherent in Judaism would be the spiritual value behind this characteristic and "the mother of success" of Jewish people.

Moreover, the Jews received another value from their religion—equality. It is noted in the Bible "let us make man in our image, in our likeness...So God created man in his own image, in the image of God he created him; male and female he created them" (Genesis 1:26-27). It is concluded that since everyone is created in God's image, everyone is equal in dignity, no lowliness or nobility, and no difference in basic human rights. Since humans are created in God's image, they shall be humble and insignificant in front of the true God; meanwhile, everyone shall be equal in essence in front of anyone else, including kings, aristocrats, and the wealthy. Only when the value of equality persists can Jewish people have enough confidence to say "no" in the face of authority and power. Only when the belief in equality persists can every Jewish person, regardless of their social class, dare to express their own views, debate equally, and pursue uniqueness and innovation. In summary, like the analysis on the view of freedom, it is impossible to understand the Jewish character of distinctiveness without viewing the value of equality *a priori*.

Compared with freedom and equality, faith in only one God is ultimately the foundation for the Jewish character of distinctiveness. The belief in the only God, YHWH, is the difference between Judaism and other religions. The theme of the Hebrew Bible, or even the whole of biblical Judaism, is to accept and maintain the faith in one God and to firmly oppose any form of idolatry, to distinguish Judaism from the polytheistic religions. Although the purpose of the Talmud is not to demonstratively substantiate monotheistic belief, its core is to provide an appropriate way of life for the Jewish people in Diaspora. After all, the oral law is the interpretation of the written law; hence it also plays a part in the maintenance of monotheism. The most important conviction in Jewish monotheism is that YHWH is the only God, no other gods before him. This is embodied in the first of the Ten Commandments and also in the Shema, the prayer read twice a day by every Jewish person. The belief in the only God serves as the final basis for the Jewish characteristic of distinctiveness. Without it, the Jewish people would not believe they were the "chosen people" of God; would not accept the Mosaic Law as obligations; would not dare to believe they are equal to the powerful Egyptians, Babylonians, Persians, Greeks, Romans, and Christians; and would not believe they are free. Based on this belief, they would hence believe that they have the right and qualification for making and upholding their distinctive quality. In other words, for religious Jews, being firm in the faith of the only God is the final basis and highest principle for Judaism and Jewish people. Without it, Judaism could not exist, and the extraordinary mode of thinking and way of life would be impossible. For Chinese, "*ansheng liming*" (get yourself settled down and get on with a pursuit of life) is often said and valued highly; for the Jews, the belief in God is the ultimate foundation on which both the Jewish lifestyle and the Jewish character of distinctiveness are based.

VI

To conclude, distinctiveness is one of the major Jewish characteristics. It is inherent in the basic beliefs and doctrines of Judaism and is revealed in the ways of Jewish life, in Jewish thinking, and in the history and presence of Jewish people. The outstanding achievements of Jewish people in various fields of religion, science, ideology, economy, politics, are closely related with this major Jewish characteristic. Meanwhile, the tragic experience of this nation, to a certain extent, was related to it as well. The aim of this distinctive character is to separate Judaism from other religions, and then the Jews from other people. As an ethnic minority, the Jews are scattered all over the world, yet without assimilating, even though they survived a great deal of suffering and affliction. An important reason for that is the unique Jewish religion and the ways of thinking and life related with it. The Jews would have been assimilated by gentiles if there were no distinctiveness and personal independence of conduct. Theoretically speaking, the Jewish character is rooted in the values of freedom and equality in the Bible and ultimately in the monotheistic Judaism, which distinguishes itself from polytheistic religions.

As for the attitude toward distinctiveness and uniformity of Chinese people, it is believed that they prefer the latter. In the Eastern Zhou Dynasty, there coexisted numerous philosophers and hundreds of schools of thought. Therefore, in a broad sense, distinctiveness was mainstream. However, in an article titled *Uphold Uniformity,* Mozi (ca. 490–403 BC), a great pioneering philosopher, advocated the establishment of a hierarchy with a strict "chief administrator" ranking system, which could convey the circumstances and opinions at the grassroots level up to the emperor. Finally, it was the emperor who governed the "righteousness of the whole world" and unified the governing orders and determinations of punishment and reward in order to rule the nation in a harmonious way. Mozi's political philosophy had its own truth under certain historical circumstances. However, the implementation of autocracy, since the Qin and Han Dynasties in China, had made political unity extend to the field of thought. Although the slogan of "upholding Confucianism only and deposing hundreds of schools of thought" had never been completed thoroughly since the Han Dynasty, the uniformity rule of politics imprisoned the thoughts of people, indeed, killed the innovative spirit and developed a psychological orientation of conforming to the vulgar and seeking for the common. The frequently mentioned proposition of "seeking common ground while reserving differences" is the reflection of this typical psychology of upholding uniformity. As a matter of fact, "to uphold uniformity," or "to seek common ground while reserving differences," is reasonable to a certain extent. For example, it is beneficial for people to find similarities among each other, reduce conflicts, make agreements, and harmonize relationships; "a unity of thoughts," as an expression of "upholding uniformity," can lead to "the unity of actions" which will accomplish what scattered individuals are incapable of. However, on the other hand, people who uphold uniformity usually lack the spirit of innovation and the courage of pursuing individuality. If upholding uniformity becomes a national common practice, this inclination would be bound to lead the entire nation to become mediocre. In the long run, people would lose their vitality and society would stagnate. It is hard to dissociate this inclination from the fall of China in the late Ming Dynasty. In conclusion, it is inspiring and significant for the Chinese nation, which is committed to national rejuvenation, to review the Jewish characteristic of distinctiveness that is inherent to Judaism and to review the experience of this unique people.

Chinese Policy Toward Kaifeng Jews

XU XIN

Nanjing University

As China is the only country in the Far East in which Jews have continually lived for more than 1,000 years, "Chinese Judaism"—referring to the religious practice and life of those Jews who had lived or are now living in China—is unique. Within this long history, a significant distinction must be made. Jews who came before modern times, in other words before 1840, became part of Chinese society and were considered as "native" Chinese or Chinese citizens; while those who arrived since 1840 have remained aliens.[1] This paper attempts to address the Chinese policy issue with a special consideration to the Kaifeng Jewry in the second half of the twentieth century, although it starts with an overall examination of Chinese policy from a historical perspective toward Jews and Judaism in order to provide a background for the issue.

Policies toward Jews and Their Religious Practices in History

During their 1,000 year residency, what, if any, has been official policy of China toward the Jews and their religious practices? Examining historical sources before the twentieth century—although documents related directly to this issue are rare[2]—a liberal policy was carried out of "respecting their religion and changing not their customs and

---

1 See Xu Xin, "Practice of Judaism in China," in *The Encyclopedia of Judaism*, eds. Jacob Neusner, Alan J. Avery-Peck, and William Scott Green, Vol. 4 (Leiden and London: Brill, 2003), 1630–1652.

2 There exist a few documents in Yuan Dynasty (1271–1368) referring to the Mongols' policy toward Jews. For details, see Donald D. Leslie, *The Survival of the Chinese Jews* (Leiden: E. J. Brill, 1972), 11–16.

traditions."³ This policy, applying to all ethnic groups and their faiths, should have naturally covered Jews and Judaism in principle regardless of whether it was made specifically toward Judaism or not. Accordingly, the governments had instituted lenient policies toward the Jews, permitting them to live within the dynasty territory and to practice normal religious activities, including building houses of worship. One would find out without too many difficulties, when examining the history, that the liberal policy was well reflected in the case of the Kaifeng Jewry. For instance, the Kaifeng Jewish stele records show that the Song dynasty emperor gave permission for Jews to live in the then capital of China and to follow their own customs and traditions.⁴

Grants of land by officials of different dynasties for the building or rebuilding of the synagogue in Kaifeng further illustrate the respect of the Chinese toward Jews and Judaism. There is a presumption that in 1163 special permission was requested and granted to construct a unique building for the synagogue in Kaifeng. Presumably, the same kind of permission was requested and granted each time the synagogue was destroyed, either by fire or by flood. The reconstruction of the synagogue in 1421 was under the direct sponsorship of Prince Zhou, who was the younger brother of Ming emperor Chen Zu. The Imperial finance office subsidized the project. The 1489 inscription records confirm this.⁵ In 1461, a flood destroyed the synagogue completely except for its foundation. After the floodwaters subsided, the Jews of Kaifeng, headed by Ai Qin, petitioned the provincial commissioner, requesting a decree confirming the right of the community to rebuild the demolished synagogue on the original site of the ancient one. The permission was soon granted, and Kaifeng Jews were able to reconstruct the house of worship, which was dedicated in 1489.

The best expression of that policy is perhaps a horizontal, inscribed plaque granted by a Qing emperor, as well as vertical plaques and scrolls

---

3   It is expressed in Chinese like this: "尊其教而不易其俗" (zun qi jiao er bu yi qi su).
4   The 1489 stele records "the three-point covenants" made by Chinese emperor with the Kaifeng Jews: "Become part of Chinese, honor and preserve the customs of your ancestors, and remain and hand them down in Kaifeng."
5   This stele is now in the Kaifeng Municipal Museum.

with couplets given the Kaifeng Jewry by local officials for the dedication of the newly completed synagogue that replaced the one destroyed in the Yellow River flood of 1642.[6]

The local government was said to enact a regulation that "strangers and carriers of pork cannot pass near the synagogue."[7] This shows that the Kaifeng Jewry enjoyed a relatively high freedom of religion and that their customs were respected by Chinese by and large. Hardly any equivalent period in the entire history of the other historical Diasporas show Jews elsewhere enjoying similar respect.

In the Republican period (1912–1949) of China, the fact that a large number of Jews (about 40,000) from Europe arrived and lived in China seem to tell us indirectly that Chinese authorities carried out a relaxed policy toward Jews and their religion. Jews received permission to stay, to establish organizations, and to build synagogues. Jewish life, including religious life, went on. Moreover, the Chinese government issued a number of statements endorsing Zionism, which should be viewed as Chinese policy toward Jews or Judaism, as Jews, Judaism and Zionism are directly related. For instance, in 1920, Dr. Sun Yat-sen, the founding father for the Republic of China, wrote a letter to N. E. B. Ezra, then secretary of the Shanghai Zionist Association, to express his support for the Jewish national cause. His letter reads:

> I have read your letter and copy of *Israel's Messenger* with much interest and wish to assure you of my sympathy for this movement which is one of the greatest movements of the present time. All lovers of democracy cannot help but support the movement to restore your wonderful and historic nation which has contributed so much to the civilization of the world and which rightly deserves an honorable place in the family of nations.[8]

During World War II, the Chinese government was particularly sympathetic to the plight of Jews in Europe and took action to assist

---

6   For the full text, see William C. White, *Chinese Jews*, second ed. (Toronto: University of Toronto Press, 1966), part I, chapter 6, 123–131.
7   Ibid., 80.
8   Sun Yat-Sen, "To N. E. B. Ezra," *The Collected Works of Sun Yan-Sen* 5 (Beijing: Zhonghua Shujiu, 1985), 256–257.

them by proposing a plan to set up a settlement in Southwest China to relocate those who were suffering in German-occupied countries in Europe in 1939. According to the plan, the Chinese government would offer Jewish refugees the same rights of residence, work, and governmental protection as Chinese citizens. The plan was proposed after a series of 1938 events spurred the victimization of helpless Jews: the annexation of Austria to the Reich in March, the fruitless Evian Conference on Jewish Refugees in July, Kristallnacht in November, and the attempt on the life of Secretary of the Legation von Rath in Paris, which resulted in massive persecution of German Jews.[9]

Although the program was never implemented, the very idea shows that Chinese and their government were sympathetic to the Jewish situation and tried to assist in time of need.

Under the Communist Rule

After the Communists took power in 1949, the newly established government, especially the local governments of the cities where Jews lived, instituted a liberal policy toward the Jewish religion, permitting the Jews to maintain their synagogues and to carry on their regular activities. The Jewish religion was recognized at that time by the government as one of the approved religions in such cities as Shanghai, Tianjin, and Harbin. For instance, the Shanghai New Synagogue remained open, and Jewish rituals were continuously observed until it was closed in 1956 because the number of Jews had decreased.[10] The Harbin Synagogue remained open until the 1960s.[11] Judaism practiced by those foreign Jews before their departure was well respected by the Communist government, although it was never on the list of officially

---

9 "Chungking National Government Programme for the Placement on the Jews in China," *Republican Archives* 3 (1993): 17–21. See also Xu Xin, "Sun Fo's Plan to Establish a Jewish Settlement in China during World War II Revealed," *Points East* 15:3 (March 2001): 1, 7–8.
10 "Report of Council of the Jewish Community Shanghai of July, 1955–July 1956," The Hoover Institution Archives, Hoover Institution.
11 Qu Wei and Li Shuxiao, eds., *The Jews in Harbin* (Beijing: Social Sciences Documentation Publishing House, 2003).

recognized religions in contemporary China as they were not Chinese citizens.

While there were almost no foreign Jews living in China from the mid-1960s to the end of 1970s, and the formal practice of Judaism ceased, the relationship between Chinese and Jews does not end there. China, which underwent dramatic changes after 1979 due to her reform and "Open Door Policy", sought foreign investments and reestablished ties with the rest of the world, especially with Western countries. This revived Jewish presence in China. Nowadays, a significant number of Jews live in Chinese cities such as Beijing and Shanghai as well as Hong Kong, which retuned to Chinese sovereignty in 1997. With more and more Jews arriving to work, invest, study, and live in China, the practice of Judaism once again has become visible in Chinese society.

For instance, in the 1980s, Jews who came to Beijing from North America to pursue careers in business, journalism, diplomacy, or for academic study, started to celebrate Jewish high holidays such as Passover. Twenty-five Jews observed a Seder in 1985 in Beijing. In the 1990s, the Beijing Jewish community took shape as more Jews lived, worked, or studied there. In 1995, Friday night services began to be held every week at the Capital Club of Beijing. Later, Sabbath prayer books and a Sefer Torah were donated to the community, which enabled them to celebrate all major holidays. Other important landmarks for the community include its first bar mitzah in 1996 and its first b'rit millah in 1997. This community was headed by Roberta Lipson and Elyse Silverberg, two Jewish businesswomen, and was affiliated with the Progressive movement of Judaism.[12]

In 2001, a new development took place in the practice of Judaism in Beijing. Rabbi Shimon Freundlich from the Chabad-Lubavitch movement came and settled in the city. His mission is to build and lead the Chabad-Lubavitch house of Beijing, an Orthodox congregation.[13] It now has its own Hebrew school and owns Dini's Kosher Restaurant.

---

12 http://www.sinigogue.org, accessed June 23, 2003.
13 http://www.chabtbeijing.com, accessed June 28, 2003.

Jews also began to return to Shanghai in the 1980s, attracted by China's Open Door Policy. As Shanghai became more and more cosmopolitan, Jewish presence in the city became more visible. Rabbi Shalom Greenberg from Chabad-Lubavitch in New York arrived in Shanghai to serve this community in August 1998. His commitment has infused new life into the growing Jewish community. Rabbi Arthur Schneier, president of the Appeal of Conscience Foundation from New York, donated the Sefer Torah to the community in 1998. There are now several hundred members of the community. They conduct regular Shabbat services and provide kosher meals. As in Beijing, there are child and adult education classes, bar and bat mitzvah training, and social brunches. On the first day of Rosh Hashanah, in September 1999, a Jewish New Year service was held at the Ohel Rachel Synagogue for the first time since 1952 when the synagogue was closed.[14]

The Jewish experience in China merits its good reputation because there is no evidence that China has ever persecuted Jews. The Chinese government seems to realize that it is necessary to create a positive cultural environment for those foreigners if China wants to keep and attract them. This kind of cultural environment includes due respect for religions.

Authorities have shown special consideration and respect to Jewish religious requirements. For instance, in 1993, to mark the historic visit of Israeli President Chaim Herzog to China after China and Israel established full diplomatic relations, the Shanghai government turned the original building of the Ohel Moses Synagogue (which had been used by Jewish refugees during World War II) into a museum. It is now open and receives thousands of visitors annually.

In 1998, the Shanghai municipal government spent over $60,000 to restore the Ohel Rachel Synagogue, which was first constructed in 1920 and is one of two remaining synagogues in the city, as a historic site. Permission to use the building for Jewish holiday celebrations is frequently granted.[15]

---

14 http://www.chinajewish.org, accessed June 28, 2003.
15 Seth Kaplan and Matthew Trusch, *Ohel Rachel Synagogue* (Shanghai: The Jewish Community of Shanghai, 2000).

Many buildings that relate to Jewish life still exist in Shanghai. The political implications of choosing and renovating original synagogues are very clear: the Chinese government understands now that a site for religious services is the core part of Jewish life.

In Harbin, the Jewish cemetery with 876 graves—the best-preserved Jewish cemetery in mainland China—is well taken care of by Chinese authorities. In the fall of 1996, at the expense of the city government, a new fence and gate were completed to better protect the cemetery. Now the city government is taking additional steps to preserve the heritage handed down by the Harbin Jewish community since it was established at the end of the nineteenth century.[16] In 2012, the Harbin Municipal Government decided to reconstruct and renovate the Harbin Main (Old) Synagogue and the Jewish Secondary School next to it, as well as two other buildings and a large square that together form a block in the heart of historical Harbin.[17] Now the project is completed and the area has a new look.

Although foreign priests are not allowed to conduct religious services in China under Chinese law, permission has been granted to the Chabad Lubavitch rabbis to conduct services in China. The Chinese government understands the uniqueness of Judaism, which means that Judaism is indigenous to the Jewish people and is inconceivable without it as Judaism and Jews entered history simultaneously. This policy also reflects the fact that Jews ordinarily do not seek converts.

Issue of the Kaifeng Jews Since 1950

When we discuss Chinese policy toward Judaism, the issue that remains the most puzzling and complicated is related to the Kaifeng Jews in contemporary China. History shows that these Jews, arriving almost 1,000 years ago, always lived according to their own ways and at their own wishes, either as observant or as assimilated Jews. Although the

---

16 Letter from Xiao Tongyan to Mr. Kaufman, *Israel-China Voice of Friendship* 17 (n.d.), 11.
17 *China Daily*, October 31, 2003 report, and based on communications between this author and Dan Ben-Canaan, member and advisor of The Old Jewish Synagogue Renovation Project, Harbin City Command Leadership Team, The Harbin Mayor and Secretary General Offices.

relations between the Kaifeng Jewry and Chinese governments were good, as we discussed earlier, we have not found any policy specifically directed at them before 1950. Nobody interfered with them and no specific policy was implemented for a long time as they were so small in number when set against the vast number of Chinese and could easily be completely overlooked.[18] Why, then, did things change during the last 60 years?

Moreover, as we have discussed above, historically speaking, the Chinese government took a very liberal policy towards Judaism as it was practiced by non-Chinese Jews only. Why did a different policy seem to exist toward the Kaifeng Jews, their identity, and their religious activities in last 60 years? Why did the government pay so much attention to them? A few available documents[19] now seem to shed some light on the issue.

Over time, Jews in Kaifeng did not lose their sense of identity even when they were not observant and their community ceased to formally exist. Today, they do not have customs and traditions different from other Chinese. While no longer practicing traditional rites, they still remember their ancestry and insist on their Jewish roots when talking about their identity. For instance, during the 1952 census conducted by the government, many classified themselves as "Jewish" when filling the census forms. As a result, their residence registration booklets and ID cards (issued in the 1980s) marked them as "Jewish" in the category of nationality. The government, at least at the local level, accepted their claims and never challenged their Jewish identity when they recorded it.

The situation started to change and Jewish identity became an issue because of political considerations after the 1952 census. This author

---

18 It is believed that the highest number of people in the Kaifeng Jewish community was about 5,000 before the Yellow River flood of 1642. In the nineteenth century, the population dropped down to 1,000 or less.
19 This author has to point out that he obtained copies of those documents under examination from an anonymous source. This author believes that the genuineness of those documents is beyond suspicion, after close examination and based on cross-references (for instance, some information and policies this author learned from a number of meetings he had with local officials in the past ten years).

believes that it was a good intention that developed into an unexpected problem.

The background is something like this: after getting rid of most of the Kuomingdang's remaining forces in the mainland and with the end of the Korean War in sight, the Chinese government started to pay more attention to the stability of the country and the unity of all ethnic groups.[20] In August of 1952, the central government of China issued three related resolutions to strengthen this unity by establishing autonomies and protecting the equal rights of all ethnic groups. One of these was the "Resolution on Ensuring That All Minority Groups That Live in China Enjoy Equal National Rights."[21] The spirit of the resolution was to insure that all minorities with the requisites for exercising regional national autonomy, irrespective of the size of their populations, are permitted to establish their own autonomous areas. Small nationalities that lack the requisites for establishing autonomous areas, or who live in mixed communities, or who are scattered across the country, enjoy national equality all the same. According to the resolution, all nationalities are given representation at the National People's Congress, each having at least one deputy.

In order to fulfill this goal, the government undertook the task of ethnic identification, as there had existed few documents to determine and clarify which were individual nationalities and which were areas inhabited by a given nationality. Until all of this was clarified, it would be difficult to ensure the rights of minorities involved in political equality, of those who were being given fair representation in the Chinese political structure.

Accordingly, the government put forward a set of traits requisite to constitute a separate ethnic group. These included the following basic requirements: a common language; an area of inhabitation; a unique set

---

20 Traditionally speaking, Chinese use the word "minority" to refer to all non-Han ethnic groups since they are all small in number compared with the majority—Han people. In fact, the word "Chinese" originally referred to "Han." Another word that is frequently used is "nationality" to refer to which ethnic group one belongs.
21 *People's Daily*, August 22, 1952. The other two are "Implementing Programme for Regional National Autonomy" and "Resolution on Measures of Setting Up Local National Democratic United Government."

of customs, attitudes, and beliefs; and traditional means of livelihood.[22] Difficult as it turned out to be, the government organized special investigation groups made up of ethnologists, linguists, historians, and other specialists to assist the local governments concerned. Any ethnic group had first to be judged by all those traits before it could be officially recognized. It is because of this set of criteria that the Kaifeng Jews did not qualify for government recognition.

It might be argued that the Chinese government was doing something impossible: to identify each and every ethnic group by one set of criteria, as there are always exceptions. However, one can hardly challenge the sincerity and good intentions of this policy as the equal rights it intended to give among all ethnic groups had never been enjoyed before.

While the ethnic identification was underway, there came the celebration of China's National Day. The theme for that year's celebration of National Day, which was one of the biggest events in Chinese political life, was also the "unity of all nationalities." Local governments across the country were asked to pick up representatives from each and every ethnic group living in their region and send them to Beijing, the capital of the country, to participate in the National Day celebration as representatives and to show the whole world that China was giving equal rights to all.

Accordingly, the Bureau of Central South[23] and the Kaifeng Municipal Government, when making their selections, chose two Jewish descendants in Kaifeng: Ai Fenming, who became a communist and worked in an air force unit in Kaifeng, and Shi Fenying, who worked in the Foreign Affairs Office of Henan Province. The reason that those two Jewish descendants were chosen was that the local governments were aware of the existence of Jews in the city and wanted to ensure equal rights for any ethnic group living in their region, including Jews.

---

22 The National Minorities Questions Editorial Panel, *Questions and Answers about China's National Minorities* (Beijing: New World Press, 1985), 144.

23 A power mechanism in Central China set up by the Central Committee of the Communist Party. The whole country was then divided into several regions to be governed by the bureau that was higher in political structure in China than provincial government.

Those two Jewish descendants were introduced as Jews while in Beijing and were well received during the celebration. They attended all activities for the National Day celebrations, including the state banquet hosted by Premier Zhou Enlai on October 16. *People's Daily*, the major newspaper run by the Central Committee of the Communist Party, cited Jews as one of 46 ethnic groups[24] that participated in the banquet,[25] an indication that the Kaifeng Jews were considered as a separate ethnic group. Seeing this, one may feel that Jews in Kaifeng were lucky in New China. They were honored simply because they were Jews. In fact, the Kaifeng Jews had rarely received such an honor previously, although they had been in China for nearly 1,000 years. As no Jews elsewhere had ever enjoyed the same honor, it seemed that their identity was not a problem at all.

In April 1953, the United Front[26] of the Bureau of Central South sent a policy-seeking telegraph to the Central United Front in Beijing to ask if it was appropriate for them to recognize the Kaifeng Jews as an ethnic group.[27] It is not clear why the issue arose at this point. Was it because of the claim by the Kaifeng Jews or simply because of the requirement of the process the local government took in ethnic identification in the region? However, one thing is clear: it would have been impossible to discuss the issue had there been no such movement of ethnic identification in the country.

In any case, this move actually raised the issue of the political and social status of the Kaifeng Jews for the first time, perhaps, in history and led to the birth of a far-reaching Chinese policy toward Kaifeng Jews. According to the policy relating to ethnic issues at the time, Kaifeng Jewry automatically would have had representation or held a seat in political mechanisms of the city, as well as in the country, had they been recognized as a separate ethnic group. This was obviously a

---

24 The number rose to 55 in the 1960s and the standard number is 56 now.
25 *People's Daily*, October 17, 1952.
26 An office set up by the Chinese government in charge of affairs of multi-party and multi-ethnic groups in general.
27 That telegraph is not available to this author, but we were able to figure out the main point from the reply document, which repeats the request. The date of the telegraph is April 3, 1953.

serious matter. It was highly necessary for the local government to seek instructions from the central government. The Central Unity Front of the Community Party of China sent an official written reply to the United Front of the Bureau of Central South on June 8, 1953, in a period of two months to give much needed instructions, which set the tone for the issue up to now and had a profound impact on the statue of the Kaifeng Jews.

This document is no doubt written in the spirit of ethnic identification, stating that Jews who scatter in Kaifeng "have no direct connections economic wise. They don't have a common language of their own and a common area of inhabitance. They have completely mixed and mingled with the majority Han population, in terms of their political, economical and cultural lives, and they do not possess any distinctive traits in any other aspect." Therefore, "it is not an issue to treat them as one distinctive ethnic group, as they are not a Jewish nation in themselves anymore."[28]

However, at the same time, the document admits that this is an intricate issue because, aside from Kaifeng, there are Jews in other Chinese cities too (it mentions specifically that there are stateless Jews in Shanghai[29]). It points out that the move "could cause other problems and put us in a passive position politically." We have no idea what "other problems" might be and why the Chinese government believes that they might be "put in a passive position politically" as nothing specific is mentioned in the document. However, the expression "in a passive position politically" means a very serious issue in political usage in China, and it is used here to warn that the local government should do everything possible to avoid that consequence.

The document conclusion is that "your request of acknowledging Kaifeng Jewry as a separate nationality is improper. Kaifeng Jewry should be treated as a part of the Han Nationality."

Nevertheless, the document stresses that the importance of the fact that "we should take the initiative to be more caring to them in

---

28 For the full text of this document, see Appendix 1 of this paper.
29 Obviously, this refers to Jewish refugees from Central Europe and still stayed in Shanghai although the majority had left after World War II.

various activities, and educate the local Han population not to discriminate against or insult them. This will help gradually ease away the differences they might psychologically or emotionally feel exists between them and the Han."

The document is hand written with many corrections.[30] For instance, originally, the document states that, in order to avoid unnecessary misunderstanding and problems, it is better not to say anything if we recognize them or not, but to keep the above principle in the mind of leaders. However, those words are crossed out before the document was sent out. The document also shows that top Chinese leaders such as Chairman Mao, Liu Shaoqi, Zhou Enlai and Deng Xiaoping had read and approved it. It is highly possible that some of corrections were made by one of them. Because of that, it becomes something untouchable. The principle drawn up in it, although originally strictly dealing with the issue of ethnic identification, became the guideline in all issues concerning the Kaifeng Jewry in years to come.

Clearly, this document is written strictly in the spirit of the policy set up for ethnic identification as one can hardly find any tone of discrimination against the Kaifeng Jews in it. It would have been a totally different story had the Kaifeng Jews then lived in the way their ancestors had lived before the nineteenth century, maintaining an observant Jewish kehillah, having a temple of their own, following the Jewish calendar and kashrut, and using Hebrew prayer—in other words, had they not assimilated.

This policy had little direct effect on the everyday life of the Kaifeng Jews, although it put an end to the possibility that the Kaifeng Jewry could be acknowledged as a separate ethnic group. They lived the same way as before the policy. Interestingly enough, the Chinese government still made some arrangements for foreigners to go to Kaifeng to meet them, which indicated that the government was still thinking that they were "Jews" even after their failure to grant them ethnic status as the goal of those visits was to meet Kaifeng Jews. For instance, Timoteus Pokora, a Czech sinologist, and Rene Goldman, a

---

30 It should be pointed out that not every word, especially those corrections, is legible as far as the copy I have is concerned.

Canadian, visited Kaifeng and met some Jews there in 1957.³¹ However, the issue seemed to die down in the following twenty years when China became more and more isolated from the rest of the world.

China underwent many changes in her policies, both in domestic and international affairs, after she adopted the Open Door Policy in the late 1970s. In January 1980, the Ministry of Foreign Affairs of China arranged for four Canadians, American journalist Aline Mosby, and Chinese reporters to make a special trip to Kaifeng with the sole goal of meeting Kaifeng Jews for the first time after the Cultural Revolution.

What made them undertake such a visit? According to Mosby, she learned on good authority that not all vestiges of Judaism had yet disappeared from Kaifeng. Thus, she made a request to the Chinese government and permission was granted.³² After the visit, the Westerners wrote and published articles about the current situation of the Kaifeng Jews, which again raised the issue both internationally and domestically. When the local government learned about it, they predicted that more and more foreigners might come and visit Kaifeng Jews with this Open Door Policy and that they should prepare themselves for this new situation. Therefore, the Unity Front of Henan Province, which was then in charge of such affairs, raised the issue of the status of the Kaifeng Jews once again by sending a report to the office of the Central Unity Front in March, 1980.³³ In the report, they asked two fundamental questions: (1) if the Kaifeng Jews should be treated as an minority group, and (2) what guidelines need attention when they deal with the issue of the Kaifeng Jews, and what kind of policy should be adopted in foreign affairs related to the Kaifeng Jews.

Why did they do this? Were they unaware of the previous policy? I do not think so. The 1953 document from Beijing should have been available to them. Were they intentionally seeking a new policy? This is highly possible, especially if we take into consideration the situation

---

31 Michael Pollak, *Mandarins, Jews, and Missionaries* (Philadelphia: The Jewish Publication Society of America, 1980), 248-49.
32 Ibid., xiv.
33 This document is not available to this author but its purpose was repeated in the reply.

in China at the end of the 1970s and the beginning of the 1980s when people in every line tried to seek new policies to make changes. However, no one knows the definitive answer.

The Central Unity Front responded to their questions on May 8, 1980.[34] Obviously, the Central Office was not ready for changes. First, the document quotes the policy made in the document of 1953 and says that, according to the information they had, Kaifeng Jews did not seek recognition as a minority people after 1953 and that, except for a few elderly, the majority of Kaifeng Jews did not have that desire. Moreover, most of the young and middle-aged people were indifferent. Therefore, based on this situation, the document says that "we believe that, as it was not necessary in the past, it is not necessary now for us to recognize Kaifeng Jewry as an ethnic group. However, when we deal with them, we should give consideration to the customs they still keep, help them to solve possible problems they may have, and more importantly, do not discriminate against them." The document suggests at the end that "some appropriate arrangements be made for representative figures among them," a typical method to deal with ethnic group or political issues in China.

We do not know the reaction of the local government. However, an increasing number of people from the West visited China. Many of them were Jewish and put Kaifeng on their itinerary in hopes of meeting some of the Kaifeng Jewry.[35]

As expected, the local authorities in charge of receiving those visitors needed a specific guideline to deal with the new situation. As a result, another document dealing directly with the policy toward the Kaifeng Jews was produced on July 2, 1984. This time, they set up three protocols as the guideline and reported it to the top authorities in Beijing. The document is written by the Foreign Affairs Office of Henan provincial government, the office in charge of those issues.

---

34 The document is entitled as "Reply for the Issue on the Kaifeng Jews" and is marked as No. (2) 401. This author holds a copy of it.
35 Pollak lists a number of such visits. For details, see Pollak, *Mandarins, Jews, and Missionaries*, xix.

The following is the full text of the three protocols laid out in the document by the office:

1. Stick to the principle of denying Kaifeng Jewry as an ethnic group of its own. Various periodicals and newspapers should carry objective reports both domestically and internationally. Recognize the fact of historical migration, but put emphasis on the freedom and happiness that they have today. Use the terminology "descendants of Kaifeng Jews" when we address them without implying any country or ethnic group in order to avoid any unnecessary controversy.

    Be lenient to foreign scholars and tourists with the request of visiting Kaifeng synagogue relics, stone tablets and meeting with Jewish descendants. The Kaifeng Foreign Affairs Office will be in charge of their visits politically.

2. From the standpoint of historical materialism, we may consider opening the original site of Kaifeng synagogue and stone tablets to the public. Kaifeng municipal museum could keep historical files of Kaifeng Jewry in one of its exhibit rooms for viewing. Related introduction could also be made in books and paintings for publicity abroad and in tourist brochures.

3. Regarding donations made to Kaifeng by Jewish persons from other countries, acceptance could be considered if the donor has no political intentions, and is only doing it out of kindness for renovating historical sites, museums or other welfare purposes. If the donor's purpose is religiously oriented or implying "a Jewish nation," the donation should be turned down with grace.[36]

As we can see here, this document shifts its emphasis on issues other than ethnic identification although the principle is kept. It puts forward a set of guidelines for tourist issues: what can be done and what cannot be done when the local people receive foreign visitors.

Obviously, the document is politically oriented and raises two fundamental issues related to the Kaifeng Jews:

1) Addressing them as "descendants," not as "Jews," in order to deny Kaifeng Jewry's connection with the Jewish people and

---

36 This author holds a copy of it.

Israel as a Jewish state, because they believed this would be controversial.
2) Making the Jewish religion taboo and anything related to Judaism not acceptable, even donations.

We have no idea what the response from the top was. However, what was ascertained is that this document provides a guideline for dealing with foreign visitors to the city. Those who are familiar with the Kaifeng issue or have been to Kaifeng would feel the policy works even today.

Appendix

The Full Text of the 1953 Document[37]

The United Front of the Bureau of Central South:

The telegraph dated Apr 3rd regarding the Kaifeng Jewry is received.

Judging from your telegraph, the Jews scattered in Kaifeng have no direct connections economic wise, they don't have a common language of their own and a common area of inhabitance. They have completely mixed and mingled with the majority Han population, in terms of their political, economical and cultural life, neither do they possess any distinctive traits in any other aspect. All this indicates that it is not an issue to treat them as one distinctive ethnic group, as they are not a Jewish nation in themselves.

Secondly, aside from the Kaifeng Jewry, there is stateless Jewish population in Shanghai. Jewish presence in some other large and mid-sized cities are also possible, however scarce it might be. It is an intricate issue. It could cause other problems and put us in a passive position politically if we acknowledge the Jews of Kaifeng. Therefore, your request of acknowledging Kaifeng Jewry as a separate nationality is improper based solely on the historical archival evidence you found. You have only seen the minor inessential differences between the Kaifeng Jews and their Han counterpart, and fail to see their commonality and the fact that they are essentially the same. (The publication found in *People's Daily* during National Day celebration time last year regarding "a Jewish nationality" was provided by the Central Ethnic Affairs

---

37 This English version of the document is kindly provided by Ningwei Xu.

Committee.) Kaifeng Jewry should be treated as a part of the Han Nationality.

The major issue is that we should take the initiative to be more caring to them in various activities, and educate the local Han population not to discriminate against or insult them. This will help gradually ease away the differences they might psychologically or emotionally feel exists between them and the Han.

The United Front of the Central Committee of the
Communist Party of China
June 8, 1953

Sukkot and Mid-Autumn Festivals in Kaifeng: Conundrums at the Crossroads of Sino-Judaic Cultural Identity

MOSHE Y. BERNSTEIN
University of Western Australia

Introduction

In September 2013, I joined the Kaifeng Sino-Judaic community for its celebration of the Jewish holiday of Sukkot (Festival of Booths), coinciding with the Chinese Mid-Autumn Festival. This coincidence was not arbitrary but rather due to inherent similarities in the Jewish and Chinese calendars. Two foreign NGOs, the Sino-Judaic Institute, and Shavei Israel (Israel Returns), were also represented at these festivities. The US-based SJI is committed to the study of the historical community of Kaifeng Jews, established during the Song Dynasty in the tenth century. It also advocates "appropriate" support for a revival of the Jewish descendants' cultural heritage and the promotion of Jewish tourism in Kaifeng. According to the website of Israeli NGO Shavei Israel, it similarly "strives to extend a helping hand to all members of our extended Jewish family and to all who seek to rediscover or renew their link with the people of Israel." However, unlike SJI, Shavei Israel has been active worldwide in facilitating the *aliyah* (immigration to Israel) and formal conversion of peripheral communities espousing Jewish identity. Along with the Jin family who immigrated in 1996, in the past decade eleven other Kaifeng Jews have undergone this process with Shavei's support and are now Israeli citizens, an apparently small number that is nonetheless a sizable proportion of the fifty families engaged in communal activities.[1]

Apart from my participant-observation during the holiday and *Shabbat* (Sabbath) celebrations, during my three-week stay, I conducted unstructured interviews to explore the foundations of the community's sense of cultural identity and perceptions of its future development. I found that the diversity of discourse globally on the constitution of Jewish identity has impacted these perceptions. Furthermore, these new articulations often conflict with the vestiges of collective memory of the community's historical identity, itself an amalgam of Confucian, Daoist and Jewish elements. These divergent views on the issue of Jewish identity have produced inherent tensions with concrete manifestations: What standards, if any, should be adopted to determine the status of Jewish identity within the Kaifeng Sino-Judaic community? Should that identity be viewed primarily as a historical narrative or a restoration of Jewish practice? Finally, is that identity best fulfilled in its autochthonous setting or in the Jewish State of Israel?

This paper does not purport to solve these questions but rather to explore, through events observed and discussions with individual community members, how these dichotomies have been translated and internalized into an emergent Kaifeng Jewish culture. It argues that divisions within the community as well as external, global rifts on the constitution of Jewish identity have triggered both confusion and communal fragmentation. Consequently, the emergent reconstruction of Sino-Judaic culture reflects and incorporates these contradictory elements, echoing similar paradoxes in the blended identity of the historical community which endured until the final demise of its synagogue in 1849.

---

1   Eichner, I. "Chinese descendants of ancient Jewish community make aliyah." *Ynetnews*, October 22, 2009. http://www.ynetnews.com/articles/0,7340,L-3793399,00.html, accessed July 17, 2014.

Arrival in Kaifeng

After an hour's drive from Zhengzhou Airport along the newly constructed S82 Zhengmin Expressway, the approach to Kaifeng is heralded by the sight of the ancient city wall dating from the later Zhou Dynasty. Its austere facade, at this time of day tinted with the crimson rays of the setting sun, obfuscated its history as having once encompassed the thriving, cosmopolitan capital of the Northern Song, then a major hub on the Silk Road and the largest metropolis in the world. As I drove north through the city centre, vendors from the night market were busy setting up displays of their assorted wares or preparing a variety of dishes at the numerous food stalls. The sizzling scents of local Hui specialties, predominated by the pungent aroma of lamb kebab and fresh *náng* bread, drifted through the open windows of the taxi. Little had changed in downtown Kaifeng since my previous visit two years earlier in 2011: the dynamic economic growth that has marked so many of China's urban landscapes continued to elude this humble backwater of Henan Province.

The taxi finally turned into the entranceway of the New Century Grand Hotel (*kaiyuan mingdu*), in the city's New Economic Zone, quite far from the Old City, where the Jewish community center, set up by Shavei two months before, was located. With a dearth of vegetarian restaurants in Kaifeng, the New Century's buffet service included an array of vegetable and tofu dishes that satisfied my kosher dietary requirements. This amenity outweighed the three kilometer distance to and from the community center, a route I traveled almost daily during my three-week stay.

Sukkot and Mid-Autumn Festival

Sukkot is one of three major Jewish festivals that commences on the fifteenth day of the seventh lunar month of Tishrei; along with Pesach (Passover) and Shavuot (Pentecost), when the Temple was standing, Sukkot mandated pilgrimage to Jerusalem. The commandment to build a *sukkah*, or booth, in which one is to reside during the period of the festival, is found in Leviticus 23:42: "You shall dwell in booths for a seven-day period; every native in Israel shall dwell in booths."

The verse that follows expounds that this specific commandment was bequeathed for future generations in order that they should know that God: "...caused the Children of Israel to dwell in booths when I [God] took them from the land of Egypt." There is a dispute in the Talmud whether this verse refers literally to the huts that offered natural protection to the Israelites in their forty-year sojourn through the Sinai Desert or, metaphorically, to the supernatural Clouds of Glory that surrounded the Israelite encampment on all sides.

Although the verse indicates a celebration of seven days, due to a rabbinical injunction adding an extra day to the observance of the festivals in the Diaspora, outside of modern-day Israel, the holiday is celebrated for eight days.[2] Among Orthodox Jews, this scriptural decree is universally observed; every household erects a structure with a minimum of three walls covered on top with branches or palm fronds. Although, like with all time-bound commandments in the Torah, women are exempted. It is customary for most religious families to eat all of their main meals during the festival inside the sukkah. Similarly, in order to fulfil the injunction to "dwell" in the sukkah, many observant Jews sleep in it, although inclement weather or adverse conditions nullify this imperative. Conservative Judaism, which adopts a more lenient view in the execution of Torah law, is less stringent on the requirement of every household to build a sukkah. Most temples, however, will construct a communal sukkah, where its congregants will

---

2   The reason for this discrepancy dates back prior to the establishment of the Hebrew calendar. When the Holy Temple existed, witnesses would come forth on either the twenty-ninth or thirtieth day of the month to testify before the Sanhedrin on the sighting of the new moon, which, when confirmed, would establish the date for any festival taking place in that month. Once the sighting was confirmed, messengers would be sent out to the outlying regions surrounding the Land of Israel to inform the Jewish communities of Diaspora. As there were many distant communities that these messengers were unable to reach prior to the start of a festival, the Sanhedrin decreed that all Diaspora communities would celebrate the festivals for two days, to account for the eventualities of both a twenty-ninth and thirtieth day new moon. Later, following the destruction of the Temple, this custom was preserved. The exceptions to this rule are the fast of Yom Kippur, the Day of Atonement, celebrated universally for one day, and Rosh Hashanah, the Jewish New Year, which even in Israel is celebrated for two days.

gather after the holiday prayers for a *kiddush*, a blessing recited over wine or grape juice followed by a snack or meal. Although Reform Jews do not recognize Torah commandments as sacrosanct, some Reform congregations will emulate the tradition of their Conservative colleagues in erecting a sukkah as a social function.

Of equal importance on Sukkot is the scriptural imperative of waving the Four Species, colloquially referred to as *lulav* (palm frond) and *etrog* (citron).[3] Nearly every Orthodox Jewish male will adhere to this imperative by purchasing, prior to the festival, a set of a citron, palm frond, three myrtle twigs, and two willow branches. The latter three are bound together; at different points in the festival liturgy the bound lulav is held in the right hand, the etrog in the left, and they are waved together in six directions as a portent for abundant rainfall in the year ahead.[4] As with the sukkah, most Orthodox households will acquire at least one set of the four species. However, because of the high cost, those unable to afford a lulav and etrog can borrow from a friend or congregant.[5]

At some time during the Shang Dynasty (sixteenth to tenth century BCE), broadly concurrent with the period when Moses is said to have received the Torah on Mount Sinai, the Chinese initiated the celebration of the harvest season at the autumnal full moon. The festival is associated with the ancient custom of offerings made to the lunar deity *Chang-e*. The festival is celebrated widely throughout China with a variety of regional customs. However, it is most common for friends and families to gather together for a meal and to eat mooncakes (*yuebing*), a symbol of harmony, under the evening sky while gazing at the beauty of the full moon. The holiday also is associated with bright lanterns and with the ritual Dragon or Lion Dances. Next to Spring Festival, Mid-Autumn Festival is the most significant occasion on the

---

3   The verse in Leviticus 23:40 instructs the Israelites to "take for yourselves on the first day the fruit of a citron tree, the branches of date palms, twigs of a plaited tree, and brook willows; and you shall rejoice before the Lord, your God, for a seven-day period."
4   The four directions of the compass as well as upward and downward. The order of the waving varies according to the Ashkenazi and Sephardi traditions.
5   The average cost of a full set in Australia is about AUD $120.

Chinese calendar, and it is celebrated ubiquitously. The government of the People's Republic of China has classified this festival as "intangible heritage"; it is also one of China's official public holidays.

The chronological convergence of Sukkot and mid-Autumn Festival during my visit was a result of parallels between the Hebrew and Chinese calendars. Both are lunar but, unlike the Islamic version, both insert seven intercalary months over the course of nineteen years. The Jewish calendar periodically inserts an extra winter month of Adar to ensure that Pesach, also referred to in the Torah as the Festival of Spring, always occurs after the vernal equinox. The Chinese include an extra month to ensure that the Northern Hemisphere's winter solstice always transpires during their eleventh month and that the Chinese New Year, or Spring Festival, will then inevitably fall after that celestial event at the conclusion of the ensuing twelfth. The upshot of the intercalations of these two congruent, lunisolar systems is that, for most years, the first night of Sukkot will also concur with Mid-Autumn Festival.

Revival, Return, or Retreat

Less than a kilometer south of the Bianjing Hotel—eponymous with the name of Kaifeng when it served as the capital of the Northern Song—is the narrow *hutong* of Caoshi Jie. Unlike the Economic and Technological Development Zone in the northern part of the city where my hotel was situated, the infrastructure in this dilapidated quarter seemed barely adequate: an odor from the sewers, a peculiar amalgam of ammonia and onions, capped the discordant mix of tobacco smoke, fresh mutton, and roasted *shaobing* (flatbreads) permeated the lane.

Just prior to the turnoff where the new Kaifeng Jewish community center was located, the steeple of a church further down the road came into view. Simultaneously, on the corner on my right, a sign with Arabic script proclaimed the location of one of the neighborhood's two mosques. That the contemporary Kaifeng Jews should find themselves in such close proximity to the representatives of the two fraternal monotheistic faiths reflects a certain historical irony. The affinity of Judaism and Islam sufficed, at least from the standpoint of the host

Han culture, to subsume any conception of distinctiveness of the Kaifeng *Yicileye* (or "Israelites")—the eponymous epithet cited in the synagogal stelae.[6] Instead, they were deemed a sub-sect of the Hui, earning them the sobriquet of "Blue Hat Hui-Hui" (*lanmao huihui*). By contrast, whereas the Hui Muslims served as a camouflage to Sino-Judaic identity, it was the Church that proved instrumental in revealing it to the Western world. Through a chance encounter in 1605 in Beijing, Cardinal Matteo Ricci "discovered" the first Kaifeng Jew, Ai Tian.[7] Subsequent missions of Jesuits over the century that followed conveyed detailed information of the religious practice, synagogal structure, and unique customs of the Yicileye. Later, at its cultural nadir with the destruction of the synagogue by flooding in 1849, it was largely Protestant missionaries who informed the West of the effective dissolution of Chinese-Jewish culture in Kaifeng. The latter also managed to purchase the waning community's Torah scrolls and Hebrew manuscripts, now displayed in various museums in the United States, the United Kingdom, and Canada.[8]

The new center is located at the end of a narrow, unpaved passageway off of the main *hutong*. I entered through an open, metallic door into a small courtyard paved with cement tiles, adorned with a fig tree on the northern wall and a pomegranate tree at its southern flank. In the middle of the courtyard, verged by the two trees, a large sukkah had been set up. It had been constructed in an imaginative engineering feat, binding a complex arrangement of long bamboo poles with steel wire fastened to a rooftop peg for support. A stretch of tarpaulin had been wrapped around this structure for the walls,

---

6   The Kaifeng stelae of 1489 and 1512 are currently on display for private viewing in the Kaifeng Municipal Museum. The stele dated 1663 was lost. Père Jean-Paul Gozani, who arrived in Kaifeng in 1698 and lived there intermittently for over twenty years, is credited with producing rubbings of the synagogal stelae, now preserved in the Vatican library.

7   X. Xu, *The Jews of Kaifeng China: History, Culture and Religion* (Jersey City: Ktav Publishing House, 2003), 1–3; M. Pollak, *Mandarins, Jews, and Missionaries: The Jewish Experience in the Chinese Empire* (New York: Weatherhill, Inc., 1998), 3–5; D. D. Leslie, *The Survival of the Chinese-Jews: the Jewish Community of Kaifeng* (Leiden: E. J. Brill, 1972), 32–34.

8   Pollak, 163.

and branches cut from the courtyard trees had been placed atop a few crossbeams for the roofing. I was later informed that it had taken two men from the community all of twenty minutes to set up the entire edifice. Inside the sukkah, there were three long tables and a dozen or so stools, with more stacks lined up against the courtyard wall. While admiring the handiwork and reflecting on the novelty of a sukkah in remote Kaifeng, Barnaby Yeh stepped out of the foyer of the main building to greet me.

Barnaby, a 25-year-old Taiwanese-American and a convert to Judaism, is a more recent import to the anomalous culture of the Chinese-Jews. Although the Sino-Judaic Institute paid for his airfare and provides a modest stipend, Barnaby's assignment to Kaifeng was largely a personal initiative. Listing his religious affiliation on Facebook as "Blue Hat Hui-Hui," an indication of his ardent identification with the Kaifeng Sino-Judaic community, Barnaby was unswervingly dedicated to reviving the historical Yicileye culture in the lives of its latter-day progenies. For the prayer service of the festival later in the evening of my visit, he had designed and printed out a liturgy based on extant Hebrew manuscripts from the Kaifeng synagogue dating to the Ming period that he had arduously translated into Mandarin Chinese. Affiliated with an Orthodox Sephardic congregation in Washington D.C., where he had undergone his conversion, he advocated the restoration of the original Judeo-Persian traditions introduced to Kaifeng by its earliest Jewish inhabitants a millennium prior. Because of his Taiwanese passport, he had an easier time than other nationals in procuring a long-term Chinese visa and, ultimately, prospective residency. His determination was such that he viewed his mission in Kaifeng as an open-ended endeavor; he even envisioned the possibility of marriage and family within the context of the Kaifeng Jewish community. In spite of his dedication and idealism, he was quick to admit that the task of instilling Jewish knowledge and values in Kaifeng was an arduous one. With the lack of any local Jewish infrastructure, persistent community squabbles and uncertainty of their future, he had his mission cut out for him, but he felt well positioned to fulfill that charge.

Barnaby gave me a brief tour of the new premises of the two-story community center rented by Shavei Israel just a month before. The center brought together two factions, the Yicileye School, founded in 2002, and the more recent breakaway *Beit Hatikvah* (House of Hope), established in 2011. The grounds for that split were allegations of the missionary tendencies of the Yicileye School's originator, the American-Israeli student and self-confessed Messianic Jew, Tim Lerner.[9] However, Lerner has suggested ancillary issues of clan allegiances and financial management also contributed to the schism. The new property consisted of a kitchen and large storage area on the western flank of the courtyard. On the ground floor's eastern verge was an entry into the foyer—normally used on Friday evenings for communal meals and prayers—which led into a small den with a computer, where Skype classes with several overseas teachers were held on Sunday evenings. Barnaby was tentatively lodging on a cot in that room until he found his own place. Along the wall of an ascending stairwell was hung an array of black-and-white photos depicting various scenes of Jewish life in early twentieth-century Kaifeng. The stairs led up to a large hall, with a lectern and plaque, meant to serve as a larger synagogue for communal services, though it had yet to be utilized in that capacity. Outside its doorway, Barnaby had posted a sign requesting the removal of shoes prior to entering, an archaic Sephardic tradition no longer in vogue. A hotplate had been plugged into an outlet, and there was already a small pot of food prepared for the evening meal resting on its surface. Two windows looked down onto the courtyard, the one on the left partially obstructed by the network of bamboo poles attached to the rooftop. Adjacent to the hall was a guest bedroom with two beds where the envoy from Shavei, Eran Barzilai, and his travelling companion and fellow rabbinical student, Shmuel Avraham, were lodging.

Later that morning, I had the opportunity to speak with Eran, who, when I first arrived, had been out with his friend on a shopping expedition for the holiday. Eran's connection to the Kaifeng Jewish

---

9   Unlike normative Jewish theology which denies both the divine or messianic status of Jesus, Messianic Jews (or "Jews for Jesus") accept these as integral to a Messianic Jewish belief.

community predates his association with Shavei Israel. In September 2009, he had enrolled as a Chinese-language student in Henan University. Eschewing the top Chinese universities normally attended by foreigners, he felt that he would learn Chinese more rapidly in a place where foreign presence was minimal. More significant in his decision, however, was his fascination with Kaifeng's Jewish descendants. Shortly after his arrival, he took on the role as Hebrew teacher at the Yicileye School and developed a close rapport with individual families and the community as a whole during the two-year period of his studies. In the aftermath of the devastating Mount Carmel forest fire in Israel in late 2010, the group presented Eran with a sum in *renminbi* equivalent to US $300 to aid those affected by the catastrophe. Knowing that most of its members were employed as low-paid factory workers or laborers, he was deeply moved at their generous gesture. Upon his return to Israel, he began his religious exploration of Judaism in a rabbinical seminary, where he subsequently met Avraham. While in Jerusalem, he arranged a meeting to deliver the group's donation to Michael Freund, the chairman of Shavei Yisrael. Thus began his association with that organization and his ongoing engagement with the Kaifeng Jews.

Freund's generosity in funding the new location had paved the way for the successful merger of the previously divided community. Apart from Eran, Shavei also had sent three other envoys to Kaifeng for short teaching stints at Beit Hatikvah. However, as mentioned above and suggested by its name, the group's focal modus operandi was facilitating the immigration of young Kaifeng Jews to the Land of Israel. It was only there, according to Eran, that, after an adequate period of study and subsequent orthodox conversion, they could experience "a full Jewish life." In 1999, Shavei Israel, in conjunction with a group of Helsinki Christian Zionists, had first facilitated that experience for the family of Jin Guangyuan, a.k.a. Shlomo, following Jin's failed attempt that same year to have the certified Jewish status of his household registry card recognized by the Israeli Embassy.[10]

---

10 N. Urbach. "What prevented the reconstruction of the Chinese synagogue? Kaifeng Jews between revival and obliteration," in *Youtai-Presence and Perception*

(The upshot of this fiasco was a police order rescinding the Jewish listing on all the registry cards of the Kaifeng Jews.) The daughter of Shlomo and Dina Jin, Shalva, became the first Kaifeng Jew to officially convert in 2002.[11] In 2006, four girls in their early twenties arrived in Israel to study Hebrew and Jewish Studies at the Bat Ayin settlement in Gush Etzion; they formally converted the following year. Three years later, Shavei further facilitated the visas for a group of seven young men, who studied at Yeshivat Hamiftar in Efrat for three years, undergoing conversion by the rabbinate in early 2013. Two of the women, Shalva Jin and Rebecca Li, have married, the former to an Israeli and the latter to a Jewish-American; each has given birth to a child. The young men were enrolled in an *ulpan* (institute) for advanced Hebrew language study. One of them, Yakov Wang, intended to pursue rabbinical studies and, following ordination, to return to Kaifeng to become its first rabbi in nearly two hundred years. In our conversation that morning I asked Eran whether Shavei would consider expediting the immigration of the older members of the community. He did not believe that was a viable option, as the processes of language shift and cultural acclimatization would prove too onerous.

One of the questions I had prepared for the subsequent interviews was whether the *aliyah* of Kaifeng's younger populace posed a demographic threat to the community's continuity. In my mind, this certainly seemed to be the case. I was therefore surprised when not a single one of the twenty-two respondents shared my concern in this regard. Whether they suffered from a collective naïveté or whether I simply failed to grasp an aspect of Chinese mentality, the unanimous view was that the departure of a substantial portion of their young demographic was positive. Some proffered the opinion that, once they understood the intricacies of Judaism, they would return to Kaifeng to impart their knowledge to the locals; others suggested that regular visits to and from

---

of Jews and Judaism in China, ed. P. Kupfer (Frankfurt am Main: Peter Lang GmbH Internationaler Verlag der Wissenschaften, 2008), 123-124.

11 M. A. Ehrlich and P. Liang, "The contemporary condition of the Jewish descendants of Kaifeng," in *The Jewish-Chinese Nexus: A Meeting of Civilizations*, ed. M. A. Ehrlich (New York: Routledge, 2008), 294.

Israel would maintain their relationship with the community. A few spoke of the still younger generation of Kaifeng Jewish schoolchildren, who would be more knowledgeable of their heritage due to the integration of their older cohorts into Jewish life in Israel. Although claims have sometimes been made among a certain segment of academia, both Western and Chinese, that the cultural revival in Kaifeng is rooted in economic opportunism, none of those whom I interviewed expressed material gain as the main benefit of *aliyah*; rather, it was, as Eran had suggested, the ability to live a fully Jewish life.

When asked about the prospects for the future of its cultural revival in Kaifeng, however, the interviewees were less sanguine. While a few expressed the hope that a continued influx of foreign teachers would enable the perpetuation of some Jewish tradition in Kaifeng, there was a general consensus that the establishment of a veritable *jiaotang*, a place of worship, was necessary. There was general discontent over the revocation of their Jewish status in the household registry cards fourteen years earlier. Even though it was acknowledged that this status was in fact a quirk contradicted by the Han ethnicity listed on their national identity cards, they nonetheless felt its annulment denied them the religious privileges of their Christian and Muslim neighbors. Surprisingly, only a few of those interviewed were aware of an attempt by the Kaifeng municipality in 1996 to rebuild the ancient Kaifeng synagogue, albeit as a museum of Kaifeng Jewish history. The suspension of that project came amidst local and international rumors that it would lead to a reinvigorated Kaifeng Jewish culture. All of my respondents agreed, however, that the current government would not be amenable to any similar project in the foreseeable future.

In a discussion I had in 2011 with Nanjing University's Xu Xin, one of China's foremost experts on the Chinese Jews, I confronted him with my concerns over the shifting demographics with the departure of the Kaifeng community's younger members to Israel. Like the descendants themselves, he did not believe that continued emigration implied a threat to the autochthonous culture. Rather, he had opined that there would be two representative and interactive poles: a practicing, integrated Sino-Judaic culture in Israel and a traditional cultural mix maintained in Kaifeng.

Convergences, Incongruities, and the Question of Authenticity

After an afternoon nap in my hotel to recover from the red-eye flight of the previous evening, I returned to the center just after five o'clock, about an hour before the festival service would commence. To my surprise, the sukkah and courtyard were still in a state of disarray: the tables, covered with a thin layer of grime, were littered with dirty dishes and food scraps. The concrete floor of the courtyard was strewn with cigarette butts. I was deliberating picking up the broom perched against a corner beside the fig tree, when I heard the sound of a bicycle from the alleyway. It was Barnaby, carrying a bag with a stack of photocopies of the redacted Kaifeng Sukkot liturgy. With obvious exasperation, he complained that Eran had informed him at this late hour that there were not enough copies of his handouts for the expected gathering. Rather than make do with the center's numerous, donated Ashkenazi *siddurim* (prayer books) commonly used by the group, Barnaby had opted to make a last-minute run to photocopy extra handouts. (Paying out of pocket, he grumbled about the steep price of photocopying in Kaifeng.) He expressed further agitation that the Israeli guests had declined to use the kitchen utensils he had properly rendered kosher subsequent to his arrival several weeks prior, interpreting their religious stringency as an offensive form of Ashkenazi chauvinism.

A few minutes after Barnaby had gone inside to shower and change for the holiday, Peng Wenxia, who prefers to be called by her Hebrew name Neta, arrived by motorbike carrying a large basket full of food for dinner that evening. Neta, a board member of the former Beit Hatikvah, was arguably one of the most active participants in the community. A 48-year-old employed full time as a toll collector, Neta has embraced her Sino-Judaic identity with unparalleled zeal. Apart from three of the young adults who have spent their high school years in Israel, Neta is the most proficient in Hebrew literacy skills. In the Mishnah classes I had taught via Skype to a few of the most advanced Hebrew students, she was the most diligent, memorizing and reciting complex passages of classical Hebrew with relative ease. Ironically, Neta's link to Sino-Judaic identity derives solely from her marriage to You Yong (or *Yoel*) whose maternal grandfather was a Li, one of the seven clan names that mark the identity of Kaifeng's Jewish descendants.[12]

Neta was pleased to see me and from her basket of tasty goodies handed me a spinach dumpling, or *jiaozi*, as a sampling from the impending feast. Although the celebratory holiday feasts usually included some dishes of beef or chicken, purchased from the local *halal* butchers (the most akin to kosher), aware of my requirements from my first visit, the women took extra care to provide me with portions of vegetarian cuisine. Neta took her basket and hurriedly retired to the kitchen, just as Gao Chao and his wife Bai Xiaojuan arrived in the courtyard, each on separate motorbikes similarly laden with cartons of food. Gao Chao is the only male member of the adult community who can read and speak some Hebrew. As such, he functioned as the *chazzan*, or cantor, leading the congregation in prayer. Many of the traditional melodies he employed, invariably of East European origin, were garnered from YouTube clips. Because of his prominent role in the community's affairs, I had erroneously assumed his lineage was as an illustrious male descendant from the Gao clan. However, earlier that morning, Barnaby had informed me that Gao also had "married in." It was through his wife, Bai Xiaojuan, or Levana, whose paternal great-grandfather was a Zhao, that Gao Chao enjoyed his current status within the community. No doubt, that status had been further cemented with his decision to undergo a circumcision procedure at the local hospital.

Neta and Gao Chao were not the only ones whose association with Jewishness derived through matrimony. Contrary to the idiom that is prevalent in the Western Jewish Diaspora of "marrying out"—where a Jew is perceived to have eroded her/his identity through

---

12 Of the seven clan names Ai, Gao, Jin, Li, Shi, Zhang and Zhao, the Li are today the most numerous. Apart from Zhang Xingwang (a.k.a. Moshe Zhang), who is regarded as a Hui imposter, there are no other known present-day members of the Zhang clan and none with a lineage traceable to the Gao.

intermarriage—exactly half of the contemporary wedded Kaifeng Jews, both male and female, have "married in" to that identity. (Today, there are no married couples of whom both are of Kaifeng Jewish descent.) Although research into the historical Yicileye noted their practice of patrilineal descent as the marker of Jewish identity, a custom that ultimately precluded their recognition by mainstream orthodoxy, that practice is no longer the marker of contemporary Sino-Judaic identity.[13] Interestingly, Chinese academics still give some credence to this historical marker, one that is confluent with the familial hierarchy in Confucianism, in authenticating the status of the present-day Kaifeng Jews.[14] For example, Chinese scholars tend to view Shi Lei, a licensed tour guide for Jewish heritage tours of China, and, more importantly, a male descendant from the Shi clan, as one of the few "genuine" Kaifeng Jews. Whether because of his adherence to the state's guidelines on the purely historical context of Sino-Judaic culture, or because of his busy touring schedule (or both), Shi is one of those Jewish descendants who have remained disengaged from the local revival of Sino-Judaic cultural identity.[15] He has, however, lectured abroad on the Kaifeng community's long history. In successfully packaging Sino-Judaic identity in the historical and touristic framework acquiescent to government policy, he has become the main reference point for Chinese scholars as well as for most foreign tourists. Of course, in terms of the Israeli Rabbinate's orthodox criteria of Jewish identity, there is no difference between Shi Lei and an

---

13 Leslie, 103.
14 Xu Xin, for example, in a discussion about the cultural activism of Guo Yan, who sources her Jewish identity through her maternal grandfather, pointed out that she was "not really Jewish" (personal conversation, October 8, 2013).
15 Shi Lei could not be reached to arrange an interview during my most recent fieldwork. In 2011, while researching my Honors thesis, I conducted a telephone interview with him. Guo Yan, another independent activist who interacts with local tourism from the Zhao family homestead adjacent to the site of the ancient synagogue, was in Hong Kong studying restauranteering during this period of fieldwork. She had previously granted me an extensive video interview in 2011.

ethnic Han who has "married in" to the community: neither is recognized as Jewish.[16]

Bai Xiaojuan, together with her younger sister, Bai Ying, had begun to clean up the tables and floor of the sukkah. Despite their protests, I grabbed an extra broom and assisted with sweeping the butt-strewn tiles. By 6:30, about twenty-five people had arrived and had begun filing into the sukkah, seating themselves on the stools set up along both sides of the U-shaped table arrangement. Barnaby distributed the copies of the traditional Kaifeng liturgy he had so diligently reproduced. On this occasion, due to variations in the holiday liturgy, Barnaby filled in for Gao Chao as chazzan with most of the group joining in a chorus of the melodic hymns that were also recited in their usual Friday night services; they also recited in unison the Chinese translation of a few of the main blessings. Compared to the service I had participated in at the Beit Hatikvah two years earlier, this one was more subdued, perhaps due to their unfamiliarity with some parts of the festival service or with the text in the handouts.

After the services were over, there was a flurry of activity, mainly of the women, to set the tables for the meal. All sorts of dishes were brought out from the kitchen—some served on the center's crockery, some on plastic throwaways—and placed on the tables in the sukkah. There was steamed bass with cabbage; marinated tofu and chilies; bok choy with garlic, honey, and soy; stir-fried spinach with chilies and Sichuan pepper; and several other recipes with unidentifiable ingredients. There were also a few dishes of braised, halal chicken feet distributed here and there across the lavish spread. Neta had set several vegetable and tofu platters close together, gesturing to me where I should take my seat, although the others were still busying themselves with preparations. Eran approached me and, speaking in Hebrew, offered to share their kosher meal with me. Apparently, Eran and Shmuel had brought kosher meat and new utensils from Shanghai. They had prepared enough food and welcomed me to join them at the

---

16 This fact has not prevented Shi Lei on his website from declaring himself "China's only Jewish Chinese tour guide" (http://jewishchinatours.com/tours/, accessed February 2, 2014).

head of the table. I voiced concern that, as I had always eaten the vegetarian dishes specially prepared for me in the past, I might cause offense if I now spurned that generosity by opting to eat thekosher food instead. He assured me that that would not be the case; despite his lack of religious observance during his student days in Kaifeng, the community displayed great respect to his present adherence to stricter kashrut standards. I thanked him but politely declined his offer.

Once everyone had seated themselves at the tables, Shmuel, wearing a dark suit and black fedora, filled his goblet with the kosher wine brought from Shanghai; the rest of the community, myself included, received small plastic cups filled from a spouted vat with homemade wine that Gao Chao had made with the help of a few others. Raising his cup, Shmuel proceeded to recite the festival kiddush, inflected with the Ashkenazi phonation, from his place at the head of the table. The kiddush and the special blessing for observing the commandment of dwelling in the sukkah were followed by the ritual hand washing before a meal. There was some commotion in the search for water faucets for the ritual hand washing preceding the breaking of bread; some went to the kitchen, others to the laundry and bathroom, while several used a large basin and cup brought out to the courtyard and situated just outside the sukkah. Finally, when everyone was again seated silently at the table, Shmuel made the blessing over two loaves of *challot* (also imported from Shanghai), then tore off two large pieces for Eran's and his consumption; he broke off several more small morsels which were distributed to the others. The *challah* had not fared well on its journey from Shanghai, particularly in the hot weather; it was stale and tasteless. Fortunately, Levana and her mother appeared in the sukkah with freshly baked *mantou* buns, served to all of the company, with the exception of the Israelis.

The meal was a gustatory smorgasbord of exquisite variety. Gao Chao and Li Bo, the most culturally active scion of the Li clan, soon appeared at the table carrying small ceramic jugs; each began tipping the limpid liquid contents into the men's plastic cups. Gao came to my place and with a knowing smile said, "*Ni xihuan he baiju ma?*" (*You like to drink rice wine, right?)* I nodded as he filled up my cup to the brim. I had learned from previous visits how *baijiu* was an essential feature—at least for those of male gender—in these social gatherings. Gao Chao, seated at the head table with Eran and Shmuel, raised his glass and gave the Hebrew toast: *L'chaim!* I raised mine in return and, in honor of Mid-Autumn Festival, offered the Chinese tribute *"Gan bei!"* downing the contents in a few gulps. The fiery fluid burned a path down my throat and esophagus, its inebriating fumes quickly dissipating upward to my brain. Feeling quite content, I helped myself to more tofu and chilies, listening to the background chatter of the women, punctuated with loud, raucous bursts of laughter from the men, joking around in the local dialect I could hardly fathom.[17] As soon as I had finished my drink, Li Bo was quick to refill my glass.

The apparition of a beaming Neta suddenly appeared before me holding a platter of delectable *yuebing*, or moon cookies. She pointed up toward the branches that formed the sukkah roof. She reminded me that it was customary to gaze at the full moon, now visibly rising above the rooftop, on the Mid-Autumn Festival. I nodded and looked up at the stars—which, according to *Halacha* (Jewish law), were meant to be visible through the sukkah's covering—and the ascending moon, which tonight seemed very large with a golden hue. Feeling a bit giddy from the liquor, I suddenly became aware of the bizarre situation of observing the Torah commandment of dwelling in the sukkah in far-flung Kaifeng while simultaneously celebrating the ancient Mid-Autumn Festival. During the course of the evening there were a lot of comings and goings in the center's courtyard. At one point, I counted forty heads; there were also a few curious neighbors who, upon hearing the din of the festivities, had entered the courtyard to get a closer glimpse of the celebrations. I wondered what they thought of Chinese men wearing

---

17 The tones in Kaifeng dialect are completely different than those in standard Mandarin or *Putonghua*. The rule of thumb is that Mandarin first tone becomes second tone in Kaifeng dialect; second becomes fourth; third becomes first; and fourth becomes third. Considering that tonal recognition and vocalization are among the more difficult aspects of Mandarin Chinese, the Kaifeng dialect poses problems for most foreign students.

yarmulkes or of the crowd huddled together under the peculiar shelter of the sukkah.

While Eran circulated among the crowd, chatting with old acquaintances, Shmuel Avraham sat alone at the head table, stroking his full beard and grinning broadly (he had also drunk his share of baijiu). He had earlier informed me that his visit to Kaifeng was for him a transit point to Southeast Asia, where he was to spend a few weeks supervising the *kashrut* (kosher certification) of food production in several factories.[18] Eran had introduced him to the group as "*labi*" or "rabbi," an appellation that boosted their self-identification as Jews and concurrently provided them with an exemplar of that coveted identity. Other rabbis representing different denominations and divergent views had made previous pilgrimages to Kaifeng. Shmuel was possibly the first *haredi*, or ultra-orthodox rabbi, to make that journey. In Israel the *haredim*, who had adopted a rigorous view of matrilineal descent, had vociferously protested the bestowal of Jewish status under the Law of Return to the Ethiopian Jews as well as to Russian immigrants of paternal descent.[19] I wondered what Shmuel thought of this throng of Chinese people emulating Jewish customs, and, conversely, how the group would view this bearded man in black coat and hat, a model of a Judaism quite unlike what they were accustomed to. Furthermore, looking around the sukkah and courtyard, I considered how the marker of authenticity of Sino-Judaic cultural identity, once embedded in paternal clan lineage, had dramatically shifted. More than half of those present for the festival celebrations staked their claim of Jewishness in either maternal or paternal clan lineage, that link sometimes regressing three or four generations; every one of this group had been informed

---

18 For more comprehensive study of kashrut supervision in China refer to M. A. Ehrlich, *Jews and Judaism in Modern China* (New York: Routledge, 2010).
19 Rather than reiterating the Jewish law of matrilineal descent, Israel's Law of Return reflected the criteria employed in Nazi Germany's Nuremberg Laws, in which any trace of ancestral Jewish blood sufficed for Jewish identity. The rationale was that anyone considered Jewish enough for the Nazi death camps should be afforded the protection provided by the State of Israel. Unlike Orthodox Judaism, Reform Judaism advocates bilineal descent, i.e. that a Jewish mother or father is the standard for Jewish identity.

as a child as to their Jewish heritage and the prohibition of consuming pork. The other half were the male or female spouses to one of those bloodline descendants.

Historical Memory and Contemporary Practice

The last recorded interviews of Kaifeng's Jewish descendants took place in August 1985. Dr. Wendy Abraham of Stanford University conducted these interviews, which are currently stored in Stanford's Hoover Institute Archives.[20] According to the SJI website, Abraham "travelled to Kaifeng to gather oral histories from six of the heads of Kaifeng Jewish clans…before being arrested and expelled."[21] Although the political situation in Kaifeng regarding the Jewish descendants had evolved somewhat since 1985, one still had to exercise a measure of caution and discretion in any dealings with the Sino-Judaic community. Apart from any residual political constraints regulating contacts with the Kaifeng Jews, in China there appeared to be a generic cultural reluctance, particularly among those old enough to remember the tumult of the Cultural Revolution, to go on record verbally with personal opinions on politically sensitive issues. The more recent proliferation of online blogging and social media in China was gradually mitigating this perspective, but provincial Kaifeng lagged far behind metropolitan Beijing or Shanghai in this emergent cultural awareness. For these reasons, I had set myself the modest goal of obtaining twelve to fifteen interviews as a sampling of

---

20 W. Abraham, "Memories of Kaifeng Jewish descendants today: historical significance in light of observations by Westerners since 1605," in *The Jews of China, Volume One: Historical and Comparative Perspectives*, ed. J. Goldstein (Armonk, New York: M. E. Sharpe, Inc., 1999), 81.

21 "About the Sino-Judaic Institute," Sino-Judaic Institute, accessed July 17, 2014, http://www.sino-judaic.org/index.php?page=about__us. The depiction of this event by Ehrlich and Liang (2008, 287) as a kind of commando raid, in which "…dozens of police officers, both plain-clothed and uniformed, were posted around the hotel," has been disputed by Dr. Abraham. She has described their portrayal of those events as "totally inaccurate" and "incredibly irresponsible scholarship" (W. Abraham, personal communication August 4, 2011). She would not, however, disclose to me a detailed account of the actual events surrounding her detainment, as she was in the process of transcribing these to her memoirs.

the active members of a group whose numbers probably did not exceed one hundred.[22] Prior to my arrival, I had emailed Gao Chao requesting that he speak to other members of the community to begin organizing interviews, but he maintained he had not had the opportunity to do so.

I arrived back at the center the next morning and performed the ritual waving of the lulav and etrog, using the set Eran and Shmuel had brought from Israel. Afterwards, I joined the two Israelis for a coffee in the sukkah and asked Shmuel for his impressions of the previous evening. He replied that he had enjoyed himself immensely and found it to be an uplifting experience. The exotic trail of history which had brought Jews to China and preserved their conviction in their Jewish identity fascinated him. This soon led into a discussion of matrilineal descent; I shared with them my hypothesis that the original Jewish settlers to Kaifeng may not have been aware of the historical shift from patrilineal to matrilineal descent, which only proliferated with the redaction of the Mishnah in the second century CE and publication of the Talmud later on in the fourteenth. Shmuel replied that, according to the Talmud, matrilineal descent had been the practice since the receiving of the Torah at Sinai. I argued that this was but one of many Talmudic anachronisms. Furthermore, scripture was replete with genealogies of Israelite men marrying foreign women whose children were likewise deemed Israelite. Scholarly research, particularly the work of Harvard's Shaye J. D. Cohen, argued convincingly for the relatively late origins, in the Hellenistic and Roman occupations, of the gradual switchover.[23] The early Kaifeng Jewish settlers had for centuries invested heavily into maintaining a synagogue and sustaining their

---

22 According to Tim Lerner, the engine behind the former Yicileye School, this was the number of Kaifeng Jews who participated in the Passover Seder of 2010, which was held in a Kaifeng restaurant. The actual number of those who might claim Jewish descent is undoubtedly more, with estimates ranging from five hundred to two thousand. Some of the descendants claim that because of political sensitivities, some who would otherwise claim Jewish descent might not record this fact in the national census forms.

23 S. J. D. Cohen, *The Beginnings of Jewishness: Boundaries, Varieties, Uncertainties* (Berkeley: University of California Press, 1999), 273.

traditions. Would they have done so, I wondered aloud, knowing that their practice of "marrying out" was excluding them from that very identity they struggled so assiduously to keep? We had moved into an uncomfortable zone in our discussion; Shmuel mechanically rejected any argument that exposed the fallibility of the Talmudic sages. We managed to shift the subject to less controversial territory, and, after finishing my drink, I returned to the New Century.

The following evening was the next gathering at the community center for the Friday night *Kabbalat Shabbat* services, again conducted outdoors in the sukkah. About twenty-five Kaifeng Jews were in attendance; prior to the service, the women lit Shabbat candles inside the foyer. Gao Chao performed as chazzan, generating greater group participation than on the first night of the festival. After the prayers ended, a few of the elders offered the customary Sabbath blessing to their offspring in attendance, the former placing their hands on the latter's heads and reciting the traditional scriptural passages. Li Xiurong, or Aviv, offered the blessing to her Han daughter-in-law, Neta.[24]

The fare that evening was not quite equal in either variety or quantity to the first night, but I was yet again presented with several tasty vegetarian dishes. Unexpectedly, and without my asking him to do so, Gao Chao stood up in the middle of the meal and announced that I had come to Kaifeng for fieldwork on my thesis on the revival of Kaifeng Jewish cultural identity, urging those present to contact me to arrange for an interview. As he spoke, I tried to gauge the crowd reaction to his exhortation. If there was indeed any enthusiasm at his suggestion, it was all but imperceptible. Milling about during the meal, I had managed to secure a date on Sunday morning to separately interview Gao Chao and his wife Levana at the community center. As Neta's work schedule precluded any availability for the coming week, she invited me to join her at her in-laws' home for interviews followed by dinner the following Monday. Shortly afterward, a newcomer whom I had not previously

---

24 Li's biological daughter, You Qing (Sarah), one of the original advanced students from my Mishnah class, had moved to New York several months prior. A divorcée, she was working in the beautification industry to support her son's college tuition.

met approached me for an interview. His name was Li Feng, a nephew to Li Xiurong. As he was leaving early Sunday morning for Shanghai, where he would be stationed on business for the next month, we organized an interview at my hotel for Saturday evening. As I was saying my good-byes, a middle-aged woman also from the Li clan, another one of Li Feng's aunts, approached me to do an interview at the center on Sunday afternoon.[25] Following those first three interviews on Sunday, the ice was broken: rather than having to solicit volunteers, I began receiving requests for participation. In the end, I was able to conduct interviews with twenty-two members of the community.

In general, as mentioned above regarding the perpetuation of Sino-Judaic culture in both Israel and Kaifeng, on most questions there was a uniformity of opinions. However, there was some divergence of opinion on the question of whether Confucianism was compatible with Judaism. A few of the respondents suggested that monotheistic belief and the notion of inviolable precepts in Judaism were irreconcilable with the pragmatic, earthly concerns of Confucian thought. Most of them, however, while acknowledging those differences, believed that in practice both systems shared many confluent values. These elements of cultural syncretism included respect for elders, honoring of parents, the centrality of scholarship, participation in ritual, and conducting relationships with humaneness and benevolence.

The widest discrepancies, however, came in response to the question as to what factors were optimal for the personal development of their Jewish identity. On the one hand, most of the participants, particularly the more active members, tended to emphasize factors related to practice: Hebrew language skills, scriptural knowledge, prayer services conducted in an actual synagogue, development of monotheistic belief, and the posting in Kaifeng of a Chinese-speaking rabbi and/or Jewish studies teachers. Practice in this regard is defined as an emulation of tradition rather than any strict observance of Halacha. By contrast, several of the respondents did not consider practice as a significant feature in their sense

---

25 The Li clan form the overwhelming majority of the Kaifeng Jewish community. Ten out of the twenty-two interviewees had the surname Li.

of cultural identity; to this group, the all-important factor was the study of Kaifeng Jewish history. Those who espoused this latter view were less engaged with concrete aspects of the revival of cultural identity such as prayer services or Judaica classes. Moreover, they were uniformly males bearing the Li clan patronymic.

While the purview of the interviews was not to establish any statistical or causative evidence, anecdotally, it would appear that those at the forefront of contemporary practice are generally those more removed from any patrilineage. These are either descendants through the maternal line bearing the surnames of Han fathers or the Han spouses of any bloodline posterities. For a Han woman marrying a male with Sino-Judaic ancestry, the adoption of his customs would not be dissimilar to the phenomenon that occurred during the early Jewish settlement in Kaifeng. Patrilocality, after all, was a prominent facet of traditional Chinese culture, which is still extant in some families. More puzzling to me was the opposite scenario, as in the case of Gao Chao, in which a Han male "marries in" to a Jewish identification through a female descendant. In 2011, I had the opportunity to discuss this anomaly with Dr. Zhang Yingchun, an expert on traditional Chinese philosophy at Zhejiang University. She explained that although the adoption of a husband's customs and ancestral line was indeed the Confucian norm, in exceptional circumstances, when the wife's ancestral line was perceived to be particularly prestigious, that custom could be inverted. This hypothesis might be supported with the perception of esteem derived from the mythos of the Yicileye, who hailed from a faraway land to which their future offspring were to one day return. Furthermore, despite the relatively recent introduction of the term *youtai*, or "Jew," into the Chinese lexicon, the inflated Judeophilia that is so pervasive in China today may also be a contributing aspect to the formation of such a view.[26] Regardless of the veracity of the hypothesis, ancestor veneration remains a prominent facet of Chinese culture; the discursive subtext of collective

---

26 Urbach, 134.

memory thus underscores and connects both polarities of practice and history.[27]

The most prominent spokesman advocating Sino-Judaic identification through history was Kaifeng businessman Li Wei. Although Li is illiterate in Hebrew and seldom attends Friday night services, he takes great pride in his Jewish identity. When I had finished questioning him for the interview, he requested that I again turn on the recorder so that he could launch into a twenty-minute oration on the history of the Kaifeng Jews (most of which was superfluous to the interview's intent). He maintained that in light of the small numbers of the community, intermarriage, rather than a prerogative, was in fact an imperative preventing genetic abnormalities in their offspring. In parrying the charge of "assimilation," a term at which many in the group took umbrage, he pointed out how Mongols or Manchus who intermarried with the Han majority lost any sense of their ethnic roots after two or three generations. The Kaifeng Jews, by contrast, had managed to preserve their unique identity for over a thousand years.

As mentioned above, it is the historical framework that is acceptable to the Chinese government. According to the policy on the Kaifeng Jews known unofficially as "the three nos" (*san bu yuanze*), there is no such entity as a present-day Kaifeng Jew.[28] The history of the Yicileye presence in China's past, however, is openly acknowledged and frequently referenced in op-eds published in the Israeli media by Chinese diplomats. The issue of practice, however, is more ambiguous. While Judaism is practiced for the benefit of Jewish expats in a few of China's major cities, a Kaifeng Jew is prohibited from taking part in these rituals or even entering the synagogues in which they are conducted, lest the rabbis of these congregations be in breach of the law forbidding proselytization.

---

27 J. D. Paper, *The Theology of the Chinese-Jews, 1000–1850* (Waterloo, ONT: Wilfrid Laurier University Press, 2012), 79–80.

28 Urbach 2008, 98. "The three nos" are: 1) Judaism is not an official religion in China; 2) Jews are not a recognized ethnicity; 3) there are currently no Kaifeng Jews.

Although the 1953 policy statement, approved by Mao Zedong and other top leaders, denied minority status to the Kaifeng Jews, it also attached a nebulous injunction to the local municipality to be "more caring for them in various activities" (Xu 2008, 205). The prayer services, Hebrew classes, and holiday celebrations are generally permitted in this ambiguous context, although periodic government reaction—usually in the form of intensified police surveillance—has occurred in the wake of any seeming transgression of a rather tenuous boundary. Moreover, in the past decade, the community has become more adept at negotiating, and thereby extending, the parameters of the cultural identification permitted to them.

Conclusion

My fieldwork in Kaifeng has led me to conclude that the attribution of the revival of Sino-Judaic cultural identity to *homo economicus* is a reductive observation based on faulty assumptions as to the meaning of "Jewishness" in the context of Kaifeng. While its association with foreign NGOs had undoubtedly provided certain material benefits to the community—scholarships, seminars, and primarily the facilitation of *aliyah*—these fail to convey the full picture of the renewal of Sino-Judaic identification. Ultimately, identity is a subjective experience that no objective observation or deduction can accurately capture. It is only through shared conversations and encounters that it is possible to glean the contours of what that identity signifies to its subjects. Anyone who has heard the enthusiasm in Neta's voice when she sings *Hatikvah*, the national anthem of Israel; seen the joyful expression of Gao Chao leading the group in a rendition of a traditional melody; or witnessed the tears in the eyes of Levana's Han mother, Zhang Xiuying, as she attests to the healing power of faith, would be able to fathom that an occurrence transcending material advantage is taking place. Internal factors—unmeasurable through mere observation—such as ancestral veneration, clan lineage, shared ritual, traditional practices, and historical memory have generated what Durkheim refers to as "collective effervescence."

Before my very first visit to Kaifeng in 2009, I met with Avrum Ehrlich, who was then a professor at Shandong University. He had recently conducted a seminar at the university for the descendants and had also visited with the group in Kaifeng. We had arranged a meeting over coffee in Beijing at the Sanlitun Starbucks to discuss his observations of the community. Prior to our farewells, he gave me parting—if paradoxical—words of advice: *Remember*, he said, *they are Jewish because they are Confucian*. Despite the various global influences and perspectives on Jewish identity extending to Kaifeng, in the end, it was impossible to extricate the identification of its Jewishness from the matrices of Chinese culture.

Sino-Judaic identity remains an amorphous mix of unresolved dichotomies, poised between irreconcilable oppositions. On the one hand, the choices they confront seem to coincide with those of Jews everywhere: whether their future lies in a return to the ancestral homeland of their Yicileye forebears or in preservation of a millennium of historical presence in China; whether the determination of their Jewishness is imposed by an external standard of Jewish law or by standards developed organically within local cultural contexts; and whether pursuing that identity entails an increase in traditional practices or an appreciation of the links to a historical past. Yet, the dynamic resolution of these generic conundrums, and the new ambiguities thus produced, are uniquely Chinese phenomena. In fact, fluidity and ambiguity are hardly novel to the Kaifeng Jews. They were not only conspicuous aspects of the ancient Yicileye culture but, more fundamentally, adaptations that enabled its preservation for a thousand years. While it cannot be predicted with certainty what the future holds in store for today's Kaifeng Jews, there is a palpable sense that, despite the many uncertainties, they will not easily be deterred from further developing their cultural identity.

Understanding of the Bible among the General Public in Mainland China: A Survey on the "Bullet Curtain" of *The Bible*[1]

MENG ZHENHUA
Nanjing University

Introduction

Many people believe that the Hebrew Bible/Old Testament is the most significant and influential contribution of the Jews to world civilizations. The New Testament, although mainly a Christian canon, was also written primarily by Jewish authors. However, compared with the millions of Chinese Christians, there are very few Chinese Jews, most of whose identity may not be recognized either by China or world Jewry. Judaism does not have official recognition in China, and Jews have never been as zealous as Christians to propagate among gentiles, and all of the current whole Bible translations into Chinese were made by Christians. Therefore, Chinese people are usually under the impression that the Bible is solely a Christian book. When Jewish stories are read and interpreted in a Christian way, readers' reception (or rejection) of the

---

[1] This paper is supported by Humanity and Social Science Youth Foundation Research Project of Ministry of Education of China (No. 12YJC752025) and the MOE Project of Key Research Institute of Humanities and Social Sciences at Universities (No. 13JJD730004). This is a revised version of an essay published in *Yearbook of Chinese Theology*, ed. Paulos Huang (Leiden: Brill, 2015).

Bible is inevitably related to Christianity, and the issue of understanding has aroused considerable academic interest.

In 1996, *Biblical Interpretation* published a series of articles that discuss how the Chinese read and interpret the Bible.[2] In June of the same year, an international workshop titled "The Bible in Modern China: The Literary and Intellectual Impact" was held in Jerusalem. More than twenty scholars from Asia, Europe, and North America participated. The proceedings of the workshop were published in 1999[3] in three parts, namely "Translation of the Bible," "Reception of the Bible," and "Appropriation of the Bible." Most of the essays in this collection discuss the history of the Chinese translations of the Bible, the strategies of the interpreters, the controversies resulting from the translations, and the appropriation of the Bible particularly in modern Chinese literature. The part entitled the "Reception of the Bible" contains two essays: the first discusses the life and work of He Jinshan (Ho Tsun-Sheen), a Chinese assistant to James Legge,[4] and the second discusses the Bible translations into Miao, the dialect of an ethnic minority, in the twentieth century.[5] In 2004, Marián Gálik, a Slovakian literary comparatist and sinologist, published *Influence, Translation, and Parallels: Selected Studies on the Bible in China*,[6] in which he points out the significance of the Christian Bible as a source for writing in China and analyzes the different ways by which several famous Chinese writers have appropriated biblical text in their works. In 2007, a conference titled "Reading Christian Scriptures in China" was held in Oxford,

---

2 Antoinette Wire, "Chinese Biblical Interpretation since Mid-Century," *Biblical Interpretation* 4 (1996): 101–123; Chenfang Lo, "Chinese Biblical Interpretation in the Eyes of a Chinese Christian," *Biblical Interpretation* 4 (1996): 124–126; Pui-Lan Kwok, "Chinese Christians and Their Bible," *Biblical Interpretation* 4 (1996): 127–129.

3 Irene Eber, Sze-kar Wan, and Knut Walf, eds., *Bible in Modern China: The Literary and Intellectual Impact* (Sankt Augustin, Germany: Institut Monumenta Serica, 1999).

4 Lauren Pfister, "A Transmitter but not a Creator: Ho Tsun-Sheen (1817–1871), the First Modern Chinese Protestant Theologian," *Bible in Modern China*, 165–198.

5 Joakim Enwall, "The Bible Translations into Miao: Chinese Influence versus Linguistic Autonomy," *Bible in Modern China*, 199–234.

6 Marián Gálik, *Influence, Translation and Parallels: Selected Studies on the Bible in China* (Sankt Augustin, Germany: Institut Monumenta Serica, 2004).

and several Chinese scholars were invited to present their theses. The proceedings were published in 2008[7] and include studies on the understanding, reception, and interpretation of the Bible by various groups and individuals from different periods. Several articles provide a panoramic view, whereas others focus on case studies. This collection represents an advanced research level in the field. Apart from the three books mentioned previously, several single articles in Chinese periodicals also investigate the understanding and reception of the Bible among different Chinese readers.[8]

The academic studies of Chinese and international researchers on the understanding and reception of the Bible among the Chinese have covered several periods, ranging from the late sixteenth century to the twenty-first century, and have shown the encounter in the fields of religion, literature, and politics, among many others. However, previous studies appear to be weak in two aspects. First, despite the numerous studies on the history of biblical understanding and interpretation in China, only a few have investigated the contemporary situation. Second, the Chinese "readers" of the Bible selected for the studies were usually limited to certain groups or individuals.

Among the sixteen essays (including the introduction) included in *Bible in Modern China*, Liang Gong's essay summarizing the achievement of studies on Chinese biblical literature[9] is the only work directly related to contemporary biblical reading. In the selected studies of

---

7 Chloë Starr, ed., *Reading Christian Scriptures in China* (New York: T&T Clark, 2008).
8 Cf. Yang Huilin, "Bendihua haishi chujinghua: Hanyu yujing zhong de jidujiao quanshi" ["Localization" or "Contextualization": Christian Hermaneutics in Chinese Context], *Shijie Zongjiao Yanjiu* (January 2003): 64–74; You Bin, "Shengjing fanyi, wenzi chuangzhi yu shehui zhuanxing—yi Zhongguo xinan shaoshuminzu de shengjing jieshou weili" [Bible Translation, Literacy Creation, and Social Transformation: Taking the Bible Reception Among the Minorities in Southwest China as the Case Study], *Jidujiao Sixiang Pinglun* 6 (2007): 286–298; Liang Hui, "Cong Zhongguo jingxue chuantong chufa quanshi shengjing: Wu Leichuan jiedu shengjing de lichang he fangfa" [Interpretation of "Chinese Classics" of the Bible: The Stand and Methods of Wu Leichuan's Biblical Interpretation], *Shijie Zongjiao Yanjiu* (February 2013): 118–126.
9 Gong Liang, "Twenty Years of Studies of Biblical Literature in the People's Republic of China (1976–1996)," *Bible in Modern China*, 383–408.

Gálik, the literature review on Chinese biblical studies include work from the 1980s and early 1990s[10] and two essays discussing the relation between the works of Gu Cheng (a contemporary Chinese poet) and Wang Meng (a contemporary Chinese writer) to the Bible.[11] From the thirteen essays (including the introduction) of *Reading Christian Scriptures in China*, only two have actually mentioned contemporary biblical interpretations and studies.[12] In fact, several hermeneutical methods proposed by contemporary ethnical Chinese scholars have been noticed by international scholars and received feedback. These methods include the cross-textual hermeneutics proposed by Archie Lee and Kwok Pui-lan, which requires the reading of the Bible in the Asian (particularly Chinese) context and searches for biblical meanings from a non-biblical world;[13] "*bijiao jingxue*" [comparative scripture], initiated by Yang Huilin and You Bin, which attempts to integrate the Chinese scriptural traditions into the Judeo-Christian scriptural reasoning;[14] and "Sino-Christian academic biblical studies in the light of the globalized

---

10 "The Reception of the Bible in the Peoples' Republic of China (1980–1992). Observations of a Literary Comparatist," *Influence, Translation and Parallels*, 93–114.
11 "Gu Cheng's Novel *Ying'er* and the Bible," *Influence, Translation and Parallels*, 271–286; "Parody and Absurd Laughter in Wang Meng's Apocalypse. Musings over the Metamorphosis of the Biblical Vision in Contemporary Chinese Literature," *Influence, Translation and Parallels*, 315–326.
12 Frederik Fällman, "Hermeneutical Conflict? Reading the Bible in Contemporary China," *Reading Christian Scriptures in China*, 49–67; Zha Changping, "Studying the New Testament in the Chinese Academic World: A Survey, 1976-2006," *Reading Christian Scriptures in China*, 81–94.
13 Cf. Archie Lee, "Biblical Interpretation in Asian Perspective," *Asia Journal of Theology* 7 (1993): 35–39; "Identity, Reading Strategy and Doing Theology," *Biblical Interpretation* 9 (1999): 197–201; Archie Lee, ed, *Yazhou chujing yu shengjing quanshi* [Asian Context and Biblical Hermeneutics], (Hong Kong: Chinese Christian Literature Council, 1996); Kwok, Pui-lan, *Discovering the Bible in the Non-biblical World* (Maryknoll, NY: Orbis Books, 1995), with further literature.
14 Cf. Yang Huilin, "Zhongxi jingwen biandu de kenengxing jiqi jiazhi" [The Possibility and Potential Value of "Scriptural Reasoning" Involving China and the West], *Social Sciences in China* (2011.1):192–205; "Jingwen biandu yu quanshi de xunhuan" ["Scriptural Reasoning" and "Hermeneutical Circle"], *Journal of Renmin University of China* (2012.5): 8–15; You Bin, ed., *Bijiao jingxue* [Comparative Scripture], Vol. 1, 2, 3, (Beijing: Religious Culture Press, 2013, 2014), with further literature.

great national studies" by Paulos Huang.[15] Nevertheless, relevant theoretical studies and practices remain in the early stages and have not stirred sufficient academic attention. Many academics still prefer to focus on historical Chinese biblical readings and interpretations.

From studies of the "more popular" history of Chinese biblical understanding and reception to the "less popular" current situation, the subjects of scholarly biblical understanding, interpretation, and appropriation are usually limited to intellectuals with religious background, such as the famous Catholics in the late Ming and early Qing Dynasties, the Protestant theologians in the late Qing Dynasty or the Republic of China, and contemporary scholars and writers. Unfortunately, the reactions of ordinary readers have often been ignored.

The explanation behind this observed phenomenon is the ability of intellectuals to express their opinions through their academic, literary, and artistic works. Moreover, their power of discourse has enhanced the influence of their ideas during their time, while their publications at present provide academia with dependable objects to analyze. By contrast, ordinary readers are unable to express their views in the form of academic, literary, or artistic work. Non-academic media in contemporary China is also limited for several reasons. A few of the articles and essays mentioned above have more or less referred to the opinions of lay Christians on the Bible but hardly pay any attention to the understanding of non-religious groups. Although Christians are usually more enthusiastic about reading the Bible than non-Christians, the possibility that non-Christians do read and interpret the Bible should never be ignored or dismissed. In his essay reviewing biblical studies and publications in China, Frederik Fällman expresses his appreciation of the work of Feng Xiang,[16] a secular literature and law

---

15 Cf. Paulos Huang, *Daguoxue shiye zhong de hanyu xueshu shengjing xue* [Sino-Christian Academic Biblical Studies in the Light of the Globalized Great National Studies], (Beijing: Minzu Press, 2012).
16 Fällman, "Hermeneutical Conflict?" 49, 63; Feng Xiang, *Chuangshiji: chuanshuo yu yizhu* [Genesis: Legend with Translation and Annotation] (Nanjing: Jiangsu renmin, 2004). Feng has published a number of other commentaries with more essays on the Bible since then: Feng Xiang, *Moxi wujing* [Torah or the Five Books of Moses] (Hong Kong: Oxford University Press China Ltd., 2006); *Kuankuan*

scholar. Fällman concludes that "non-Christian readings of the Bible are also extremely interesting." He also points out that "the Bible is more and more becoming a text that anyone can read in China, and anyone can interpret."[17] However, similar to most scholars, Fällman primarily focuses on traditional publications and rarely pays attention to Bible readers who lack the ability and opportunity to write and publish books or articles.

In this regard, it is necessary to employ the research methods of the social sciences to examine the attitude of ordinary people toward the Bible. Scholars have conducted research on the rapid propagation of Christianity in mainland China in the past 35 years from various perspectives. Despite the significant achievement, these studies primarily focused on the number, composition, and distribution of Christians, the propagation of Christianity, the reception of Christian doctrines and the religious experience of believers, and the effect of the religion on religious and non-religious groups. Only a few studies put forth questions directly regarding the biblical text in their fieldwork and surveys.

However, how the general public in contemporary China understands the Bible deserves scholarly attention. Although the holy scripture of Judaism and Christianity has been widely disseminated in the Middle East and Europe in the past 2000 years, even reaching China as early as the pre-modern ages, the biblical religions never had a widespread following in Chinese society. Regardless of people coming to China with science and technology in the sixteenth and seventeenth centuries, with warships and cannons in the nineteenth century, and financial capital and political ideas in the modern ages, Christianity has always remained an alien culture that the majority of the Chinese population cannot wholeheartedly accept. Such an attitude toward Christianity is closely related to their attitude toward the

---

xinxiang yu Chu'aijiji [Letters to Kuankuan & Exodus] (Beijing: SDX Joint Publishing Company, 2007); *Zhihuishu* [The Books of Wisdom] (Hong Kong: Oxford University Press China Ltd., 2008); *Xin yu wang: Yuebo fuyin ji qita* [Faith and Oblivion: the Gospel of Job and Others] (Beijing: SDX Joint Publishing Company, 2012).

17   Fällman, "Hermeneutical Conflict?" 63.

Bible. Thus, it is important to identify which specific biblical texts and ideas influence them to accept or reject biblical religions. Given the long history of the Chinese and their rich culture and traditions, their understanding of the Bible is contextual and can be compared to that of the intellectuals. Such understanding, although usually neither systematic nor professional, may also enlighten the professional cross-textual and cross-cultural biblical hermeneutics.

Needless to say, conducting a survey on the understanding of the Bible by the Chinese public is a difficult task. The first concern is about defining "general public," as it will determine the sample selection process, particularly how to avoid the selection bias in terms of educational levels, areas, and religious faith. The survey should not be limited to the believers of Christianity because the percentage of non-Christians among the Chinese population is much higher. In addition, the willingness of respondents to cooperate with the investigator and express their true opinions affects the result of the survey. In a survey held in 2005 about the Christian faith and its effect on religious experience, the investigators claim that ordinary people clearly have no particular reasons "to shun the questions concerning their own religious faith…Therefore, self-description can be taken as an effective way for us to see the real situation of religious faiths."[18] In my personal experience distributing survey questionnaires during my teaching career in a secular university in mainland China in the past six years, despite the anonymity of the research instrument asking students about their personal religious background and views on the Bible, the reliability of the results may be questionable. Based on presentations and examination papers, the Christian background of some students is evident, although this observation may also be a result of the effect of Christian propagation materials. In addition, the percentage of documented Christians is usually much higher than that deemed from the questionnaires. Furthermore, although the samples are suitable and all respondents are willing to express their real thoughts, a survey is very costly. Considering that Bible-reading, although it can be done in

---

18 Xinzhong Yao and Paul Badham, *Religious Experience in Contemporary China* (Cardiff: University of Wales Press, 2007), 75.

fellowships or groups among Christians, is usually more individualized for the readers, particularly among the non-believers, investigating their understanding of the Bible may require prohibitive manpower and material resources in addition to the possible danger of being misunderstood and suspected by certain departments.

Survey Samples and Explanations

Considering the practical difficulties mentioned above, this study attempts to generate a new type of study samples. The concept of "biblical text" has been expanded from the scripture itself to the Bible-based films and television programs, particularly the 2013 American TV series, *The Bible*. For the readers' reactions, the data were collected from the comments posted by the Chinese audience of *The Bible*.

A television miniseries produced by Roma Downey and Mark Burnett, *The Bible* was broadcast weekly between March 3 and March 31, 2013 on the History Channel. It is divided into five parts and ten episodes. Based on the New International Version and the New Revised Standard Version, it narrates "Genesis to Revelation" in "one grand narrative" in five two-hour parts, each part containing two or three biblical stories told through live action and computer-generated imagery.[19] The most classic stories of the Hebrew Bible/Old Testament are told in the series, including the creation story (Genesis 1-3) and Noah's ark (Genesis 6-8), Abraham's life and his covenant with God (Genesis 15), Hagar and Ishmael (Genesis 16), the birth of Isaac (Genesis 21), Aqedah (Genesis 22) and the destruction of Sodom and Gomorrah (Genesis 19), Moses and the story of Exodus, including the miracles and the receiving of the Ten Commandments at Mount Sinai (Exodus 2-20), Joshua's conquest of Canaan (Joshua 1, 2, and 6), the story of Samson and Delilah (Judges 16), the reign of Saul and David, as well as the establishment of the United Monarchy (1 and 2 Samuel), the decline of the Kingdom of Judah (2 Kings 24-25), the legend of Daniel (Daniel 3 and 6), and the return of the Judahites to Jerusalem (Ezra 1). The second half of the series mainly describes the life of Jesus based on the

---

19 See http://en.wikipedia.org/wiki/The_Bible_(TV_miniseries) for more details and further references.

Gospels, including the Nativity, the miracles during his mission in Galilee and Jerusalem, the crucifixion and resurrection, and a few stories of his disciples (Acts) in the last episode.

Both Roma Downey and Mark Burnett are pious Christians,[20] and they stated in an interview that they hope "this series will affect a new generation of viewers and draw them back to the Bible."[21] Thus, they exerted effort to ensure biblical accuracy. Downey told the media, "We had a team of over forty respected theologians and scholars. We sent them scripts for feedback and to ensure accuracy. We have been sending clips and episodes to experts, scholars, and to various pastors and faith leaders. This is our sacred text, and we wanted to ensure an accurate depiction."[22] Under this principle, the final version of the TV series may be somehow different from the biblical text[23] but remains very close to the scripture overall. According to Dr. Helen Bond, senior lecturer in New Testament at the University of Edinburgh and director of the Center for Christian Origins, this series "is an excellent dramatization of the Bible—it is historically credible, put together with sensitivity and imagination, and at times truly moving."[24]

Clearly, no matter how close to the original text, the TV series should be different from the real biblical text in several ways. However, in a country such as China which lacks the traditions of biblical culture and where the Bible is unavailable except in church, watching *The Bible* can be an approach to get a full picture of the structure of the biblical

---

20 Roma Downey was raised as, and remains, a Roman Catholic. Cf. http://www.washingtonpost.com/posttv/local/actress-roma-downey-on-religion-faith-219/2012/02/09/gIQATJNT1Q__video.html, accessed August 30, 2014. Mark Burnett's father was a Roman Catholic, his mother was a Presbyterian, and he has strong Christian faith. Cf. http://en.wikipedia.org/wiki/Mark__Burnett, accessed August 30, 2014; http://www.huffingtonpost.com/roma-downey-and-mark-burnett/making-the-bible-series__b__2782643.html, accessed August 30, 2014.
21 Robert Crosby, "From Survivor and Touched by an Angel to the Bible," *Christianity Today*, February 25, 2013. http://www.christianitytoday.com/ct/2013/february-web-only/from-survivor-and-touched-by-angel-to-bible.html, accessed August 30, 2014
22 Ibid.
23 For details, see a summary of http://en.wikipedia.org/wiki/The__Bible__(TV__miniseries)#Differences__from__the__Bible, accessed August 30, 2014.
24 http://www.bibleseries.tv/what-faith-leaders-are-saying-about-the-final-episode, accessed August 30, 2014.

narrative and to learn the details directly and conveniently. TV shows and films may attract bigger audiences than traditional books and may arouse the interest of many non-religious people. In addition, they can lower the knowledge requirement of the audience, such that understanding and thinking about the Bible is no longer a privilege of intellectuals but rather a basic education that almost everyone can enjoy. Moreover, the slight differences between the TV series and the biblical text have hardly any influence on the stand and thinking of the audience, based on the reaction of the Chinese audience of *The Bible*. Therefore, *The Bible* can be regarded as an extension and complement of the biblical text, from which we can collect the real reaction of the audience to the Bible through the "bullet curtain."

The "bullet curtain" is based on video sharing websites with the function of simultaneous comments. A special feature of this kind of website is the simultaneous posting and appearance of comments like subtitles of the videos that are running and being watched. These comments are visible to other members of the audience, and the audience can give their own feedback and/or interact with others while watching videos. Numerous simultaneous comments sliding over the screen give the appearance of a curtain of intensive bullets in shooting games, hence the term "bullet curtain" (*danmu* in Chinese). This system was first applied in animation works but soon extended to all videos.

The most popular bullet curtain sites in China are AcFun (http://www.acfun.tv) and bilibility (http://www.bilibili.com). Bilibility was established at the beginning of 2010 and had soon taken the lead owing to its abundant videos, convenient registration, and easy procedure when posting bullet curtain. As of June 2014, *The Bible* has been viewed 250,000 times on bilibility and less than 10,000 times on Acfun. The number of views served as the basis for our selection of the bullet curtain of bilibility as the survey sample.

The bullet curtain poses clear advantages over the traditional survey types (i.e., paper questionnaire and interviews). The rapid development in science and technology in recent years has resulted in a rapid increase in the number of Internet users in China. By June 2014, Internet users in China reached 632 million, accounting for 46.9% of

Understanding of the Bible among the General Public in Mainland China   109

the total population.²⁵ The Internet is no longer a privilege of the few elites but has become a common and important platform for ordinary people to gain knowledge and exchange information. In addition, the fact that any registered user can post simultaneous comments, taking the bullet curtain as the sample can effectively exclude selection bias in educational level and location or area of the respondents. Moreover, everyone in the audience can post their comments voluntarily without giving their names²⁶ so they can freely express their real opinions without any interference from external factors. Thus, they do not hesitate and do not need to conceal their religious background and views on the Bible. From the perspective of management and censorship, although both managers of bilibility and the uploaders reserve the right to delete the bullet curtain, the diversity of the content does not give any clue or indication if any certain comment has been deleted or screened because of political or religious reasons. Further, given that the bullet curtain is posted simultaneously while the audience watches the video, it represents and demonstrates the first reaction of the audience upon seeing parts of the video. The initiative, freedom, and timeliness of expressing opinions make the bullet curtain a relatively ideal data source for the survey of Chinese understanding of the Bible.

Internet users can continue posting comments as long as the videos are still on the website. Therefore, a time limit should be imposed with regard to data collection. In this survey, data collection ended on January 31, 2014, or almost one year after the broadcast of *The Bible*. A total of 12,892 comments, most of which were posted in the first

---

25 China Internet Network Information Center (CNNIC), "Di 34 ci zhongguo hulian wangluo fazhan zhuangkuang tongji baogao" [The 34th Report of China Internet Development Statistics], July 21, 2014. http://www.cnnic.net.cn/hlwfzyj/hlwxzbg/hlwtjbg/201407/t20140721__47437.htm, accessed August 30, 2014.

26 It required certain technical means to download and analyze background data to get to know the author of every comment. Thanks to Mr. Tang Xiao, who helped solve some technical problems in collecting data, and thanks to Miss Rong Yu and Sun Rong, who assisted with data processing. These data only contain the author's screen names for each comment to connect comments posted by the same author, but the real names and identities of the authors still remain anonymous.

three months after broadcast, were posted by 2,415 IDs.[27] These comments serve as the sample of this survey. A few comments were posted after January 2014 but have hardly any influence on the analysis.

However, using the bullet curtain as samples also has disadvantages. For instance, given the anonymity of users who post comments, knowing their exact age and educational level is impossible and a follow-up study may not be an option. In regard to content, the most difficult problem is comments that are too short and without context; the meaning of such comments cannot be easily determined and classified. Some comments have only several characters such as "amen" or "God bless" and do not indicate whether the authors are Christians or not. Some comments may contain sarcasm, but no one can be sure since there are few words. In this study, such unclear comments are not classified. Despite that, we cannot totally preclude the danger of over-interpretation of some comments, just like there is subjective over-interpretation of biblical and other classical texts.

Analysis of the Bullet Curtain Data

Religious background

Taking the bullet curtain of the TV series *The Bible* as the basic sample has very clear advantages, as stated above, such as excluding selection bias in educational level and physical locations of the respondents. However, this series was produced based on the holy scripture of the Judeo-Christian religions, and the primary purpose of the producers, who are deeply religious, was propagation. Therefore, the first issue to discuss is whether the audience and the commentators of this series are basically Christians, given that the number of Chinese Jews is almost negligible. If yes, can they really represent the general public of China?

---

27 Technically, it is possible for one person to log in and post comments with more than one ID, and it is also possible for more than one person to share one ID, though one may not find any necessity of doing this. In this study, the word "commentator" equals one "ID" on bilibility.

And how does the non-religious audience understand the biblical stories shown in *The Bible*?

Unlike many other series, in which lots of comments on the bullet curtain are about the stars, their personal lives, and other relevant works, the comments on *The Bible* mainly focus on the plot and seem to be more serious. However, most comments do not really reflect the religious backgrounds of the commentators. For instance, one comment says, "maybe the Bible should not be understood literally...I believe many people will agree with me on this" (2-b). This can either be an opinion of a religious person or an idea of a non-religious individual. Some short comments with typical religious words (such as amen, God bless, repent, etc.) may be natural implications of a believer, but a non-believer can "borrow" it, too.

In general, the criteria used to judge whether a commentator is a Christian or not is at least one of the following: (1) he/she clearly and seriously expresses his/her own religious belief; (2) he/she posts relatively long and systematic comments or views by using emotional religious language; or (3) he/she directly criticizes the agnostic and/or atheist comments on the bullet curtain from the perspective of a religious individual. Based on any of these criteria, very few commentators can be identified as believers of other religions and none of them seem to be Jewish. As for the bullet curtain that visibly shows that the commentators are not religious, dividing them into two more specific groups (namely, agnostics or skeptics and atheists) may be helpful. Agnostics or skeptics may initially state that they are non-religious; strongly question the historicity of biblical accounts, especially the miracles; and post comments that clearly reflect that they do not believe in the existence of the Judeo-Christian God. Atheists are not only non-religious but are also highly critical of religions. Atheists condemn every event and idea shown in the series that they do not agree with, as well as the canon, doctrines, and impact of Christianity and other monotheistic religions by using relatively aggressive words.[28] Further, a

---

28 This division is inspired by the study of Yao and Badham, who conclude that most Han Chinese "regard themselves as neither religious believers nor firm atheists, but non-religious" (Yao and Badham, *Religious Experience in Contemporary China*,

lot of comments discussing and summarizing the plots of *The Bible* are posted like banter or filled with sarcasm. However, since believers may also express opinions in this manner, such comments and the authors are generally not identified.

According to these principles, out of the 12,892 simultaneous comments, 2,163 (or 16.78%) posted by 734 IDs (30.39% of the total) can be identified as clearly reflecting religious backgrounds of the authors. The composition is as follows (see Table 1).

The composition of the commentators is quite different, as shown in Table 2.

Within the observed value of the surveyed data, the percentages of comments and IDs of Christian background are almost identical, and both numbers are higher than that of the Christians in the total population of China.[29] This may imply that Christians are more interested in watching and discussing *The Bible* than non-Christians. In spite of this result, the comments and the IDs of Christians are a small portion of those clearly expressing their religious background, and the percentages are smaller than those of the agnostics and firm atheists, who have many more IDs (over 50% and 30%, respectively) and posted more comments (over 40%). Consequently, in the interactions and disputes of the commentators, the Christians are usually at a disadvantage and

---

153). While in agreement that those who are not religious should be divided into different groups, pointing out that Yao and Badham's research focuses on the religious activities and experiences of people is necessary, but this mainly deals with their understandings of the Bible. Following the analysis on the content of the bullet curtain, "agnostic" or "skeptic" may be more precise in this case to identify the "non-religious."

29 A long-term dispute on the number of Christians in China without reaching any consensus exists. The estimations vary from 20 million to 1,300 million. According to the recent official statistics, the number of Chinese Christians ranges from 23 million to 40 million and are 1.7% to 2.9% of the total population. Cf. Jiang Hongbin, "Zhongguo jidujiao sanzi aiguo yundong weiyuanhui chengli 60 zhounian jinianhui juxing" [The 60th anniversary commemoration of the Chinese Christian Three-Self Patriotic Movement Committee was held], *People's Daily*, August 6, 2014, 11. In the 2005 survey mentioned above, 91 out of the 3,196 adult samples are self-claimed Christians, accounting for less than 3% (Yao and Badham, *Religious Experience in Contemporary China*, 72). The estimations of religious and academic institutes overseas are usually higher, but none exceeds 10% of the total population.

Table 1: Religious backgrounds indicated in the comments

	Number of comments	%
Christian	310	14.33
Other religions	2	0.09
Agnostic or skeptic	905	41.84
Firm atheist	946	43.74
Total	2163	100

Table 2: Religious backgrounds of the commentators

	Number of IDs	%
Christian	108	14.71
Other religions	2	0.27
Agnostic or skeptic	396	53.95
Firm atheist	228	31.06
Total	734	100

sometimes become so angry that they tell agnostics and firm atheists repeatedly "don't watch this series if you don't like God, there is a red cross in the upper right corner (for you to close)" (2-c). Moreover, the percentage of firm atheist IDs is not as much as that of their comments, suggesting that this group is more zealous in criticizing religions, particularly monotheism.

Knowledge of the Bible

Many Western viewers who have grown up in Judeo-Christian cultures are quite familiar with the plot of *The Bible*, but most Chinese viewers may not have relevant background knowledge. Watching *The Bible* may have been their first opportunity to hear biblical stories, and thus, some of them ask questions in the bullet curtain regarding plots or ideas that they are not familiar with. However, in the bullet curtain of *The Bible* on bilibility, a number of comments reflect that the authors are knowledgeable beyond the TV series and are rather professional. These comments show acquaintance with biblical texts, including some plots that are not mentioned in the TV series (such as the incest between Lot and his daughters, the stories of Jacob and Joseph, and the reign of Solomon and the kings). A number of comments bring them up and express disappointment that these events are excluded, or they summarize the stories for other viewers.[30] Regarding the plots in the series, some comments affirm the nuances from the biblical text. Some knowledgeable comments show acquaintance with biblical languages, history, and culture: many comments suggest that the figures in the series speak Hebrew or Aramaic, and some point out that "Jehovah" (which is still in most Chinese Bible translations) is an incorrect translation and that "Elohim" is a masculine plural form in Hebrew. Occasionally, comments in the bullet curtain introduce relevant background and culture, including the relationship between/among the figures, the geographical environment, and the household items of ancient Israelites/Jews. Several commentators also express familiarity with biblical scholarship, including the achievements of biblical archaeology and their significance, the parallels between the creation story and the Mesopotamian civilizations, and even the scholarly controversy over how the Israelites entered Canaan. Some comments also compare the plots of crossing the Red Sea, Samson and Delilah, and King David in *The Bible* with other versions in previous movies and point out their similarities and differences, which implies the authors' acquaintance with biblical films.

According to Table 3, comments showing knowledge of the Bible and IDs posting these comments account for 13.15% and 9.61% of the total, respectively, which indicates that these commentators are more enthusiastic in posting comments.

Although this investigation is independent from the one above, it is worth integrating the two. Among the commentators with relevant knowledge of the Bible, 46 IDs present their religious background (as shown in Table 4), of which Christian commentators account for more than 20%. However, agnostic and firm atheist commentators still account for more than three-fourths, which is not far lower than their

---

[30] Many comments in the bullet curtain announce the succeeding plots of the TV series in advance but do not reflect whether or not the authors know them from watching the series earlier. Thus, these comments are not reckoned with in this category.

Table 3: Comments and commentators with knowledge of the Bible

	Number	%
Comments showing relevant knowledge of the Bible	1695	13.15
Total comments	12,892	100
IDs posting comments with biblical knowledge	232	9.61
Total number of IDs	2415	100

Table 4: Religious background of commentators with knowledge of the Bible

	Number of IDs	%
Christian	10	21.74
Agnostic or skeptic	22	47.83
Firm atheist	14	30.43
Total	46	100

proportion in the total number. Therefore, this implies that knowledge of the Bible does not necessarily have absolute and direct relationship with religious background. Non-religious people, including agnostics and firm atheists, also can gain biblical knowledge by studying.

Connecting with Chinese context

The TV series *The Bible* shows biblical stories that are strictly based on the Hebrew Bible/Old Testament and New Testament and never directly mentions China or its surrounding areas and civilizations. However, while watching the series, many Chinese viewers initially relate the biblical plots with the context of Chinese literary and artistic works. Thus, the audience usually views the biblical accounts and ideas from a Chinese perspective.

Given that *The Bible* has hardly any Chinese elements in theme, content, production, starring, and distribution, it is totally a foreign work to the Chinese audience. Therefore, not many comments in the bullet curtain are related to the Chinese context (see Table 5). However, observing the content of these comments, which are really insightful for later discussions, is worthwhile.

Table 5: Comments related to Chinese context and their commentators

	Number	%
Comments related to Chinese context	650	5.04
Total comments	12,892	100
IDs posting comments related to Chinese context	125	5.18
Total number of IDs	2415	100

Table 6: Attitudes toward Jews and Israel expressed in the comments

	Number of comments	%	Number of IDs	%
Pro-Jewish/Israel	24	23.76	10	20
Anti-Jewish/Israel	77	76.24	40	80
Total	101	100	50	100

Attitude toward Jews and Israel

In China, although the Bible is widely considered solely as a Christian canon and many people in the religious and non-religious audience would equate the biblical stories with Christianity and its doctrines and ideas, there are a number of comments associating the biblical plots directly with Jews and Israel. Out of the 12,892 simultaneous comments, 277 (2.15%) posted by 146 IDs (6.05% of the total) directly talk about Jews, Judaism, the situation in the Middle East, and other related topics, among which 101 comments posted by 50 IDs show a clear attitude toward the Jews and Israel. To my surprise, anti-Jewish/Israel opinions are much more common than the pro-Jewish/Israel ones.

The "Jewish myth" in contemporary China[31] does not seem to be popular here. Instead, the audience harshly criticizes Jews and Israel in reaction to the plots of *The Bible*. And in the pro-Jewish/Israel camp, most comments simply show sympathy for the miserable destiny of the Jews but seldom praise "Jewish wisdom" as many best-sellers do.

---

31 Cf. the last chapter of this book for more details, "Reflections on Chinese Jewish Studies: A Comparative Perspective" by Song Lihong.

Examples of Comments on the Bullet Curtain

The statistics above reveal that many more agnostic or atheist viewers post comments in the bullet curtain on *The Bible* on bilibilitv than Christian viewers. The agnostic and atheist comments are mainly on the stories of Aqedah, the ten plagues, the Israelite conquest of Canaan, and the Nativity, which are "popular" stories in the series that received many more comments than others on the bullet curtain.

In the story of Aqedah, God's testing of Abraham is widely questioned by the audience. Many of them say God was "overly suspicious" or "toying with human beings" (1-c)[32] and argue that even if it was God that created human beings, He should not have offhandedly tortured them, just like a mother should not torture her children (1-c). Many in the audience blame God in this story, saying He was "evil," "brutal," "insane," "abnormal," and "foolish." These viewers call him "god of death," or "tyrant," and believe "he would be punished for this" (1-b; 1-c). As for Abraham in this story, only a few comments praise his "faith," as many churches would usually advocate. The audience accused Abraham of cruelty (to Isaac and to Hagar and Ishmael before), and say that "he was sold, but then counted money for the abductor." Although Abraham did not kill Isaac, thanks to the angel, some viewers recall the story of Jephthah's daughter and point out that such tragedies might have occurred (1-c). Meanwhile, the audience shows great sympathy for Sarah, who was totally forgotten in the biblical text but who appears at the beginning of this story in the TV series. A few viewers even sigh with emotion that the scapegoat replacing Isaac is absolutely innocent.

Also in the story of the ten plagues in Exodus, God's behavior is criticized by the audience. They question the accusation of the then Pharaoh and the Egyptian infants and why they were slaughtered by God. Some viewers also blame Moses for his double-crossing practice (2-b). Similar comments appear in the story of the Israelite conquest of Canaan. Most in the audience cannot accept the ideology of justifying

---

32 The numbers and letters of the episodes and sections are based on the version on bilibilitv: http://www.bilibili.com/video/av525765

massacres in the war under the name of God, and they ask, "is this the way the LORD teaches people how to occupy territories?" Some go further and assert that the groups believing in this LORD are not different from terrorist organizations (3-a).

In discussing these plots, many viewers express their strong indignation on biblical religions, and even all monotheistic religions, and accuse them of being narrow, cruel, evil, and controlling the believers' minds through imaginary stories and through brainwashing them by using fear. Many commentators even define monotheism as an "evil cult" and strongly condemn the idea of "if you believe, then…, if you don't believe, then…"

It should be recognized that these reactions are not unique among Chinese readers and audiences in the twenty-first century. Even within the Judeo-Christian civilizations, those narratives have long been questioned, especially after the Enlightenment Movement. However, for the Chinese people, who grew up with their own cultural traditions without the mindset and premise of "God is one" or "God is always correct," and who tend to regard biblical religions as alien and strange, the feelings of rejection and disgust can be stronger when coming across the stories of Aqedah, the ten plagues, and the narrative of violence in the conquest of Canaan. At this point, the response of the Christian audience to the comments by atheists seems to be somewhat weak. Aside from repeating biblical texts, or slogans of propagation, or arguing that "the Egyptians also slaughtered the Israelite infants," and "the Canaanites are extremely evil," they keep on telling the repudiators "not to watch it if you don't like" and "respect others' faith." Such comments are soon replied to by non-Christian viewers, who suggest that Christians are acting as if they were superior and assert that everyone has the right to watch *The Bible* and give comments, and some mention that some Christians do not respect non-Christians either (2-b; 3-a).

When coming across plots of conflicts between nations, the Chinese audience shows empathic concern not for the protagonists (the Israelites) but for the villains (the Egyptians or the Canaanites). A number of viewers regard the biblical Israelites as the Eight-Power

Expeditionary Force, which invaded China a century ago and ask, "Will China become Jericho in the Bible?" (3-a). As for one of the heroines in biblical text and the series, Rahab the prostitute, some commentators identify her as a "traitor" and express anger at elevating such a figure (3-a).

When the religious viewers emphasize in their comments on the bullet curtain the great impact of the Bible in raising human moral standards and promoting social development, other viewers with agnostic or skeptical views, and especially firm atheist views, criticize the idea of binding morality with religions. They claimed that the Chinese knew nothing about the Christian God or the Bible in ancient times, but they did have ethics and virtues. The "morality" shown in the series, however, looks absurd and unacceptable in modern times. Some further propose that during the ancient period, China could also be very strong without the Bible; therefore, the influence of the Bible might be limited. Regarding the critiques on the ten plagues and the narrative of violence, besides the opinions mentioned above, many viewers refer to Buddhism and praise it for helping everyone, including those who do not believe, and express thoughts that the God in the Bible seems to be barbarous and selfish (3-a). As for equal retaliation in the plot, one comments, "Does this mean I become a devil exactly like you?" (2-b).

Compared with the Old Testament, the New Testament part of *The Bible* has fewer critics in the bullet curtain on bilibility, and they are also less harsh but maybe more sarcastic on the life of Jesus. The virgin birth is one of the greatest and most significant miracles in the Bible, and the TV series portrays this story in a touching way. However, most of the commentators question the reality of this event and affirm it was to conceal the adultery of Mary. Many describe Joseph in this story with popular Internet terms such as "NTR,"[33] "happy to be a father," (*xi dang die*)[34] or "hero of taking over (pregnant woman)" (*jie*

---

33 An abbreviation from Japanese ねとられ (ne to ra re), meaning one's spouse was raped by or committed adultery with others.
34 It means a man marries a pregnant woman and becomes the father of another's child very soon.

pan xia), etc., meaning being sexually betrayed (6-a; 6-b; 6-c). The other stories of Jesus, for example curing patients and propagation, nevertheless do not really resonate with the Chinese audience, and some of the commentators even regard them similar to stories of magic doctors[35] and pyramid sales, both of which are common in present China and are widely despised by the people.

As for the anti-Jewish comments, they have little to do with the traditional anti-Semitic views in the Christian world. Only several of them suggest that the Jews "should have paid for killing Jesus" (1-c), as medieval Christians would have claimed, but most of the commentators criticize the behavior of the Jews simply because of their violent actions. And they regard the modern Israeli-Palestinian conflict as a repetition of the biblical Israelite conquest of Canaan and assert, "the Jews were persecuted but now are persecuting others," or "to occupy others' land and make them silent, this is what the Israeli(te)s[36] did in the past and are doing today" (2-c). While suspecting the historicity of the biblical accounts, some audience members express that they think the Jews were "super narcissistic" (1-a, 3-a), and others say *The Bible* is proof of Jews controlling the USA, especially the media (5-a, 6-b, 7-a, 8-a).

Notes on the Content of the Bullet Curtain and Its Reasons

From the statistics and content of the bullet curtain listed above, it is noted that for *The Bible*, which is a TV series with a religious theme, the majority of comments from the mainland Chinese general public are not from believers of biblical religions. On the contrary, agnostic and firm atheist viewers not only contributed more comments on the bullet curtain, but also made sense with their remarks, including both traditional critics of some biblical accounts and their assessments based on Chinese context.

These comments on the bullet curtain were posted initially and anonymously by the audience without any political or religious

---

35 A deception in which one pretends to be a patient and claims to have been cured by a magic doctor, who is actually a fraud, to attract real patients to that doctor to gain money.
36 In Chinese, Israelite and Israeli are the same word.

organization or mobilization. From the content, it is clear that they were contributed by different commentators and reflect their actual thoughts. The statistics show that the agnostic and atheist camps in the audience have taken the advantage. Atheism has been the official ideology in mainland China since 1949, and most Chinese are raised and educated in an atheist environment in which religions are marginalized. But atheism does not serve as the only communist ideology, and now that the government does not really emphasize it as it did before, since the reform and the opening policy were launched, why is it still widely accepted by the general public?

This may be explained in several aspects.

From a historical point of view, China has suffered from the invasion and oppression of Western countries since the mid-nineteenth century. Although this may not have absolute and direct relations with Christianity, it is difficult for the Chinese to separate the Western missionaries from the imperialist invaders, both of whom came to China with canon or cannon, and worship or warship. Nevertheless, a number of invaders were indeed believers of Christianity and considered themselves like the Israelites conquering Canaan under God's instructions in the Bible. Given this context, it is not surprising for Chinese people to take the side of the Egyptians in the narrative of the ten plagues and the Canaanites in the Israelite conquest, whereas figures like Rahab, who gave up her own traditions and embraced the foreign power, are condemned.

Official atheist education is one of the reasons, from the perspective of reality. The "evil cult" has been severely and continuously condemned in official media in the past fifteen years, and this idea has penetrated deeply into people's mind. However, owing to the lack of general knowledge about religions, ordinary Chinese people usually confuse "normal religion" and "evil cults," both of which believe and worship deities. Therefore, some people equate Christianity to an evil cult and reject it. In addition, some sects of Christianity propagate regardless of time, place, figures, and occasions, and thus arouse antipathy in people. Another point is that some terrorist attacks carried out by extreme religious organizations (though usually not by Christians) leave ordinary people with an impression that "monotheism brings violence."

Given the ideological background of influential Chinese thoughts, different views regarding miracles can also be an obstacle for people to accept Christianity. Miracles serve as evidence of the existence of God and human finitude and are a basic essence of Christianity. However, mainstream Chinese culture generally lacks this idea, although such ideas can be somewhat popular in certain folk religions and faiths. In Confucianism (including neo-Confucianism), the idea of integration between human and nature (*tian ren he yi*) is undoubtedly more significant. Now that the universe is an entirety that cannot be separated, humans can therefore exist without relying on supernatural beings or events. Buddhism, which calls miracles "shentong," admits their existence and functions. In addition, Buddhism encourages the belief in deities, ghosts, and ordinary human beings that can gain more or less "shentong" through the retribution system and practice. However, in the Buddhist theoretical system, the core principle is karma. Life and death, disaster, and reward are all from karma, which cannot be interrupted by "shentong." Hence, those who have "shentong" seldom exhibit them to common people. Given this background, the first reactions of many viewers to the miracles shown in the series (crossing the Red Sea, the Nativity, etc.) were of distrust.

Despite the aforementioned explanations, the comments on the bullet curtain on *The Bible* on bilibility show that quite a lot of the audience, most of whom may be non-religious, have compelling knowledge of the Bible. This suggests that even in a society where atheism is the dominant ideology, people still have interest in the Bible, although it may be considered as a book (or collection of books) about humanity rather than about faith and as an opportunity to gain relevant biblical knowledge. More and more academic publications on the Bible have been released in mainland China in recent years, including both original and translated research works and textbooks. Readers can easily get a full picture of the Bible and learn about the research on specific topics. Also, the Internet has made it possible for people to search for relevant biblical knowledge of their interest. While watching *The Bible* series online, people can either look up answers to their questions in a new window and post the result as a comment, or they can inquire in the bullet curtain for others to answer. The difficulty of gaining knowledge, including biblical knowledge, has been reduced to a great extent. Needless to say, some online information may not be reliable (particularly in the Chinese network), but with the development of the Internet, users are expected to have better ability to discriminate.

This is, therefore, an important point for the Jews, and especially for the Christian church interested in propagation, to notice. It will be impossible for them to only talk about the "Jewish wisdom" or gospels of the New Testament and stay away from the "difficult chapters" of the Hebrew Bible/Old Testament. In this age of the Internet, it is convenient for almost everyone to get the knowledge they are curious about. Thus, one should rather face those texts than evade them. Scholars have discussed the tricky problems in biblical texts and published important books and articles. However, given that the audience may not actually study the professional and theological arguments, it is also necessary to make answers and explanations concise. Moreover, the original purpose of the TV series is propagation; as such, the pious producers present only the biblical stories and ideas they found self-evidently correct. However, the result was ineffective among the Chinese people, who may completely miscomprehend the meaning of the biblical stories. This case is a good example to demonstrate that ideas considered "absolutely right" among some people may not work well with others. In the process of spreading a culture, regardless of how strange biblical or non-religious messages may be to different communities, many obstacles will emerge. As such, communicators need to learn how to think from the perspective of the audience.

In conclusion, this study attempts to employ sociological methods and a new sample to survey the understanding of the Bible among the general public in mainland China. Needless to say, this study is preliminary research, and we have a lot to do in the future. For example, we may conduct a diachronic study to compare the statistics in different periods, or a synchronic study to compare the reactions of a Chinese audience with the reactions of an audience of Western Judeo-Christian background to a specific film or TV series, or a deep study of the comments on certain plots. Of note is that this survey is based on the comments in the bullet curtain on *The Bible* and only shows the religious stand or tendency of the audience while watching the series.[37] Nevertheless, through the present study, we obtain insight into the status of Christianity as one of the lesser ideologies in China. The Bible, especially some parts of it, can be one of the reasons why the Chinese have rejected this foreign religion. However, this does not prevent the Chinese from reading the Bible and gleaning relevant knowledge from it. Moreover, it is also interesting to observe the comments regarding the Chinese context and intelligent connections between the Bible and Chinese classic works and reality. Such comments may shed light on cross-textual reading of both texts. In addition, an ironic phenomenon may arouse our interest—although the Jews are proud of their scripture, the Bible does not really improve the image of Jews in China but may have the opposite effect. Therefore, the study of reader reaction becomes particularly significant.

---

37 In other words, their religious beliefs may vary in different situations. Religious beliefs and religious activities cannot be automatically equated "because of the gap between believing and belonging." (See Yao and Badham, *Religious Experience in Contemporary China*, 153. For more detailed discussion based on the survey, cf. chapter eight, "Religiosity of the Religious, the Non-religious and the Atheist," 152–177.)

The Changing Image of the State of Israel in *People's Daily* during the Cold War

SHE GANGZHENG[1]
Brandeis University

Abstract

In this essay, the author analyzes the reports related to the State of Israel in *People's Daily*, an official newspaper of the Chinese government as well as a representative of China's mainstream media, from 1948 to 1991 and argues that Israel's image in China during the Cold War had roughly gone through five stages: 1) 1948–1954; 2) 1955–1964; 3) 1965–1976; 4) 1977–1985; and 5) 1986–1991. Generally speaking, such change presents a U-shaped curve in accordance with concurrent changes in domestic and foreign circumstances of the People's Republic. The changing image of Israel in China not only reveals the twists and turns in the development of Sino-Israeli relations from early statehoods of both countries till the establishment of their diplomatic relations in the wake of the Cold War, but also reflects the position of the State of Israel in China's overarching strategy of foreign policy and its subtle relationship with China's domestic affairs.

---

1 I owe special thanks to my former advisor at Peking University, Wang Yu, for discussing with me the idea of writing this article at the very beginning. For their thoughtful comments on earlier drafts, I am also grateful to Song Lihong (Nanjing University), Amber Taylor (Brandeis University), Li Wan (Harvard University), and Zhang Shujian (Peking University). All remaining errors, however, are mine alone.

Introduction

It is a challenging project to conduct a historical analysis about the change of Israel's image in Chinese media during the Cold War, not only due to the voluminous collection of news reports, but also because some of the early texts around the founding of the People's Republic in 1949 are difficult to find today. However, *People's Daily* (*renmin ribao*), which is an official newspaper of the Communist Party of China (CPC) and later also of the Chinese government, provides us with a relatively feasible entry point. Founded in 1946, *People's Daily* became China's most widely circulated newspaper after the founding of the People's Republic, and has always been considered the mouthpiece of the leadership of the communist China.

Examining and comparing the reports on issues related to Israel in *People's Daily* during the Cold War allows us not only to understand how the image of Israel evolved in the Chinese mainstream media at this period, but also to observe the subtle transition between each phase of changes. Perhaps more important, it can help us, through those "simple" wording of newspapers, to analyze the twists and turns in the interaction between China and Israel in more than 40 years, and the inextricable connection between Sino-Israel relations and those domestic and international affairs China was dealing with.

Literature Review

State of Israel, but also the Berlin Blockade and Airlift which marked the first major international crises of the Cold War. On the other side of Eurasia, the Nanjing Nationalist Government led by the Kuomingtang (KMT) was facing a precarious situation in the Chinese Civil War, which would result in its retreat from the mainland to Taiwan and the victory of the Communist Party a year later. Therefore, it is totally understandable that Israel studies had no chance of existing in China before 1949. From the establishment of the People's Republic till the year 1978, China and Israel didn't have any diplomatic relations and were actually in a long-term state of hostility. Coupled with the "leftist" radical ideology and the impact of the ten-year "Great Cultural Revolution," there was little academic research on Israel, let alone studies on the image of Israel in Chinese media.[2] Since Deng Xiaoping launched his reforms in the late 1970s, Israel studies in China have made considerable progress, but still, few scholars or journalists were involved in studies regarding the image of the State of Israel in China at that period. Since the year 2000, research on this field began to increase gradually, and more and more scholarly articles with novel viewpoints and profound conceptions have been published: one example is Ma Xiaolin's "Chinese Media Reports on the Middle East in Six Decades" published in 2010. The strengths and weaknesses of these publications could be summarized as follows.

First, more and more researchers are increasingly aware that the media reports in the People's Republic didn't take the pro-Arab and anti-Israel stance from the outset, but most of them do not provide evidence regarding whether the media in China expressed a favorable opinion of Israel during its early statehood or not, nor the impact of that opinion. Chinese scholars often choose the founding of the State of Israel or the People's Republic of China as the starting point on the timeline for their research on Sino-Israel relations, and they generally believe that these two countries had a promising prospect of deepening mutual understanding or even establishing diplomatic relations in the late 1940s, but this process was interrupted due to the outbreak of the Korean War in 1950. For example, one of the academic authorities on Jewish studies in China, Pan Guang, wrote an article titled "On the Historical and Current Situations of Sino-Israel Relations" in 2009. In this article, the author mentions that the media of CPC had "generally welcomed" the birth of the State of Israel and quotes a report in 1948 from *Jizhong daobao* [*Jizhong Herald*].[3] Nevertheless, *Jizhong daobao* was just a temporary newspaper of the CPC Central Hebei District, and both its circulation and influence are difficult to assess because of its short-lived history. Moreover, the report quoted in the article is

---

2   Pan Guang, ed., *Youtai yanjiu zai zhongguo: sanshinian huigu* [*Jewish Studies in China: A Retrospect of Thirty Years*] (Shanghai: Shanghai Academy of Social Sciences Press, 2008), 59.
3   Pan Guang, "Zhongguo-yiselie guanxi de lishi yanjin yu xianzhuang fenxi" [On the Historical and Current Situations of Sino-Israel Relations], *Shehui kexue* [*Social Science*] (2009.12).

merely a newsletter without any in-depth or follow-up reporting, which makes it difficult to infer whether the Chinese Communist Party and its affiliated media had any coherence in the reports regarding Israel in this period.

Second, scholars usually point out that events like the Bandung Conference and the Suez Crisis were major turning points for the image of the State of Israel in China, but many ignore the foreshadowing of such "sudden change" in the Chinese media. Many Chinese scholarly articles, including "Chinese Media Reports on the Middle East in Six Decades," discuss the relationship between the government and the media in China. They generally argue that, at least before the Chinese economic reform in 1978, most media outlets in China belonged to different levels of the government or the communist party, which "highly politicized" those reports concerning foreign affairs, and imply that the stances of the Chinese media are always subject to the change of Chinese foreign policy.[4] However, this seemingly perfect explanation is also debatable since it not only underestimates the possibilities of tensions and contradictions between the directives from political leaders and the response of journalists/commentators,[5] but it oversimplifies and exaggerates the suddenness of the change of Israel's image in the Chinese media under different circumstances.

Third, many articles make observations about the role of Israel and China's overarching strategy in the international arena, but few of them pay attention to the impact of the domestic situation or political movements inside China on the changing image of Israel in Chinese media. Most articles try to demonstrate that the reports about Israel in the Chinese media during the Cold War were in accordance with Chinese foreign policies toward the greater Middle East at the same period, but they often overlook that at this period China was also

---

4   Ma Xiaolin, "Liushinian lai woguo meiti guanyu zhongdong wenti de baodao" [Chinese Media Reports on the Middle East in Six Decades], *Alabo shijie yanjiu* [*Arab World Studies*], (2002.2).

5   Wu Guoguang, "Command Communication: The Politics of Editorial Formulation in the *People's Daily*," *The China Quarterly* 137, 1994, 194–211.

experiencing significant fluctuations on the domestic level.⁶ Although it is disputable whether China's external behavior has always been shaped primarily by domestic concerns,⁷ it is certain that without the analysis on domestic affairs, any explanation of the change of Israel's image in Chinese mainstream media like *People's Daily* would be incomplete.

The First Stage: 1948–1954

In the first two years after the State of Israel was founded, the image of the State of Israel in *People's Daily* was quite positive. In this period, the reports in *People's Daily* not only expressed sympathy for the suffering of the displaced Jewish people, but they also unequivocally showed support to the newly-founded State of Israel during its "War of Independence."

On May 28, 1948, two weeks after the founding of the State of Israel, the word "Israel" appeared for the first time in *People's Daily*: a report on the fourth page was titled "The Wandering Life of the Jews for Two Millennia Was Ended. The State of Israel Was Established in the Near East. The Soviet Union, Poland, Yugoslavia, Czechoslovakia, and the United States Granted Official Recognitions." This report mentions that modern Israel is "the first Jewish state for more than two thousand years," and bluntly claims that the founding of Israel symbolizes "the total failure of the so-called 'UN trusteeship' conspiracy of dominating Palestine."⁸ The report also briefly describes the formation of Israeli provisional government and the diplomatic recognition granted by several countries, giving the readers an impression that this

---

6   Wang Yufeng, "Guojia liyi shiye xia de zhongyi guanxi" [Sino-Israel Relations from the Perspective of National Interests] (MA diss., Shanghai International Studies University, 2009).
7   Chen Jian, *Mao's China and the Cold War* (Chapel Hill and London: University of North Carolina Press, 2001), 279.
8   Xinhua News Agency, "Youtairen jieshu erqiannian liulang shenghuo jindong chengli yiselie guo su bo nan mei zhuguo jun zhengshi chengren" [The Wandering Life of the Jews for Two Millennia Was Ended. The State of Israel Was Established in the Near East. The Soviet Union, Poland, Yugoslavia, Czechoslovakia, and the United States Granted Official Recognitions.], *People's Daily* (Handan, Hebei) (May 28, 1948).

new state was methodically moving forward in both its domestic and diplomatic affairs.

At that moment, the CPC hadn't achieved its revolution victory on a national scale in China, and thus it had few direct interests in Palestine or throughout the Middle East. However, a deeper analysis on the news coverage in *People's Daily* reveals that the CPC's attitude toward Israel was heavily influenced by the Soviet Union. Although the CPC and the Communist Party of the Soviet Union (CPSU) disputed many issues relevant to the future of China and of the communist revolution in East Asia at that moment,[9] regarding Middle East issues the communists in China still considered the Soviet Union's support for the UN partition plan and Resolution 181(II) broadly in line with the interests of both the Arabs and the Jews. Moreover, the support for Israel expressed in *People's Daily* seems to be more logical when considering the different inclinations in the respect of ideologies between Israel and the Arab states: before it aligned completely with the Western powers in the mid-1950s, Israel was widely considered a Jewish state with a socialist nature. During the same period, however, most Arab states were either under the colonial rule of Great Britain or France or governed by monarchies that traditionally held an anti-communist stance.

The reports around the founding of Israel could still be argued as relatively neutral and objective since they don't have too many particularly emotional or striking expressions. However, in the following months, the wording in *People's Daily* shows a stance that fully supports Israel's war effort and finds fault with the Arabs. The first report in *People's Daily* about the war itself was published on June 5, 1948, titled "War Broke Out between the Arabs and the Jews because of the Evil Foreign Policies of Great Britain and the United States. The Soviet Union Sympathizes with the State of Israel which Was Invaded." It is written, soon after "The Jewish people finally achieved their long-term just aspiration of Zionism," "armies from seven Arab states made massive invasion and threatened to overthrow the State of Israel," and

---

9 Chen, *Mao's China and the Cold War*, 44–46.

"the Jewish side offered firm and just resistance to the aggressors." Correspondingly, the words describing the Arabs are negative or even "reactionary" in many aspects. For example, it says that many soldiers in the Arab armies were transformed from Anders' Army, which "had all kinds of connections with the German Nazis."[10]

In its subsequent reports, *People's Daily* continues such rhetoric. Israel is depicted as a peace-loving, courageous, and self-defensive state, while Arab countries are usually defined as "aggressors" or the "puppets of the imperialists." For example, referring to the truce proposal in the UN Security Council on May 29, 1948, *People's Daily* claims that the proposed truce is "in favor of the Arab Aggression," while against "the interests of the self-defensive Israeli Army."[11] By early 1949 as the war waned, *People's Daily* straightforwardly claims that "the war of aggression against the nascent State of Israel waged by Egypt, Transjordan, and seven other Arab countries—which was manipulated by Anglo-American imperialism since mid-May last year—has been subjected to abject failure."[12]

It should be noted, however, that although the reports in this period had a seemingly anti-Arab and pro-Israel stance, the coverage of the conflict itself is not the core purpose of *People's Daily*. Most pro-Israel reports have the clear intent of justifying the stance of the Soviet Union, which opposed the invasion against Israel at this period, while the anti-Arab rhetoric was indeed a criticism of Great Britain, which kept its presence in many Arab states and especially in their armies, and

---

10 Anders' Army refers to the Polish Armed Forces in the East in the period 1941–1942. Xinhua News Agency, "Zai yingmei zuie waijiao zhengce gudong xia, jindong ayou liangzu baofa zhanzheng yingmei maodun qu jianrui sulian tongqing yiselie guo zao qinlue" [War Broke Out between the Arabs and the Jews because of the Evil Foreign Policies of Great Britain and the United States. The Soviet Union Sympathizes with the State of Israel which was Invaded.], *People's Daily* (Handan, Hebei), June 5, 1948.
11 Xinhua News Agency, "Bugu yiselie guo heping yuanwang alabo jundui pohuai tingzhanling" [Regardless of the Peace Aspiration of Israel, the Arab Army Broke the Truce.], *People's Daily* (Handan, Hebei), June 23, 1948.
12 Xinhua News Agency, "Yingdi fuzhi qinlue zhanzheng shibai hou you tu wuzhuang ganshe yiselie" [The British Imperialism Considers a New Armed Intervention against Israel after the War of Aggression was Defeated.], *People's Daily* (Handan, Hebei), January 18, 1949.

of the United States, which then had an ambiguous attitude toward the Middle East.[13]

Since the founding of the People's Republic of China in October 1949, most CPC media, including *People's Daily*, maintained this style in reporting the issues related to the Middle East. However, from the outbreak of the Korean War till the eve of the Bandung Conference, the attitude of *People's Daily* toward Israel became more and more neutral. This is mainly because, on the one hand, the Israeli government, led by David Ben-Gurion, gradually changed its non-identification policy between the Eastern and Western blocs during the Korean War and aligned itself with the United States in enforcing the embargo on China;[14] on the other hand, in order to break through the containment placed by the United States in the international society, the nascent communist government of China planned a charm offensive toward different countries in the Middle East and also around the globe in the early 1950s.

The Second Stage: 1955–1964

In the mid-1950s, the image of Israel in the Chinese mainstream media, like *People's Daily*, experienced a dramatic change. From the perspective of macro-history, it is often considered a sudden change, but in fact it can still be divided into two phases.

1) The Bandung Conference in 1955 and the exclusion of Israel from the "Progressive Camp" (jinbu zhenying)

The Bandung Conference was a watershed in the history of Sino-Arab relations in the twentieth century, not only since the State of Israel was

---

13 Xinhua News Agency, "Yingmei zhengduo jindong liyi zaocheng ayou liuxue chongtu sulian zhenlibao fabiao shelun qianze" [Great Britain and the United States Are Competing in the Near East and Causing Bloodshed between the Jews and Arabs. *Pravda* Editorializes to Condemn.], *People's Daily* (Handan, Hebei), June 5, 1948.
14 Young Sam Ma, "Israel's Role in the UN during the Korean War," *Israel Journal of Foreign Affairs*, 2010.IV.3, 82. See also Michael Brecher, *Israel, the Korean War, and China: Images, Decisions and Consequences* (Jerusalem: Jerusalem Academic Press, 1974).

excluded from this so-called "Asian-African Conference" due to obstruction from the Arab side, but also because, at the same time, this conference provided a platform for the first time for communist China and the Arab states to get to know each other. As both the Chinese and the Arab peoples viewed themselves as the victims of Western imperialism, it was natural that communist China supported the efforts of the Arab people to get rid of colonial rule and seek independence. It was at this moment that the leaders of China, like Mao Zedong and Zhou Enlai, began to notice the profundity, complexity, and chronicity of the Arab-Israeli conflict. Considering winning the support of multiple Arab states, China adopted the policy of postponing the establishment of diplomatic relations with Israel, which was also reflected in *People's Daily*. In the news feature titled "The Struggle for the National Independence in the Near East" published on April 20, 1955 during the Bandung Conference, for the first time Israel was not included in the list of "progressive countries."[15] What was worse for Sino-Israel relations was that five days later in a report about the closing remarks of Zhou Enlai, the journalists of *People's Daily* wrote that the Premier made special mention of "the struggle for human rights" of the Arabs in Palestine.[16]

2) The Suez Crisis in 1956 and the condemnation of Israel as the "proxy of imperialism"

The Suez Crisis and the Israeli invasion of the Sinai Peninsula caused Israel's image to suffer a disastrous decline in China. There is no doubt that the main targets of condemnation by the Chinese media were Great Britain and France; however, since Israel fired the first shot in the battlefield, it still incurred severe criticism. Two days after the war broke out, a report titled "The Israeli Invasion Was Bitterly Hit by the

---

15 Gao Hong, "Jinzhongdong renmin zhengqu minzu duli de douzheng" [The Struggle for the National Independence in the Near East], *People's Daily* (Beijing), April 20, 1955.
16 Xinhua News Agency, "Yafei huiyi shengli bimu zhouenlai zongli zai bimu huiyi shang fayan" [Asian-African Conference Has Successfully Concluded. Premier Zhou Enlai Made a Speech in the Closing Ceremony], *People's Daily* (Beijing), April 25, 1955.

Egyptians. Israeli Government Is Sending Reserve Forces to the Border. Egyptian Newspapers Condemn the Western Countries for Supporting Israel" clearly determines the nature of Israel's operation as an aggression.[17] The next day, for the first time, the State of Israel appeared on the front-page headlines of *People's Daily*: an editorial entitled "Don't Set Fire, Don't Commit Aggression" devotes most sections to condemning Great Britain and France, but it also talks about Israel for a whole paragraph:

> It must be noted that Israel gets no benefit by acting as the foot soldier of the western colonists, and if it continues to provoke Egypt by the orders of western colonial powers, it will definitely be cast aside by the peace-loving people around the world.[18]

It can be argued that this editorial sets the tone for the image of Israel in China for many years to come—Israel began to be repeatedly depicted as the invader in the Middle East. Nevertheless, *People's Daily* didn't exaggerate too much in vilifying Israel at that moment. On November 8, 1956, an article titled "Israel—the Tool of Imperialism to Break the Peace in the Middle East" was published in *People's Daily*. The author argues that Israel "has become a tool of imperialism," but still makes it clear that "Great Britain and the United State have the primary responsibility for the endless Arab-Israeli conflict today" and expresses pity for Israel, which "was abandoned by other states in the Middle East."[19] Also, in the column of "Letters to the Editor" in the same month, a reader writes, "I hope the Israeli youth who were driven to the battlefield might realize that you are used as cannon fodder by

---

17 Xinhua News Agency, "Yiselie jundui qinfan aiji zaodao tongji yi zhengfu dongyuan houbeibing miji bianjing chunchunyudong ai bao qianze xifang guojia zhichi yiselie dongwu" [The Israeli Invasion Was Bitterly Hit by the Egyptians. Israeli Government is Sending Reserve Forces to the Border. Egyptian Newspapers Condemn the Western Countries for Supporting Israel.], *People's Daily* (Beijing), October 31, 1956.
18 Editorial Office, "Buxu fanghuo buxu qinlue" [Don't Set Fire, Don't Commit Aggression], *People's Daily* (Beijing), November 1, 1956.
19 Gao Jinyuan, "Yiselie—diguo zhuyi pohuai zhongdong heping de gongju" [Israel—the Tool of Imperialism to Break the Peace in the Middle East], *People's Daily* (Beijing), November 8, 1956.

the Western imperialists, you should drop your weapons, stop your sins and stop killing your neighbors."[20] Therefore, it could be argued that at that moment, Israel was still occasionally viewed as a victim of swindlers, which was still different from its image in the 1960s when China began to be obsessed with the idea of "world revolution" and called for the destruction of the "Zionist Regime."

Although in the following years after the end of the Suez Crisis, Israel had been playing a relatively negative role in the reports of *People's Daily*, China's mainstream media shifted its criticism away from Israel at the beginning of the 1960s. This was primarily because in the early days of the 1960s, China and the Soviet Union split and ended up in rivalry, with China fighting against both "American imperialism" and "Soviet revisionism" simultaneously, and thus caused China to reduce its focus on the Middle East for a while. China not only faced threats from the Soviet Union and the United States but also underwent a hard time as some countries, which had close relations with the Soviet Union, gradually distanced themselves from China. Egypt, Iraq, and Yemen were among those countries that had a bumpy relationship with China throughout the early 1960s.[21] On the other hand, China's economy encountered great difficulties in the early 1960s because of the "Great Leap Forward" (*da yuejin*) movement, resulting in a sharp decline in foreign trade. Moreover, the decrease of China's aid to foreign countries also severely impacted Sino-Arab relations and led to the decline of China's influence in the Middle East.

Under such circumstances, it was unlikely that *People's Daily* and other Chinese mainstream media would widely cover reports on the Middle East as they did in the Suez Crisis and afterwards. A set of data from the *People's Daily* might substantiate China's decreasing interest in the Middle East during the early 1960s: there was only a total of 35 reports with "Israel" included in their titles from January 1, 1960 to

---

20 Yang Ruiqi and Wan Zhijing, "Zhichi aiji renmin fandui yingfa qinlue" [Supporting the People of Egypt to Fight against the Anglo-French Aggression], *People's Daily* (Beijing), November 2, 1956.
21 Yitzhak Shichor, *The Middle East in China's Foreign Policy 1949–1977* (New York: Cambridge University Press, 1979).

December 31, 1964; by comparison, as many as 136 reports focusing on Israel appeared on the newspaper in the year 1957.

The Third Stage: 1965–1976

In contrast to China's low profile in the early 1960s, however, reports in the Chinese media on Israel and on the Middle East have increased significantly from 1965 onward. Taking *People's Daily* as an example, there were a total of 71 reports mentioning Israel from 1965 to the eve of the Six-Day War, which was more than twice of the number of reports from 1960 to 1964. This phenomenon was not only closely related to the tensions between Israel and the United Arab Republic at that time, but it also could be connected to the domestic political movements in China. The Great Cultural Revolution, which would break out a year later and severely deteriorate the foreign relations of China, was now on the way. More important, the fanaticism of the "continuous revolution" in the mid-1960s aroused China's expectation for the world revolution, which would underline "the unity of revolutionaries worldwide" against those two superpowers, the United States and the Soviet Union.

In practice, China not only paid lip service to the "national liberation movement of the Third World" including the Arab states in the Middle East, but it also offered substantial foreign assistance to those parties or organizations which carried out armed struggles, for example the Palestinian Liberation Organization (PLO) which was founded in 1964. China treated the PLO office in Beijing with the same level of embassies and helped it train all kinds of personnel. Moreover, in 1965 when meeting with the delegation of the PLO, Mao Zedong said, "Israel, like Taiwan, is one of the military bases of the American Imperialism in Asia. The United States inserted Israel into the Arab land, just like they created the Taiwan issue for us—with the same purpose."[22] Since the leaders of CPC viewed the Arabs as China's natural allies, there is no doubt that Israel was seen as China's archenemy in the international arena.

Not surprisingly, therefore, when China shifted its attention back to the Middle East again in 1965, its mainstream media began to vilify

---

22 Wang, "Guojia liyi shiye xia de zhongyi guanxi."

the State of Israel in accordance with China's foreign policy toward this region. For example in the news feature titled "Israel—the Tool of Invasion of the United States," published on May 17, 1966, the author wrote, "On the next day of its founding, the State of Israel began to wage war against its neighboring Arab states."[23] This stance is totally different from the reports in *People's Daily* in 1948.

Half a month later, the Six-Day War broke out in the morning of June 5, 1967, which fundamentally reshaped the geopolitical structure of the Middle East, and its repercussions remain until today. Despite the numerical disadvantages of Israel against Egypt, Jordan, and Syria in terms of troops and weaponry, the fledgling Jewish state fought for its survival by launching preemptive strikes against the Arabs. Israel not only unexpectedly defeated the Egyptian, Jordanian, and Syrian armies within six days, but it also reversed its position among Middle Eastern countries. Correspondingly, however, the image of Israel in China's mainstream media also suffered another disastrous decline and was depicted as the "demon" because of its relentless war effort against the Arab countries. During the Six-Day War and afterward, the image of Israel in *People's Daily* was always connected with negative terms such as "invaders," "war machine," or "proxy of the United States," while the Arab side always appeared as the "just defenders."

Moreover, a report after the Six-Day War in *People's Daily* was entitled "Uprooting Strongholds, Raiding Barracks, Planting Mines and Bombing Military Vehicles: Palestinian Guerrillas Launched Series Attacks Heavily Beating Israeli Invaders," which could easily arouse the history of guerrilla warfare led by the CPC during the anti-Japanese war among the Chinese readers, evoking a mood of sympathy with the Palestinians/Arabs and also abhorrence of Israelis.[24] Generally speaking, during this period, the Chinese media adopted

---

23 Rong Jiu, "Yiselie—meiguo de qinlue gongju" [Israel—the Tool of Invasion of the United States], *People's Daily* (Beijing), May 17, 1966.
24 Xinhua News Agency, "Ba judian xi junying mai dilei zha junche balesitan youjidui guangfan chuji tongjian yiselie qinluejun" [Uprooting Strongholds, Raiding Barracks, Planting Mines, and Bombing Military Vehicles: Palestinian Guerrillas Launches Series Attacks Heavily Beating Israeli Invaders.], *People's Daily* (Beijing), September 14, 1968.

the terms and rhetoric of the age of revolution. Negative terms were exclusively directed to Israel, such as aggression, barbarity, cruelty, turpitude, crime, brutality, brazenness, looting, extremely atrocity, provocation, insanity, arrogance, and killing. Positive terms always related to Arab countries and people, such as bravery, fearlessness, sacrificing, revolutionary masses, people, and absolute justice.[25]

Besides, in accordance with China's grand strategy of both "anti-Soviet" and "anti-America" during this period, Chinese mainstream media always attacked these two superpowers when criticizing Israel. In addition to criticizing the Johnson administration of the United States for supporting Israel, Chinese media like *People's Daily* also claimed that the Soviet Union betrayed the Arabs since it allowed the Jews to immigrate to Israel during the reign of Brezhnev. Therefore, Israel is depicted as the mixed blood of the Soviets and the Americans, "Israel is so audacious to oppose the 100 million Arabs only because it gets the support from both superpowers. The United States gives it money and armaments, while the Soviet Union provides it with human resources."[26]

In addition to vilifying Israel, in 1973, the *People's Daily* claimed that the October War was a deliberate invasion launched by Israel, which is obviously different from the fact that Egypt and Syria fought this war in order to gain back the lands they lost in 1967. In general, the numbers of reports about Israel reached a new height in *People's Daily* during the early 1970s, and on average there was a news report relevant to Israel every two or three days. Immediately after the October War, readers could find more than one report about Israel in *People's Daily* every day and most of them followed the same style: Israeli Defense Force continues to provoke the Arab front and is bitterly hit by the Egyptian/Syrian Army or by the Palestinian guerrilla groups.

The Fourth Stage: 1977–1985

The next change of the reports on Israel in *People's Daily* began to occur in 1977. In the decade before 1977 when China was experiencing

---

25 Ma, "Liushinian lai woguo meiti guanyu zhongdong wenti de baodao."
26 Xinhua News Agency, "Shi shui tong yiselie 'gongkai goujie'" [Who Is "Overtly Colluding" with Israel], *People's Daily* (Beijing), March 26, 1976.

the devastating "Great Cultural Revolution," few reports could be defined as "objective" or "neutral" by the standards of today. However, in 1977, the first report with a relatively neutral stance toward Israel appeared in *People's Daily*. It was about Egyptian President Sadat's visit to Jerusalem and the reception from the Israeli side.[27] Similar reports could also be found regarding the peace talks that followed, the Camp David accords negotiated by the United States President Jimmy Carter in 1978, and the signing of the peace treaty between Egypt and Israel in 1979.

Such change reflected in reports was not only related to the progress of peace negotiations between Israel and Egypt during the late 1970s, but also closely connected to the political atmosphere in China itself. After Mao Zedong died in 1976, the Cultural Revolution finally drew to an end. After abandoning the fanaticism of world revolution, the communist leadership of China became more and more pragmatic and mild in international disputes. Besides, as China shifted its focus to domestic economic developments, it reduced its foreign aid to those "revolutionary states" of the third world and helped create a more peaceful environment in which China could build normal commercial ties with more countries.

However, such change doesn't mean that China completely abandoned its former stance regarding Israel. There is no doubt that most reports in *People's Daily* about Israel in the late 1970s and early 1980s were still severely critical, especially when Israel announced plans to annex East Jerusalem in 1980 and the Golan Heights in 1981. Moreover, after Israel invaded Lebanon in 1982, the *People's Daily* began a new wave of criticism, which climaxed in the news reports about the massacre that took place in the Palestinian refugee camp of Sabra and Shatila in West Beirut.[28]

---

27 Xinhua News Agency, "Aiji zongtong sadate fangwen yiselie" [Egyptian President Sadat Pays a Visit to Israel], *People's Daily* (Beijing), November 28, 1977.
28 Xinhua News Agency, "Yiselie qinluejun qinzhan beilute xiqu zhihou canku tusha yiqianduo ming balesitan nanmin" [More than One Thousand Palestinian Refugees were Mercilessly Slaughtered after the Israeli Invading Troops Occupied West Beirut], *People's Daily* (Beijing), September 20, 1982.

Another interesting aspect of the reports in *People's Daily* in this period is the differentiation of "the Israeli people" from the Likud government. In contrast to the previous reports, which just focused on the "belligerent" Israeli government, the voice of the Israeli left began to be heard in China. For example, a report titled "Tens of Thousands Israeli People Demanded Begin's Ouster" published on September 27, 1982 covered in detail the mass protest held by Peace Now in Tel Aviv two days earlier in which many people pressured the government to establish a national inquiry commission to investigate the massacres and called for the resignation of the Defense Minister Ariel Sharon.[29] Moreover, many other reports in *People's Daily* during this period were focusing on the complaints from ordinary Israelis about the worsening economic conditions and recurring crises in Israel.

The Fifth Stage: 1986–1991

After the year 1985, as Mikhail Gorbachev became the leader of the Soviet Union and began his economic and political reform, the tensions of the Cold War in the international arena were gradually lowered. It was under such circumstances that China and Israel realized a new opportunity to develop relations. This rapprochement between China and Israel at the end of the 1980s was also reflected in Chinese mainstream media like *People's Daily*. Some reports with positive attitudes toward Israel began to appear in *People's Daily* again after more than 30 years. One of the most obvious examples was the coverage of Shimon Peres' visit to Morocco in 1986, which was described by *People's Daily* as "a compelling event" in the Middle East.[30]

---

29 Xinhua News Agency, "Yiselie shushiwan qunzhong shiwei yao beijing xiatai" [Tens of Thousands Israeli People Demanded Begin's Ouster], *People's Daily* (Beijing), September 27, 1982.

30 Chen Jichang and An Guozhang, "Zhongdong xingshi fazhan zhong yige yinrenzhumu shijian yiselie zongli peileisi turan fangwen moluoge mo guanfang jianmo meiguo gandao gaoxing yue yu ai xu shate chuoshang" [A Compelling Event Occurs in the Middle East. Israeli Prime Minister Peres Pays a Visit to Morocco. Moroccan Government Remains Silent. The United States Is Happy about the Development. Jordan Exchanges Views with Egypt, Syria, and Saudi Arabia.], *People's Daily* (Beijing), July 23, 1986.

There were still many reports critical of Israel, especially during Israel's crackdown of the first *intifada*, but the numbers and levels of such critical reports were significantly reduced compared with the last three decades. Instead, more "appeals" appeared in *People's Daily*, which called for peace talks between Israel and the Palestinians. And more and more reports focused on the domestic situation and political structures of Israel, as well as scientific developments, which meant that the image of Israel was in transition from an "enemy state" to a "normal state." For example, on September 21, 1988, *People's Daily* reported with a positive tone that Israel launched its first man-made satellite and mentioned that "this means Israel becomes the eighth country around the globe having the ability to send satellites into space, and thus becomes one of the members of the 'space satellite' club in the international community."[31]

Perhaps the most important aspect about the change of Israel's image in *People's Daily* in this period is that there were more and more reports about direct contact between China and Israel on an official level, which would have been unimaginable before the mid-1980s. First is a report published on July 2, 1987 about a visit of the leaders of the Israeli Communist Party to Beijing, in which *People's Daily* reported that "the relations between Israeli Communist Party and Communist Party of China have been normalized."[32] Later, there were more reports about the meetings between delegation members and also between the foreign ministers of China and Israel inside the United Nations headquarters in New York.

At the end of 1991, journalists from Xinhua News Agency, the official news agency of China, interviewed the Israeli Prime Minister for the first time. *People's Daily* reported this interview and quoted Yitzhak Shamir's words that "Israel is interested in developing normal and friendly relations with China," and "cooperation between China and

---

31 Lv Zhixing and Wu Wenbin, "Yiselie fashe diyike renzao weixing" [Israel Launches its First Man-Made Satellite], *People's Daily* (Beijing), September 21, 1988.
32 Feng Zhaoyang, "Yigong zongshuji zai beijing da jizhe wen" [General Secretary of the Communist Party of Israel Answers Questions in Beijing.], *People's Daily* (Beijing), July 7, 1987.

Israel would not only be good for two countries, but also for two peoples."³³

The Cold War came to an end when the Soviet Union collapsed in the last month of 1991, while the relations between China and Israel, as well as the image of Israel in Chinese media like *People's Daily*, were also ready for the beginning of a new chapter. One month later, on January 24, 1992, China and Israel formally established diplomatic relations, with the signing of the communiqué in Beijing by the foreign ministers of both countries, David Levy and Qian Qichen.

Conclusion

From the materials and analyses mentioned above, we could argue that an examination of the reports about Israel in *People's Daily* during the Cold War could not only help us understand many aspects of Sino-Israel relations at the same period, but it could also enable us to analyze the inner connections between the image of Israel, Sino-Israel relations, and the domestic and foreign events China experienced in those 40 plus years. Several conclusions could be drawn.

1) The changing image of Israel in China during the Cold War is a reflection of China's changing foreign policies during the same period. The foreign relations of China were constantly changing during the period of the Cold War, and the reports in *People's Daily* became a mirror to reflect the different stances and orientations of China's diplomatic strategies since it served as perhaps the most important official newspaper of the Chinese government. Therefore, no matter whether *People's Daily* praised Israel's struggle during its "War of Independence" in the late 1940s or condemned Israel's "aggression" against neighboring Arab countries in the 1960s and 1970s, we could always trace relevant sources in China's foreign policies. It is totally understandable that the attitudes of *People's Daily*, the mouthpiece of the

---

33 Zhou Zexin and Gao Qiufu, "Yiselie zongli jieshou xinhuashe jizhe caifang tan zhongdong hehui deng wenti" [Israeli Prime Minister Is Interviewed by Journalists of Xinhua News Agency and Talks about Issues Including the Middle East Peace Conference], *People's Daily* (Beijing), December 5, 1991.

CPC, seemed to be synchronous with the stances of the Chinese government during the Cold War.

2) Israel has often been a focus of China's foreign strategies in the international arena, but it hardly served as the core interest of China during the Cold War. China's policies toward Israel were always influenced, or even determined, by its policies toward other regions or countries in the same region, i.e. the Middle East. During the first Arab-Israeli War in 1948–1949, most reports in *People's Daily* about Israel were followed by the viewpoints or comments from the Soviet government, *Tass*, or *Pravda*. And, after mid-1950s, when criticizing Israel, *People's Daily* usually included condemnation of the United States or the Soviet Union in the same articles. By the mid-1980s, when China withdrew step-by-step from the Cold War structure and focused on its domestic developments, *People's Daily* gradually began to treat Israel as a normal state in its reports.

3) The changing image of Israel in the Chinese media is also closely connected to the domestic affairs in China during the Cold War. According to the sociology of news production, the essence of producing international news is the process of domestication, localization, and even nationalization, which is inevitably influenced by the domestic political structures, cultural traditions, and economic interests.[34] And the core of such kind of domestication and localization is to establish correlation between external/foreign events with the internal/domestic readers. Therefore, it is not surprising that when Israel appeared in *People's Daily* as the just defender against the Arab armies helped by the British personnel in the late 1940s, the CPC was at the same time calling the Chinese people to fight against the KMT which was assisted by another "imperialist" country—the United States; when in the late 1960s and early 1970s *People's Daily* condemned Israel day after day as the archenemy of the

---

34 Gan Xianfeng, "Meiguo zhuliu meijie wenben zhong de zhongguo xingxiang bianqian" [The Transitions of China's Image in the American Mainstream Media], *Xinwen daxue* [*Journalism Quarterly*], 2010.2.

"revolutionary" Arab people, China was undergoing the so-called "Cultural Revolution" and obsessing with the idea of pushing forward the "world revolution"; and finally when *People's Daily* began to focus on the domestic situation, especially the scientific developments, in Israel in the late 1980s, China also was shifting its attention to its economic reform and developments.

The Reception of Contemporary Israeli Literature in China

ZHIQING ZHONG
Chinese Academy of Social Sciences

In an essay titled "Modern Hebrew Literature in China" published in Chinese,[1] I clarified the terms of "Jewish Literature," "Hebrew Literature," and "Israeli Literature" for the first time to the Chinese speaking world. "Contemporary Israeli literature" means the literary products produced in the modern Jewish-nation state, the State of Israel.

The cultural contacts between China and Israel grew dramatically after the establishment of diplomatic relations between China and Israel in 1992. To some extent, the reception of contemporary Israeli literature in Chinese should trace back to this historical moment.

The Translation of Contemporary Israeli Literature into Chinese

"The single most important invention in the history of human civilization is the translation," said the distinguished Israeli author Amos Oz in a seminar devoted to his writings and held by the Institute of Foreign Literature at Chinese Academy of Social Sciences (CASS), the highest research institution in China, at the turn of summer and autumn 2007. As the great step in the process by which a work of literature written in

---

1 First it was published in a collection of a series of conference papers by Peking University; then it was reprinted by *Journal of Suzhou Technological College*, No. 2, 2007; and then it was published in *Dialogue Transcultural*, eds. Yue Daiyun and Alain le Pichon (Nanjing: Jiangsu People's Press, 2007), 308–317.

one language and culture reveals itself to another language and culture,[2] translation indeed played an important basic role for Chinese to get in touch with and to accept contemporary Israeli literature and culture.

Similar to America, in which it is difficult to argue that Israeli literature has enjoyed anything more than very limited success,[3] Israeli novels in Chinese translation did not sell very well in general compared to equally important English and American writers. The reason, I argue, is that Chinese were still not familiar with Israeli culture and Israeli society, which shaped the settings of its literature at the beginning of the 1990s. Some readers claim that it was hard for them to enjoy reading those texts due to their strange and alien contexts. Also, America is more influential on the ideology in China than Israel. However, in contrast to America, when it comes to the generality of committed Jewish laypeople who are affiliated with Jewish institutions and are involved with the life of the community, it is difficult to find much recognition of the names of Israeli writers, not to mention experience reading their works.[4] Some big names in Hebrew literature, such as Amos Oz, Yehuda Amichai, and David Grossman, are gradually becoming more and more popular among Chinese intellectuals and even among common readers.

Before focusing on the peculiar phenomenon of Amos Oz's popularity in China, I would like to give a general map of contemporary Israeli literature in China. In retrospect, according to the recent statistics of the Institute for the Translation of Hebrew Literature in Tel Aviv, the decade of 1986–1996 saw the publication of 12 Hebrew books in Chinese translation, while the decade of 1996–2006 was much more fruitful with 48 titles published. Up to now, 114 books and anthologies have been translated from Hebrew into Chinese. More specifically,

---

2   Alan Mintz, *Translating Israel: Contemporary Hebrew Literature and Its Reception in America* (New York: Syracuse University Press, 2001), 15. See also, Zhong Zhiqing, "Modern Hebrew Literature in China," in *The Jewish-Chinese Nexus: A Meeting of Civilizations*, ed. M. Avrum Ehrlich (London and New York: Routledge, 2008), 164–172.
3   Alan Mintz, *Translating Israel: Contemporary Hebrew Literature and Its Reception in America*, 3.
4   Ibid., 3.

there are 74 books of prose, 5 books of poetry, 27 books for children, and 10 anthologies. The growing number is prominent in contemporary literary works of world literature. Perhaps the publications of contemporary Israeli literature rank second only to Japanese literature in the field of Eastern literary studies in the last decade. Among these titles, there are collections of Hebrew short stories and poetry, including *An Anthology of Hebrew Short Stories*, edited by Xu Xin, 1992; *Songs of Jerusalem*, a collection of Hebrew poetry by Yehuda Amichai, translated by Fu Hao, 1992; "Three Days and a Child," a short story of A. B. Yehoshua translated by Chen Yiyi, 1992; as well as a series of Hebrew novels including S. Y. Agnon's *The Bride Canopy*, translated by Xu Xin and others, 1995; Amos Oz's *My Michael*, 1998, and *Black Box*, 2004, both translated by Zhong Zhiqing; and David Grossman's *See Under: Love*, translated by Zhang Chong and Zhang Qiong, 2005.

The translation of modern Hebrew fiction is more impressive. As they began to introduce contemporary Israeli literature to the Chinese speaking world, the publishers and the people involved in this cultural distribution paid more attention to Hebrew classics. Early collections of Israeli literature published both in Taiwan and in mainland China mainly included the writings of S. Y. Agnon, S. Yizhar, Moshe Shamir, Haim Hazaz, and Yehuda Amichai. The mainland collections came out later than those published in Taiwan in the 1970s; therefore, the publishers had a chance to include several world famous Hebrew authors who came onto the literary scene in the 1960s, such as Amos Oz, A. B. Yehoshua, and Aharon Appelfeld. Meanwhile, some literary magazines, such as *Contemporary Foreign Literature* (vol. 2, 1991) and *Journal of World Literature* (vol. 6, 1994), published special issues on contemporary Israeli literature. For instance, *Journal of World Literature*, a leading literary translation magazine in China, published a special issue on contemporary Israeli literature and included "The Continuing Silence of a Poet" by A. B. Yehoshua, "Where the Jackals Howl" by Amos Oz, and "Momic," an excerpt from David Grossman's masterpiece *See Under: Love*.

The Institute of Translation for Hebrew Literature played a key role in the first and second stages of promoting contemporary Israeli literature in mainland China. More recently, the Devorah Harris Agency has been very active in distributing Hebrew books in the Chinese market. Mrs. Nilli Cohen, the director of the Institute, came to the Beijing International Book Fair (BIBF) almost every year to meet with Chinese publishers and translators. The Institute provided humble subsidies to help publish most of the Hebrew classics mentioned above. In cooperation with the Institute for the Translation of Hebrew Literature, Anhui Literature and Art Publishing House published a best Hebrew Fiction Series in 1998. It included Yosef Haim Brenner's *Breakdown and Bereavement*, translated by Luo Han and Meng Jian; David Vogel's *Married Life*, translated by Yang Dongxia and Yang Haihong; Yossel Birstein's *A Face in the Clouds*, translated by Liao Huixiang and Xiao Yaozhen; and Ruth Almog's *Tiny Coat*, translated by Diaso Haifeng and Wang Mingqian. Also supported by the Institute for the Translation of Hebrew Literature, in 2000, Baihuazhou Literature and Art Publishing House published a series of contemporary Israeli novels edited by Mr. Gao Qiufu, former deputy President of Xinhua News Agency. These four books are Yehoshua Kanaz *After the Holidays*, translated by Zhong Zhiqing; Birstein's *Collector*, translated by Sui Lijun; Yoram Kaniuk's *Aunt Shlomzion the Great*, translated by Shen Zhihong and Gao Sui; and Aryeh Sivan's *Adonis*, translated by Dai Huikun and Xiaodai. This series of books were reprinted and also received the national book prize in Foreign Literature in China. In addition, China Social Sciences Publishing House published Ruth Almog's *Death in the Rain*, translated by Zhu Meihui; Orly Castel-Bloom's *Mina Liza*, translated by Yang Yugong; and Benjamin Tammuz's *Minotaur*, translated by Zheng Yalan, in 1998.

Later on, Shanghai Translation Press was working on ten Hebrew classical books sponsored by the Eisenberg family through the Institute for the Translation of Hebrew Literature. Among them are Amos Oz's *Black Box*, translated by Zhong Zhiqing, 2004; S. Y. Agnon's *A Simple Story*, translated by late Xu Chongliang, 2004; Meir Shalev's *Blue Mountain*, translated by Yu Haijiang and Zhangying, 2005; David Grossman's *See Under: Love*, translated by Zhang Chong and Zhang Qiong, 2005; Yehuda Amichai's *Open Closed Open* translated by Huang Fuhai, 2007;

Aharon Appelfeld's *The Age of Wonders*, translated by Yang Yang, 2009; A. B. Yehoshua's *Lover*, translated by Xiang Hongquan and Feng Xia, 2009; Haim Be'er's *The Pure Element of Time*, translated by Wang Yibao, 2010;Yoram Kaniuk's *Adam Resurrected*, translated by Lu Hanzhen and Guo Guoliang, 2010; and Yehoshua Kenaz's *Returning Lost Loves*, translated by Huang Fuhai, 2010. The publication of these series signified that Hebrew literature in Chinese translation has become more and more accepted.

Special issues on Hebrew literature in periodicals are also well organized, which marked the fact that Chinese editors and translators were professionally furthering development of the genre. As one of the editors for *Journal of World Literature* at that time, I gained professional training in Hebrew language and literature at Tel Aviv University and started my PhD program in modern Hebrew literature under the supervision of Prof. Yigal Schwartz at Hebrew University and then continued at Ben-Gurion University in Israel so that I might try to combine the literary value in Israel with the reader's taste in China. In 1999, *Journal of World Literature* published a special issue on the young generation of prominent Israeli writers who emerged on the literary scene in the 1980s and 1990s. This includes an excerpt from Meir Shalev's *The Blue Mountain* and short stories and essays by David Grossman, Orly Castel-Bloom, Nava Semel, and Etgar Keret. In 2003, this *Journal of World Literature* published a special issue on Israeli Holocaust literature including the writings of many eminent Hebrew Holocaust writers and poets, such as Aharon Appefeld, Ka-Tzetnik, Haim Gouri, Yehuda Amichai, Dan Pagis, Itama Yaoz-Kest, Natan Zach, Abba Kovner, as well as second generation Holocaust writers such as Savyon Liebrecht and Nava Semel. To a certain extent, these two issues showed a more professional selection, with a specific theme by both Chinese and Israeli editors and a good review essay, or preface. Meanwhile, the editor's thinking and motives were published in *The Scorch Land: A Selection of Modern Israeli Stories*, edited by Gao Qiufu, People's Literature Publishing House, 1998, and *The Mediterranean Rose: A Selection of Israeli Women Writers*, Chinese Women's Press. Meanwhile, some publishers started to import bestsellers. For instance, People's Literature Press bought the copyright of Zeruya Shalev's *Love Life*, and the first print was 8,000 copies. But it will take time to see whether the bestsellers in Israel and other European countries can be appreciated by Chinese readers.

To some extent, 1996 was the turning point in introducing contemporary Israeli literature to China when Yilin Press in Nanjing bought the copyrights for, and published, five books of Amos Oz: *Elsewhere Perhaps*, translated by Yao Yongcai, 1998; *My Michael*, translated by Zhong Zhiqing, 1998; *To Know A Woman*, translated by Fu Hao and Ke Yanbin, 1999; *Perfect Peace*, translated by Yao Yongqiang and Guo Hongtao, 1999; and *Fima*, translated by Fan Hongsheng, 2000. This was the first time a single Hebrew Israeli author was introduced on a large scale in China by an independent Chinese publishing house. Another Hebrew writer who was published by an independent Chinese publisher was Uri Orlev. Three of his novels, including *The Man from the Other Side*, translated by Yang Hengda and Yang Fan; *Lydia, Queen of Palestine*, translated by Yang Hengda and Yang Rong; and *The Island on Bird Street*, translated by Li Wenjun were published by Anhui Children's Publishing House in 2000.

The visit of Amos Oz to the Institute of Foreign Literature at CASS in 2007 could be seen as a breakthrough in the literary exchange between China and Israel. In cooperation with the Israeli Embassy in Beijing and the Israeli Consulate in Shanghai, we arranged a series of events and activities which brought great attention to contemporary Israeli literature from Chinese publishers, intellectuals, and common readers. In addition to launching *A Tale of Love and Darkness*, translated by Zhong Zhiqing, lectures at CASS, Beijing University, and elsewhere, and cultural activities both in Beijing and Shanghai, a seminar was held on the works of Amos Oz by the Institute of Foreign Literature at CASS. This was the first time such a seminar devoted to the writings of a single Hebrew writer had been held in China. Three generations of Chinese scholars and writers attended. Among them was Mo Yan, a Nobel Prize laureate, who delivered a speech. More than forty leading Chinese newspapers and magazines published articles, reports, or review essays related to these events. Ms. Cao Jie, the associate editor-in-chief for Zhejiang Literature and Art Publishing House, negotiated with Liu Feng, the editor-in-chief for Yilin Press which owns Amos Oz's copyright in mainland China, and decided to buy the rights for *Rhyming Life and Death* and *Where the Jackals Howl* after meeting with Amos Oz at the BIBF. Tong Baomin from the People's Literature Publishing House decided to republish Zhong Zhiqing's translation of *Black Box* after the rights of Shanghai Translation Publishing House expired. These three novels appeared on the market in 2010 and 2011. Yilin Press continued to publish Amos Oz's *The Same Sea*, translated by Hui Lan, 2012; *A Panther in the Basement*, translated by Zhong Zhiqing, 2012; *The Story Begins*, translated by Yang Zhengtong; and *Suddenly in the Depth of Forests*, translated by Zhong Zhiqing, 2012.

In March 2010, David Grossman, another distinguished Israeli author, came to visit Beijing and Shanghai, invited by the Bookworm Festival. I wrote a long interview for a leading Chinese newspaper. Zhengjiang Literature and Art Publishing House and Yilin Press consulted with me about Grossman's books. They bought the rights to *Her Body Knows, Frenzy, The Internal Grammar, Someone to Run With*, and *Zigzag Child*. Three of them are available on the market now. Meanwhile, China CITIC Press and Nanhai Press published Meir Shalev's *A Pigeon and a Boy*, translated by Mao Lu, 2008, and Sami Michael's *A Trumpet in the Wadi*, translated by Li Huijuan, 2009.

The Canonization of Amoz Oz in China

Until now, Amos Oz is the most widely translated and best recognized Hebrew writer translated into Chinese. In his influential work *The Western Canon: The Books and School of the Ages*, Harold Bloom selected Amos Oz's *A Perfect Peace* in his reading list of classics.[5] Originally published in 1982, *A Perfect Peace* has been translated into Chinese based on Hillel Halkin's English version by Harcourt Brace Jovanovich in 1985. Set in a fictional kibbutz, the novel portrayed the gap and the ideological tensions between the founding fathers of the

---

5   Harold Bloom, *The Western Canon, the Book and School of the Ages* (New York: Riverhead Books, 1994), 528.

kibbutz and their children. The son, Yonaton Lifshitz, decides to leave the kibbutz where he was born and raised, and his sterile marriage, to start a new life. But the arrival of Azariah Gitlin, a Russian, brings about a painful reconciliation of their different destinies in a society struggling with changing realities. It is "Oz's strangest, riskiest, and richest novel," wrote *Washington Post Book World*. "Oz is a peerless, imaginative chronicler of his country's inner and outer transformation," from *Independent*; and "handles his narrative with great agility," from *Sunday Times*. Amos Oz told me he mostly appreciates *The Same Sea*, originally published in 1998, and *My Michael*, originally published in 1968.[6] As a literary professor and critic at Yale, Harold Bloom selects authors for "both their sublimity and their representative nature." It seems to him that "originally the canon meant the choice of books in our teaching institutions, and despite the recent politics of multiculturalism."[7] As for the canonical status of a literary work, he pointed out that an originality is a strangeness.[8] At this point, he values *A Perfect Peace* for its portrayal of peculiar kibbutz life and the conflicts between the pioneering Zionists and the native-born Israelis. In contrast, as a representative New Wave writer, Amos Oz seems to value his personal literary techniques and the readers' responses to the books, so he favors *My Michael*, which changes the face of modern Hebrew literature, and *The Same Sea*, which combines poetry and prose.

At the beginning of the 1990s, three short stories by Amos Oz, including "Nomad and Viper," "The Way of the Wind," and "Where the Jackals Howl," were translated into Chinese, but there was almost no response from readers. As mentioned above, Yilin's edition of five books of Amos Oz published in the second half of the 1990s brought attention from circles of Chinese academics, writers, and common readers.

---

6 From one of the conversations between the author and me in the autumn of 2010 in Tel Aviv.
7 Harold Boom, *The Western Canon, the Book and School of the Ages*, 15.
8 Ibid., 4.

Although *A Perfect Peace* has received some good reviews since publication, it has not achieved the reputation of literary classics in China. Among the five titles of Amos Oz by Yilin Press, *My Michael* was best received both critically and commercially. Immediately after it came out in 1998, the leading women writers Chi Li and Xu Kun commented positively about Amos Oz's understanding of women; Chi Li mentioned many times the influence of Amos Oz's poetic and concise language on her own writing.[9] Prof. Ding Fan, a leading literary critic at Nanjing University, identified with Oz and the culture he represented.[10] In 1999, *My Michael* received a national book prize in Foreign Literature in China; it was also the first Israeli book that won a prize in China. Later on, *My Michael* and *To Know a Woman* were reprinted and republished by Crown Publishing Company in Taiwan in 2004. Just before Oz's first visit to China in 2007, these two novels were republished in mainland China by Yilin Press. In the seminar on Amos Oz in 2007 at CASS, both Xu Kun and Yan Lianke, another leading Chinese writer and the 2014 Kafka Prize winner, delivered a lecture on *My Michael*. In the year of 2012, *My Michael,* together with another three Oz titles in this series, were reprinted. According to the publisher, altogether *My Michael* was reprinted five times in mainland China and sold more than 20,000 copies.

My Michael has several characteristics of a canonical work in the eyes of Chinese readers and literary critics. First, it is of great aesthetic value. As Chi Li said, the essence of literature is that it is the art of word. The most charming characteristic of *My Michael* lies in the texture of language, which is clear, terse, and with the beauty of rhyme. The opening paragraph of the novel reads, "I am writing because people I loved have died. I am writing this because when I was young I was full of the power of loving, and now that power of loving is dying. I do

---

9 Chi Li, "Juemiao de jianyue zhimei" [The Perfect Beauty of His Terse Style] in *Dongfang wenhua zhoukan* [Oriental Culture Weekly], vol. 8, 1999; Xun Kun, "Yelusaleng, Yelusaleng" [Jerusalem, Jerusalem] in *Zhonghua Dushubao* [Chinese Reader Weekly], March 24, 1999.
10 Ding Fan, "Tupo Wenhua Goutong de Pingzhang" [Bridging the Gap between the Cultures] in *Zhonghua dushubao* [Chinese Reader Weekly], March 24, 1999.

not want to die." Readers can't help being touched and locked into reading.[11]

Second, Amos Oz shows the vivid life and people of Jerusalem in the 1950s to people outside Israel. Xu Kun recognized that the genius of Oz comes from his successful portrayal of Israeli women's everyday life and psyche. Through daily routine, he shows the gloomy family life and society of Jerusalem in the 1950s.[12] At the seminar on Oz's works, Yan Lianke claimed that the detailed elements of family life form the tissues full of literary life and literary blood and passion in Amos Oz's novel. Beneath Hanna and her family's anxiety and restlessness lies the anxiety of Jerusalem. Through the passionate and poetic narrative, a Chinese writer may sense the harmoniousness and rupture.[13]

Third, scholars made connections between Israeli women, family, and national politics through reading *My Michael*. As I pointed out in my latest essay on Oz, the first perception of this poetic novel is a love story, and it drew the attention of many Chinese readers for its fluent and beautiful writing. However, it actually reflects the social and political myths of the 1950s through the telling of a young couple's family life and their love tragedy. I argued that Hanna Gonen, the heroine, is an anti-social and anti-political figure through analyzing her complex attitude toward family, the Arabic twins, and Jerusalem.[14]

Another novel by Amos Oz that has been accepted very well is *A Tale of Love and Darkness*. The book was first introduced to China in 2007, and I translated it.. It has been republished twice, both in mainland China and in Taiwan, and reprinted three times. In the past seven years, the novel has received dozens of reviews and essays. Readers

---

11   Chi Li, "Juemiao de jianyue zhimei" [The Perfect Beauty of His Terse Style] in *Dongfang wenhua zhoukan* [Oriental Culture Weekly], vol. 8, 1998.
12   Xun Kun, "Yelusaleng, Yelusaleng" [Jerusalem, Jerusalem] in *Zhonghua dushubao* [Chinese Reader Weekly], March 24, 1999.
13   Yan Lianke, "Yelusaleng jiaolv de chuiyan" [The Cooking Smoke of Jerusalem's Anxiety] in *Journal of World Literature* 1 (2008), 287–291.
14   Zhong Zhiqing, "Nvxing, jiatingyu guozuzhengzhi: aozi de 《wode mihaier》 [Women, Family, and National Politics: Reading Amos Oz's *My Michael*] in *Journal of Jewish Studies*, 12 (2013), 151–159.

were deeply touched by Amos Oz's personal stories and Jewish experience.

Chinese writers represented by Mo Yan, the Nobel Prize laureate in 2012, wrote that it is a personal bible, which shows Bible-like tolerance and sincerity: Amos Oz is a Jew, but what he has done is beyond simply being a Jew; he is an Israeli, but he embraces the whole of mankind. His voice is clear and wise.

Mo Yan also said that he mostly appreciated Amos Oz's great talent as a writer. In his opinion, Amos Oz put a Jewish family, a cell of a Jewish nation, into the background of Jewish history and family. As a novelist, Mo Yan said he admired Amos Oz's literary technique of creating characters and scenes. As he said, we followed the pen of Amos Oz and his characters, we crossed through the streets of Jerusalem and entered the Joseph Klausner's library; we met with the little Arab girl and her little brother. We moved with him into that soul-stirring night when the General Assembly of the United Nations voted for a Jewish State and an Arab State in Palestine; the dark streets, the bright starry sky, and the trembling air are beset with crisis and hope. We seem to see his father, who spoke many languages, an elegant and polite man, stand there shouting, as if words had not been invented. We seem to see his mother, a restrained and indifferent woman, embraced with her stranger-like husband for the first time. The fates of nation, state, and normal family are merged so stirringly. However, outside the Jewish neighborhood, the countless Arabs were in a silence, preparing to meet the miserable fate of being exiled from their homeland, shedding blood, fighting, and sacrificing. Such a scene is the great contribution of Amos Oz to world literature, and it has already become a canon.[15]

Almost all the Chinese newspapers in 2007 nominated *A Tale of Love and Darkness* as one of the annual best sellers. *China Reader Weekly* recommended it as one of the year's best ten books. Chinese graduate students work on Amos Oz's writings for their master's theses. The subjects include Amos Oz's views on life in a kibbutz, female

---

15   Mo Yan, "Yigeren de shengjing" [A Personal Bible] (speech at the seminar on Amos Oz's works, Institute of Foreign Literature, Chinese Academy of Social Sciences, Beijing, September 3, 2007).

characters in his novels, and an analysis of *A Tale of Love and Darkness*. A textbook published by Beijing University recommended it to students. In 2012, Muses Publisher in Taiwan published *A Tale of Love and Darkness* in complex Chinese. In 2014, Yilin Press republished *A Tale of Love and Darkness*. Altogether, it has been published three times and has sold more than 16,000 copies. Perhaps *A Tale of Love and Darkness* will become part of the canon selected by Chinese educational institutions.

Creating the Image of another Side of Israel through Literature

Modern Hebrew literature is a conveyance of the writer's thoughts and ideas. It has a special ability to help create positive images of Jewish people, both culturally and politically. At the same time, reading Hebrew literature in Chinese is a good way to enter or approach the heart of the Jewish world, to understand their culture and living conditions.

During the recent conflict in Gaza, an editor from *Xin Jingbao* (*Beijing News*) invited me to contribute a long article to their newspaper on the Israeli writings about war. I selected three generations of Hebrew writers in Israel to make an argument that most Israeli writers are peacemakers who are trying to oppose war. The literary texts I selected were the short stories "Khirbet Khizeh" and "The Swimming Contest" by the first generation Israeli writers S. Yizhar and Benjamin Tammuz, respectively. Both Yizhar and Tammuz had personal contact with Arab inhabitants in Palestine in their early years. The central concern of Yizhar's writing is the expulsion of Palestinian villagers from their homes by Israeli soldiers, acting under orders in the last months of the war of 1948. He exposes the conflict between moral value and national obligations. In "The Swimming Race," Tammuz considers the elusive dream of Arab and Jew in all its tragic complexity and ends the story with the sentence, "It was I, all of us, were losers."

As for the writings of second generation Hebrew writers in Israel, known as the New Wave writers, I selected Amos Oz's *A Tale of Love and Darkness* and A. B. Yehoshua's *The Lover*. Set in the Yom Kippur war, *The Lover* creates a symbolic allegory of communication, even though it is not so successful, between Jews and Arabs inside Israel through the love between Dafi, a Jewish girl, and Naim, an Arab boy. In *A Tale of Love and Darkness*, Amos Oz memorializes his personal contacts with an Arab worker, who rescued him from the cellar in a shop, and Aisha and her little brother, whom he accidentally injured. He also describes the long conflicts between Jews and Arabs with literary imagination. In the lives of individuals and of peoples, too, the worst conflicts are often those that break out between those who are persecuted. It is mere wishful thinking to imagine that the persecuted and the oppressed will unite out of solidarity and man the barricades together against a ruthless oppressor. In reality, two children of the same abusive father will not necessarily make common cause nor be brought close together by their shared fate. Often, each sees in the other not a partner in misfortune but rather the image of their common oppressor. That may be the case with the hundred-year-old conflict between Arabs and Jews.[16]

Due to limited space in the newspaper, the only literary text I selected from the third generation of Hebrew writers was David Grossman's *To the End of the Land* (Hebrew title, *A Woman Fleeing from Tidings*). The novel was conceived in 2003 when Grossman's first son, Yonathan, was in the army and his second son, Uri, was due to join the army in one and a half years, and it was completed after Uri's death during the Second Lebanon War in 2008. In this novel, a middle-aged Israeli woman runs away from home, to the end of the land, holding to the idea that as long as her son is alive in her own recalling and narrating of his life, he will survive the lethal dangers of military service.[17]

I viewed these texts from the perspective of the conflicts between Israelis and Palestinians. All the authors mentioned here are against the war, peacemakers by showing consciousness, human concern, and moral values. In a way, we might say that Chinese readers see another side of Israel and its people who are not fighters on the battlefield nor

---

16 Amos Oz, *A Tale of Love and Darkness*, trans. Nicholas de Lange (London: Chatto & Windus, 2005), 329–330.
17 Yael S. Feldman, *Glory and Agony: Isaac's Sacrifice and National Narrative* (Stanford: Stanford University Press, 2010), 317.

politicians who support war, but rather normal human beings with morality, consciousness, and sympathy. My editor added several subtitles to every book to stress the pain and suffering of the Arabs. It shows the significance of the literature in a certain way through the motives of the author and the editor.

An image of another side of Israel also has been established through literary seminars and conferences. In the seminar on Amos Oz's works in 2007, Chinese writers Mo Yan, Yan Lianke, Xu Kun, and Qiu Huadong contributed a special understanding to Amos Oz's *A Tale of Love and Darkness, My Michael,* and Amos Oz's image in China. Scholars including Chen Zhongyi, the director of the Institute of Foreign Literature and an expert in Latin American literature, Lu Jiande, an expert in English literature, and Zhong Zhiqing, who specializes in Hebrew literature, presented a paper on Oz's *Fima, My Michael, Elsewhere Perhaps,* and *A Tale of Love and Darkness.* Gao Qiufu, a former deputy president of Xinhua News Agency, and Fu Hao, an expert in English literature and a translator of Yehuda Amichai, talked about their experiences with Israeli culture. The literary characters of Amos Oz discussed during the seminar, such as Noga in *Elsewhere Perhaps*, Fima in *Fima,* and ,the father, mother, and the little child in *A Tale of Love and Darkness* were revived, and they travelled to China through literary translation and discussion. That is why Oz is deeply convinced that literature contains a certain magic, "the more local it is, the more universal it might become; the more provincial the story is, the more universal it might become."

The last examples I would like to cite here are the academic conferences which bring together Chinese and Israeli scholars. In October 2006, Prof. Yigal Schwartz, the director for Haksherim, the Center of Jewish and Israeli Literature and Culture at Ben-Gurion University, and the Institute of Foreign Literature at CASS co-organized a conference titled "Literature and National Awareness." A dozen Chinese and Israeli scholars came together for the first time to discuss literary issues. On July 8–9, 2014, scholars from these two institutions met with each other again in China to discuss "Nation and Narration in China and Israel." In the opening session, Prof. Chen Zhongyi, the director of the

Institute of Foreign Literature, discussed the contradiction between cosmopolitanism and national identity, Prof. Yigal Schwartz presented a paper titled "Sleeping with the Enemy: On the 'National Matchmaking Agency' in Modern Hebrew Literature," Prof. Sun Yu, the dean of the School of Liberal Arts at Renmin University, dealt with several remarks on Lu Xun's ideas of nation.

Both China and Israel have long cultural traditions and face many challenges and clashes with the modern world. Literature interprets all these situations in a special way. In the panel on "Tradition and Modernity," Prof. Dang Shengyuan presented, "The Aesthetic Spirit in Traditional Chinese Culture"; Dr. Amir Banaji gave a new look at the modern story of the Hebrew Melitsah; Prof. Tu Weiqun explored the narrative strategy of *Dream of the Red Chamber*, and Nirit Kurman discussed the solitary sex in the poetry of Esther Raab, Israel's first native woman poet.

Both China and Israel have encountered other cultures in different historical periods. The two cultures have a variety of similarities and differences, which left us many inspiring questions to reckon with. In the panel titled "The Encounter of the Cultures," Dr. Haviva Ishay examined a special meeting between Jewish nation and Arabic narration in the Middle Ages, Prof. Ye Jun talked about German Dichtung (literature) to the east and the reestablishment of Chinese national drama in modern times, Prof. Fu Hao discussed the difference between Jewish and Chinese attitudes toward knowledge, Prof. Zhong Zhiqing made a cross-cultural reading of the *Lamentations* and "The Lament for Ying," an ancient Chinese poem by Qu Yuan, a poet in the Warring States period. In the panel on "Nation and Narration in China and Israel," Prof. Yitzhak Ben-Mordechai discussed a new Jewish nation according to the Jewish writer-critic-thinker M. J. Berdyczewski, Prof. Cheng Wei presented a paper titled "From 'Empire' to 'Multination-state': The Transformation of the Political Discourse in China in 1912," Prof. Nitza Ben-Dov examined the train as a symbol of the renewal of the Hebrew language and of Jewish fate. In the session on dialogue between Chinese and Hebrew writers and poets, the leading Chinese writer Yan Lianke, the Israeli novelist and poet Shimon Adaf, and the young and promising Chinese writer Xu Zechen exchanged ideas on the writings between tradition and modernity.

The conference was well publicized. Both sides learned a lot from each other. Prof. Schwartz announced plans to organize another similar conference in the near future in Israel. He concluded, "Jews are always on the way to the Land of Israel, and so, in a certain sense, the closer they get to it, the more distant it becomes." That inspired us to give more thought to the past, the present, and the future of Israel.

Zhong Zhiqing is a research professor for the Institute of Foreign Literature at Chinese Academy of Social Sciences and is a visiting scholar at Tel Aviv University, the British Academy, and Harvard Yenching Institute. She holds PHD from the Department of Hebrew Literature at Ben-Gurion University. Her doctoral dissertation is "A Comparative Study of Hebrew and Chinese Literature in Response to the Catastrophe of World War Two." She is the author of two monographs, *20th Century Hebrew Literature in Transition*, which has been selected by the National Achievements Library of Philosophy and Social Sciences in 2012, *A Study of Contemporary Israeli Authors*, and a collection titled *"To Put a Finger on the Wound": Reading Hebrew Literature and Culture*. She is also the translator of *Modern Hebrew Fiction* by Gershon Shaked; Amos Oz's *My Michael, Black Box, A Tale of Love and Darkness, Rhyming Life and Darkness, A Panther in the Basement*; and more.

Currently she chairs a Study of Biblical Literary Criticism sponsored by CASS and Hebrew Narrative and Jewish Identity sponsored by the National Social Science Foundation of China.

China's Relationship with Israel, Opportunities and Challenges: Perspectives from China

CHEN YIYI[1]
Center for Middle East Peace Studies, Institute of Arts and Humanities, Shanghai Jiao Tong University

Historiography

This author is certainly not the first to write about Sino-Israeli relations. There is a vast amount of multilingual literature on this subject based on the extensive work of Israeli, American, British, United Nations, mainland Chinese, and Taiwanese archives. The extant literature includes the life work of Yitzhak Shichor[2] plus books and articles

---

1   I wish to thank Quint Simon, a former undergraduate student at Georgetown University under Professor Maina Singh's supervision who kindly shared with me the final version of her Program for Jewish Civilization senior thesis, "An International Relations Detective Story: The Mysterious Case of Modern Sino-Israeli Relations, 1948–2011." I had the opportunity to provide a partial reading list for her thesis work, to read a draft version of the thesis, and to comment on the draft. There are substantial amounts of overlapping references on the historical facts part of Simon's paper and the current chapter.
2   "China and the Role of the United Nations in the Middle East: Revised Policy," *Asian Survey* 31:3 (1991): 255–269; "China and the Gulf Crisis: Escape from Predicaments," *Problems of Communism* 40:6 (1991): 80–90; "China and the Middle East since Tiananmen," *Annals of the American Academy of Political and Social Science* 519 (1992): 86; "Israel's Military Transfers to China and Taiwan," *Survival* 40:1 (1998): 68–91; Reuven Merhav and Yitzhak Shichor, "The Hong Kong Connection in Sino-Israeli Relations," in *China and Israel 1949–1998: A Fifty Year Retrospective*, ed. Jonathan Goldstein (London: Praeger, 1999); "A China Diary: Towards the Establishment of China-Israel Diplomatic Relations," *The China Quarterly* 158 (1999): 492–493; "Blow Up: Internal and External Challenges of Uyghur Separatism and

by P. R. Kumaraswamy,[3] Pan Guang,[4] Jonathan Goldstein,[5] Lillian Craig Harris,[6] John Garver,[7] Yin Gang,[8] and many others.[9]

These authors collectively have answered several important questions about Sino-Israeli relations. For example, the history of the Sino-Israeli relationship, both before and after the establishment of the formal diplomatic relationship; the role that the United States and Taiwan played in the quadrilateral relationship between China, Israel, the United States, and Taiwan; the achievement in political, economic, and cultural relations between the two countries; and the crucial role military technology transfer from Israel to China played in the relationship.

Islamic Radicalism to Chinese Rule in Xinjiang," *Asian Affairs, an American Review* 32:2 (2005): 119–135; "Ethno-Diplomacy: The Uyghur Hitch in Sino-Turkish Relations," *Policy Studies* 53 (2009); "The U.S. Role in Delaying Sino-Israeli Relations: Two's Company, Three's a Crowd," *Jewish Political Studies Review* 22.1 (2010): 136.

3   P. R. Kumaraswamy, *China and the Middle East: The Quest for Influence* (New Delhi, 1999) *China Report* 34: 3–4; "Israel-China Relations and the Phalcon Controversy," *Middle East Policy* 12.2 (2005): 93–103; "The Vital Triangle: China, the United States, and the Middle East," *Pacific Affairs* 82.4 (2009–2010): 699–701.

4   Most publications by Guang Pan focus on the Shanghai Jewish Diaspora, touching occasionally on the Sino-Israeli relationship, for example "Zhongguo-yiselie guanxi de lishi yanjin he xianzhuang fenxi" [On Historical Evolution of Sino-Israel Relation and Analysis on the Present Situation] *Shehui Kexue* [Journal of Social Sciences] 12 (2009): 156–163.

5   Jonathan Goldstein, ed., *China and Israel 1949–1998: A Fifty Year Retrospective*; "The Republic of China and Israel, 1911–2003," *Israel Affairs* 10.1-2 (2004): 223–253; "A Quadrilateral Relationship: Israel, China, Taiwan, and the United States Since 1992," *American Journal of Chinese Studies* 12.2 (2005): 177–202; "'Not Just Another Country' The Olmert Family Sojourn Through China," *Chinese American Forum* 24.1 (2008): 15–21.

6   Lillian Craig Harris has not published actively in the past decade; for some earlier publications, see "The People's Republic of China and the Arab Middle East, 1948–1996: Arab Perspectives," in *China and Israel 1949–1998: A Fifty Year Retrospective*, ed. Jonathan Goldstein; "China and the Middle East: The Quest for Influence," *Pacific Affairs* 74.1 (2001): 98–101; "Xinjiang, Central Asia and the Implications for China's Policy in the Islamic World," *The China Quarterly* 133 (1993): 111–129.

7   See relevant discussions in *China and Iran: Ancient Partners in a Post-Imperial World* (Seattle, WA: University of Washington Press, 2006).

8   See articles below and his recent article, "Zhongguo yu yiselie guanxi liushi nian shuping" [Overview of Six Decades of Sino-Israel Relationship], *Xiya feizhou* [West Asia and Africa] 4 (2010): 31–35.

9   See the various authors quoted in this chapter.

Despite extensive scholarly literature, there are some older questions that remain to be answered, or at least that need to be discussed from a different angle. Moreover, due to recent developments in China and the Middle East, as well as the shifting balance among the world powers, the Sino-Israeli bilateral relationship is an "old" topic that calls for a new approach based on additional sources of information.

For example, none of the existing works took into full consideration the profound implication of China's dramatic economic growth during the past decade. Being the second largest economy in the world, exerting more and more direct influence over the economy of the United States and the European Union, some significant shifts in China's international political role are taking place faster than many had expected. These shifts are not only happening in the West, but also in developing countries where China has often been "demonized" as a natural-resources plunderer, local-order destroyer, and dictator supporter by both Western media and academia.

With systematic surveys conducted by Chinese think-tank scholars in a large number of countries, China learned to judge its own influences and images based on firsthand knowledge and data from the local people; this knowledge and data tend to be much more positive than those given by academia and the media.[10] This type of new knowledge is to be considered when discussing China's diplomacy. Arab League countries' attitudes and reactions to China's changing role in the world in general, and in the Middle East in particular, also significantly affect the Sino-Israel relationship, not to mention the attitude of the many Muslim countries that are not members of the Arab League.[11]

---

10   The statement is based on the results and analysis of dozens of large-scale surveys on China's international image, conducted by the Institute of Arts and Humanities, Shanghai Jiaotong University, and headed by Professor Liu Kang, with multiple partners in various countries. The survey covers all regions of the world. This author plays an important role in this team. Parts of the data are still unpublished but are being heavily analyzed internally.

11   This statement is based on many public diplomacy activities this author initiated or played a crucial role in. Additional information is based on discussions with many Chinese and Muslim diplomats, including many members of the Council of Arab Ambassadors to China, China's Special Envoy to the Middle East Issue Ambassador Wu Sike, officials in the Chinese-Arab countries' Friendship Associations,

Even more important than the view of China's international friends is China's own view regarding its role in the international arena in general and in the Middle East in particular. Besides the aforementioned information, China's domestic political nuance and public opinion change regarding its international role, and especially its investment in other countries and areas affects its diplomacy. China has already exhibited flexibility regarding Taiwan and is readjusting its "black cat/white cat" theory to a more finely tuned approach toward others that well reflects its ancient culture as well as its efforts to exercise more effective soft power on the world. When China recalibrates its Middle East strategy and its power balance and interest equilibrium with the United States, the Sino-Israel relationship could well be at the top of the list affected.

This author wishes to shed some light on these new factors and on potential future development regarding the Sino-Israel relationship by drawing on unclassified sources.[12] Starting with an overview of the history between the two countries is necessary; albeit repeating much known information, the following has a distinctive focus on the Chinese perspective.

An Overview of History

The People's Republic of China was established in October 1949, about 17 months after Israel announced its independence. On January 9, 1950, Israel extended recognition to China. However, the two countries did not establish a formal diplomatic relationship until January 1992, so the following review of historical events is divided by this year. Systematic discussions on the significance of these events are found in various publications.[13]

Chinese think-tank scholars, and government officials, with information that can be disclosed.

12 Sources will be duly noted where possible; I choose to obviate names and sources in some cases, especially those in personal communications, private interviews, and discussions in both Israel and China, held under the Chatham House Rule.

13 Aron Shai, "Sino-Israeli Relations: Current Reality and Future Prospects," *Institute for National Security Studies*, Memorandum 100 (2009); Zev Suffot, "Israel's China Policy 1950–1992," *Israel Affairs* 7 (2000): 94–118.

In the beginning, the Arabs did not come in between (1949–1955)

There was a small time window (about five months) for Israel to establish a formal diplomatic relationship with China, but Israel missed the opportunity. Initial contacts between the two countries were established in their Moscow embassies. When China's Ministry of Foreign Affairs sent a cable to its embassy in the Soviet Union on January 28, 1950 asking whether Israel, after acknowledging China, had sent documents for establishment of formal diplomatic relationships, Israel did not answer. Israel decided not to establish direct contact and instead tried to keep using the Moscow embassy to maintain contact with China. On June 13, China again asked Israel to send a direct mission to China. While China was waiting for an answer, the Korean War broke out on June 25, and Israel decided to sit on the sideline to keep the status quo due to "budgetary constraints."[14]

The Arab League passed a resolution in August, much later than several rounds of contact between Israel and China, to forbid any Arab country from acknowledging China. Therefore, in the beginning, it was not the Arab countries' pressure on China that prevented formal relationships between the two countries, but rather Israel's indecisiveness that caused them to miss the opportunity, a point often ignored by politicians and scholars today when discussing the relationship between the two modern countries.

It is easier, when looking back, to blame the pressure on the Arabs or the United States for not setting up missions immediately and for ignoring the small five-month window of opportunity. The fact is, in the beginning, Israel was not aligned with the United States, and thus there was no U.S. pressure; the Arabs were never a factor influencing China. Israel was beginning to distance itself from the Soviets while getting closer to the United States, and the intimacy between the Arabs, the United States, and Europe was starting to crack.

---

14 Yin Gang, "Zhongguo-yiselie guanxi liushi nian: zhiyue yu quehan" [Restraint and Regret, Sixty-Year Relationship between China and Israel], *Journal of Sino-Western Communications*, special issue on Jewish and Israel studies in China, V2SI1 (2010): 225–32, especially 228.

China's stance against terrorism (1955-1975)

In 1955, Foreign Minister Zhou Enlai convinced the countries present at the Bandung Conference that China was more committed to opposing hegemony than spreading Communism or supporting the Soviet Union.[15] Because Arab states had managed to exclude Israel from the conference, Israel started to face hostility not only from the Middle East, but also from South and Southeast Asia and China.[16] By the time Egypt abandoned Taiwan on May 30, 1955 and established a formal relationship with China, Israel had lost all opportunities. The 1956 joint invasion of Egypt by Israel, Britain, and France severed connections between China and Israel for 20 years. Nevertheless, China never agreed with the Palestinians or other Arab countries with regard to denying the survival right of Israel in the region. Premier Zhou criticized terrorism activities of the Palestinians and rejected the idea of throwing the Israelis into the Mediterranean.[17]

Black cat/white cat: military deals (1975-1987)

The 1969 border clashes between China and the Soviet Union effectively convinced the Chinese that it was the Soviet Union, not the United States, that was the main hegemonic power threatening China's national security.[18] Thus, China sought reconciliation with the United States in the early 1970s.[19]

Mao published his "Three Worlds Theory" in 1974, in which he placed China at the forefront of the third world; the United States and the Soviet Union in the first world, and semi-developed countries in an amorphous second world.[20] When Middle Eastern third world countries complained about China's growing contact with the United

---

15 Zhang Shuguang, "Constructing 'Peaceful Coexistence: China's Diplomacy toward the Geneva and Bandung Conferences, 1954–1955," *Cold War History* 7.4 (2007): 514.
16 Suffot, "Israel's China Policy 1950–1992," 103.
17 Gang, "Zhongguo-yiselie guanxi liushi nian: zhiyue yu quehan," 230.
18 Herbert Yee, "The Three World Theory and Post-Mao's China Global Strategy," *International Affairs* (1994): 244.
19 Harry Harding, *A Fragile Relationship: The United States and China since 1972* (Washington, DC: Brookings Institution Press, 2002), 77.
20 Yee, "The Three World Theory," 239.

States, China argued that taking a practical approach when dealing with the United States and the West in general is the correct way to move forward.[21]

As early as 1975, starting from recorded contact between a Chinese delegation and the Israeli pavilion at the Paris Air Show, clandestine military exchanges between the Israeli Defense Forces and the People's Liberation Army ensued.[22]

Another reason pushing China to conduct a flexible foreign policy is its need to take advantage of all the resources available to help develop its fragile economy right after its decade-long Cultural Revolution. Foreign investment and technology transfer have played an important role since China's 1977 Open Door Policy. Israeli and Jewish investments played a role as well. Since Israel could help China promote its economic and military modernization goal, the new practical foreign policy effectively gave a green light to Sino-Israeli relations.[23] This is the foreign policy version of Deng Xiaoping's "black cat/white cat" theory.[24]

Anwar Sadat's 1977 historic visit to Israel allowed for a "timely adjustment in China's regional foreign policy."[25] China decided to portray itself as a disinterested and honest broker in the Middle East peace process. In doing so, it hoped to forge a contrast between itself and the United States. On one hand, China had credibility among Arab countries as a leader of the non-alliance movement; on the other hand, forging stronger ties with Israel would balance its position as a middle man in Middle Eastern issues.

China believed it could simultaneously emulate and compete with the United States in its newly assumed role of "pushing forward the

---

21 Craig Harris, "The People's Republic of China and the Arab Middle East, 1948–1996: Arab Perspectives," in *China and Israel 1949–1998*, 51.
22 Yossi Melman and Dan Raviv, "Israel 'in Weapons Deal with China'," *The Guardian*, December 3, 1986.
23 Zev Suffot, A China Diary: Toward the Establishment of China-Israel Diplomatic Relations (London: Frank Cass, 1997), viii.
24 The theory goes that "no matter if it is a black or white cat, as long as it catches the mice, it is a good cat."
25 Gang, "Zhongguo-yiselie guanxi liushi nian: zhiyue yu quehan," 231.

ongoing Middle East peace process."²⁶ This stance has changed little in at least the past four decades.

Although both governments have denied all such deals, by the early 1980s, Israeli technology in the fields of agriculture, solar energy, advanced technology, and construction made their way to China.²⁷ From the Chinese perspective, acknowledgement of such dealings would "undermine the friendly relations between China and Arab countries and the Palestinian people."²⁸ Therefore, China always denied any hints in the media about this type of activity. Israeli officials never publicly contradicted the denials of their Chinese counterparts.

In September 1987, a meeting between Chinese and Israeli officials was held at the United Nations. Following this meeting, Israel and China worked transparently towards the full normalization of relations. Steps included the liberalization of China's restrictions against Israeli passport holders and the establishment of a variety of mechanisms for academic, scientific, and touristic exchanges.²⁹ The final establishment of diplomatic relations on January 24, 1992 represented the culmination of a careful and deliberate five-year process toward full diplomatic ties.

After Establishment of Formal Relationships (1992)

Achievements

All of Israel's presidents and prime ministers have visited China. Before 2000 (see the Phalcon incident below), all of China's presidents and prime ministers visited Israel. China's rhetoric and actions in the Middle East reflect a conscious effort to balance the interests of Israel

---

26 Zhang Ping, "China and Israel Start Diplomatic Relations," *China Daily*, January 25, 1992.
27 John Burns, "Israel and China Quietly Form Trade Bonds," *The New York Times*, July 22, 1985.
28 Ibid.
29 Andrew Higgins, "Small flag of Israel flutters diplomatically in China, Israel's first official presence in China, ostensibly for academic exchanges, highlights a discreet relationship which depends heavily on secret military deals," *The Independent*, June 6, 1990.

and the Arab world.³⁰ Most official statements on Israel focus on proliferating ties between the two countries. Those dealing with the Israeli-Palestinian conflict do so without the accusatory tone that characterized such statements in the past.

For example, in October 2010, China's Special Envoy on the Middle East Issue Wu Sike stated that China sought "efforts from all parties to show flexibility and compromise on various issues."³¹ This language places the responsibility for improvement in the laps of both the Israelis and the Palestinians.

Israel has been careful not to offend the sensibilities of the Chinese government with regard to Taiwan. Prior to normalization in 1992, the basis of Israel-Taiwan relations was military transfers.³² As soon as China and Israel normalized relations, Israel put an end to these military exchanges. Israel has also been careful never to dispute the "One-China Policy." The fact that four Chinese migrant workers in Israel (total number peaked at 40,000)³³ have been killed in terrorist attacks organized by Hamas has brought home to China the severity of the terrorist problem in Israel.³⁴ The attacks fundamentally "altered for the better both official and non-official Chinese views of Israeli policies towards Palestinians suspected of planning terrorist actions in Israel."³⁵

In terms of trade, the value of the total bilateral imports and exports reached $7.65 billion in 2010, nearly 150 times the 1992 value.³⁶ China has risen to become Israel's fifth largest export destination, and exports in certain key industries increased by more than 200% between

---

30 For an interesting case study of the Chinese media's coverage of Israel in the period prior to having a friendly relationship, see She Gangzheng in this volume.
31 Bi Mingxing, "Chinese Mideast Envoy Urges Israel-Palestine Talks Back on Track," *Xinhua News*, March 25, 2011, http://news.xinhuanet.com/english2010/china/2011-03/25/c_13798256.htm, accessed July 28, 2014.
32 Shai, "Sino-Israeli Relations," 31.
33 Gang, "Zhongguo-yiselie guanxi liushi nian: zhiyue yu quehan" [Sixty Years of Sino-Israeli Relations: Limitations and Problems], 231.
34 Shai, "Sino-Israeli Relations," 31.
35 Ibid.
36 "China to Expand Economic Ties with Israel," *China Daily*, March 3, 2011, http://www.chinadaily.com.cn/china/2011-03/03/content_12106851.htm, accessed July 28, 2014.

2008 and 2009.³⁷ China has become a big buyer of Israeli agrotechnology, water purification, and telecommunications systems. Israel imports a variety of mechanical, electronic, chemical, and textile goods from China.³⁸

In terms of cultural exchange, within a few years of normalization, the Israeli Philharmonic Orchestra visited Beijing, and the Israel Museum hosted an exhibition on traditional China.³⁹ Since 2007, Tel Aviv University has been home to one of China's Confucius Institutes, a government-sponsored organization that promotes Chinese language and culture through a variety of cultural programs. Notable programs have included the 2009 "Experience China in Israel" festival and the 2011 "Chinese Culture Week", which included performances by China's modern dance and kung fu masters.⁴⁰

Tourism has also grown exponentially since 1992, especially after the easing of visa restrictions, the establishment of a direct Tel Aviv–Beijing flight, and the opening of an Israeli tourism bureau in China. The $11.1 million Israeli pavilion at the 2010 Shanghai world's fair also proved to be a great hit among the Chinese. In 2010, China worked with Israel to create a TV special, called "The Land of Milk and Honey," through which Chinese citizens could be exposed to Israeli society, politics, and geography.⁴¹

Considerable cooperation exists between Israeli and Chinese universities, research institutes, and scientific academies in all areas. Every Israeli university has established a program in China, and the number of students abroad in the other country at any given time numbers in the hundreds.⁴² There are Jewish studies or Hebrew/

---

37 Israel-China: 2009 & 2010 H1 Bilateral Trade Figures, *Israel Chamber of Commerce in China*, 2010, http://beijing.ischam.org/business-in-china/useful-information, accessed October 2, 2011.
38 Ibid.
39 Shai, "Sino-Israeli Relations," 29.
40 "Chinese Cultural Week Kicks Off in Israel," *Xinhua News*, February 15, 2011.
41 Liang Jun, "China-Made Documentary Spotlights Israel," *The People's Daily*, July 30, 2010.
42 "Fact Sheet: China-Israel Relations," *The Israel Project*, 2010, http://www.theisraelproject.org/site/apps/nlnet/content2.aspx?c=hsJPK0PIJpH&b=883997&ct=8971845, accessed October 2, 2011.

Israel-related programs in several universities and research institutes in China, with Beijing University leading the field since 1985. Chinese authors have taken it upon themselves to explain Jewish civilization to their Chinese compatriots by compiling books with titles such as, "Crack the Talmud: 101 Jewish Business Rules," "The Illustrated Jewish Wisdom Book," and "Know All of the Money-Making Stories of the Talmud."[43]

Setbacks

Despite the growth of these overwhelmingly positive avenues of exchanges, the path of Sino-Israeli relations has not been entirely smooth since 1992. Two incidents are most prominent. In 1999, Israel agreed to sell China the Phalcon, an Israeli-developed sophisticated reconnaissance aircraft. As this technology would allow the Chinese to gather intelligence from an aircraft at a distance—a critical ability for the Chinese if there were ever an outbreak of hostilities in the Taiwan Straits—the Pentagon raised serious objections.[44] Ultimately, Israel had no choice but to forgo the deal and pay $319 million in compensation.[45] In 2004, Israel agreed to repair and update the Harpy drones, which were laser-guided unmanned aircrafts it had sold to China in 1994. Although servicing had been part of the original deal, U.S. Defense Secretary Paul Wolfowitz raised major objections on the grounds that the upgrade would make it technologically superior to that of the U.S. military.[46] Israel ultimately reneged on the deal and paid a large sum of compensation.

Following the Harpy controversy, Washington dictated to Tel Aviv a new set of rules regarding the transfer of technology to China.[47] Not only have these rules effectively precluded *any* bilateral weapons exchange, but Chinese officials also regularly complain that harsh restrictions on dual-use technology impede purely civilian trade, too.

---

43 Isaac Stone Fish, "Selling the Talmud as a Business Guide," *Newsweek,* December 29, 2010.
44 Kumaraswamy, "Israel-China Relations and the Phalcon Controversy."
45 Shai, "Sino-Israeli Relations," 28.
46 Ibid.
47 Ibid., 29.

The two incidents above, together with allegations that Israel had transferred "Patriot" anti-missile technology to China and had helped China in building the F-10 multipurpose fighter aircraft incorporating Israel's "Lavi" technology in addition to the later cancelled "Einstein Exhibit" incident as a cultural repercussion of the previous incidents, need to be viewed in the context of a quadrilateral tug-of-war. The four parties are China, Taiwan, Israel, and the United States. Since 1979, all American administrations, both Republican or Democratic, have been committed to the defense of Taiwan under the U.S. Congress's Taiwan Relations Act. It is precisely because of that Act that the United States forced Israel to pull the plug on its export to China of the "Phalcon" reconnaissance airplane and on the upgrading of the "Harpy" drone from a spy plane to a predator aircraft. U.S. intervention would have happened irrespective of any alleged transfer of American technology from Israel to China.[48]

The stalemate changed for the positive recently with Israel Defense Minister Ehud Barak's June 2011 visit to China and China's chief of staff General Chen Bingde's visit to Israel in August, although this high-level exchange may not result in immediate direct hardware sales. The roles of the two sides are very different from a decade ago, when China was seen solely as a military hardware buyer. Today, China is influencing Israel's security situation much more than it did a decade ago.[49]

As a Jewish state, Israel's national image in China has suffered some damage due to the import of Western anti-Semitic stereotypes into China. The most influential manifestation is in the *Currency War* book series.[50] The books can be best described as a copy and paste job

---

[48] For an excellent account of the five incidents and analysis of the quadrilateral relationships, please see Jonathan Goldstein, "A Quadrilateral Relationship: Israel, China, Taiwan, and the United States Since 1992," American Journal of Chinese Studies 12.2 (2005): 177–202.

[49] See, for example, the carefully worded news releases at http://usa.chinadaily.com.cn/china/2011-06/12/content__12678387.htm by China Daily and http://www.usatoday.com/news/world/2011-08-14-military-chief-israel-visit__n.htm, both accessed October 2, 2011.

[50] Song Hongbing, *Huobi zhanzheng* [*Currency War*], Vols. 1-5, (Beijing, 2007–2014).

from widely available Jewish conspiracy theories over the Internet. What brought credibility to the Chinese readers was that the author was trained in the United States, worked for Fannie Mae and Freddie Mac, and now is a financial advisor in China. These types of books are becoming more and more popular among the Chinese elites.

The growing popularity of Christianity among ordinary Chinese, on one hand, brings more knowledge about the evangelical version of the "Promised Land," which is "pro-Israel." On the other hand, various Christian groups transmitted anti-Semitic concepts to many Chinese people. The Muslim population in China has increased contact with their Middle Eastern brethren during the past two decades. A higher percentage of the Muslim population takes pilgrimage trips to Mecca. Some brought back the Muslim versions of Jewish conspiracy theories to their local communities. However, both types of developments are not yet very prominent, thus, hardly noticeable to the Chinese government or to many Israelis visiting China today.

Why Sino-Israel Relationships Are at a Crossroad

Shared national mentality among modern Jews, Chinese, and Palestinians

One cannot understand the People's Republic of China or the State of Israel well without reading into the mentality of the two nations before their founding. For the Jews engaging in Zionism movements in order to create a new State of Israel, the years of exile and anti-Semitism culminating in the Holocaust during WWII are the fundamental elements of its national consciousness. In every Chinese mind, there is engraved the national humiliation embodied in their string of losses to Western imperial powers starting from the first and second Opium Wars (since the 1840s) and culminating with the Japanese invasion between 1937 and 1945. That the two ancient nations share mutual sympathy based on their recent history of suffering is far more powerful than their more commonly quoted long history of civilizations and cultural values. To both Israel and China, having a delineated territory and the power to protect their people is the only way to ensure these tragedies never happen again. Dr. Sun Yat-sen, the founding father of the Republic of China, sympathized with the Zionism movement because of this exact shared mentality between these two peoples.

Similar to the Holocaust to the Jews and the Opium Wars to the Chinese, the Naqba to the Palestinians, and probably to the entire Arab nation, is a shared national tragedy and humiliation. To the Arabs, the Naqba and the Opium Wars are more comparable because both historical events took place on the respective nations' own homeland. The Holocaust fell upon the Jewish people in Europe, which is not the native land of the Jews. However, according to the Palestinians, one consequence of the Holocaust—such as seeking the establishment of a modern Jewish nation by the Zionists—took place upon the then homeland of the Palestinians, which has nothing to do with the Holocaust itself. Consequently, the sufferers of the Naqba, i.e., the Palestinians, were "punished" for a crime they did not commit.

China never took revenge for the humiliation of the Opium Wars on another nation's land—not in Britain, France, or Japan. By the same token, the Palestinians claim that it is not fair for the Jews to be compensated for their suffering in Europe and in the Middle Eastern region of Palestine. According to many Arab nations, the Palestinian refugee problem needs to be solved on the land of the Palestinians. Leaving these people in the countries where they are now, even letting them be absorbed, will not solve the issue permanently since this will create a Palestinian Diaspora, just like the Jewish Diaspora before it. If the Jews do not want to go back to the Diaspora, there is no reason to force the Palestinian refugees to stay in a Diaspora, unless they want to.[51]

China's Changing Role in the International Arena

The rapid economic advancement in the past several decades has forced China to be more proactively involved with international affairs since its enterprises and economic interests are present all around the world.

---

51 Information gained from personal communications with multiple Arab countries' ambassadors to China.

The Middle East region is crucial to China's overall energy security.[52] Besides, the previous non-interference policy, combined with investments in countries without conducting extensive political risk assessment, created losses during the Arab Spring. One case in point is Libya, where China invested heavily. The civil war and overthrow of Gaddafi led to gigantic investment losses,[53] forcing China to subsequently change its political stance almost 180 degrees. China started to welcome and interact with the anti-governmental coalition as well as tone down and eventually completely end support for the Gaddafi regime in the media so that some of the losses could be recouped in the future regime.[54]

In order to build a more constructive relationship with the majority of nations in the region, China cannot avoid discussing Israeli-Palestinian conflicts with Arab nations. As one of the permanent members of the United Nations Security Council, China's stance on the issue will make a big difference for both sides of the conflict.

Many of China's activities in the international arena are seen as more and more closely affecting Israel directly. For example, China has held recent joint military exercises with Turkey, has sent ships to the Gulf of Aden to fight pirates there, and has pledged a large number of troops to the peacekeeping force in Lebanon, making it one of the largest contributors to the multinational force dispatched in the aftermath of the 2006 war between Israel and Hezbollah guerrillas. Israel suspects some Chinese-made rockets have reached Palestinian militants

---

52 Christina Lin, "The New Silk Road: China's Energy Strategy in the Greater Middle East," *Policy Focus* 109 (2011).
53 The amount of losses in investment by China is hard to gauge, the numbers revealed by different authorities change along the development of the event. For an earlier version, see "China Counting Financial Losses in Libya," http://english.sina.com/china/p/2011/0303/362644.html; for a different (relatively later) version, see "China's investment in Libya is more than $20 billion and the amount of loss is difficult to estimate," http://chonzfashion.hubpages.com/hub/Chinas-investment-in-Libya-is-more-than-20-billion-and-the-amount-of-loss-is-difficult-to-estimate, both accessed October 2, 2011.
54 The change in the Chinese government's attitude and discourse is easily traced in all Chinese media; for a sample of the English media, see "Fall of Gaddafi: Policy Challenge for China and Russia," http://www.eurasiareview.com/07092011-fall-of-gaddafi-policy-challenge-for-china-and-russia-analysis/, accessed October 2, 2011.

in Gaza. Israel is also concerned about China's ties with Iran, a strategic threat to Israel because of the Iranian leadership's rhetoric towards Israel and China's vetoing of sanctions on Tehran at the United Nations.

However, China is not exempt from various difficulties when it tries to play up its role as an international power. China's concept of a "peaceful rise," a development theory aimed at assuring the world that China will not use its increasing national power to interfere in the domestic affairs of other nations, has been greeted with doubt by many countries. More particularly, its "non-interference" foreign policy has been accused of being a "supporting whoever is in power" policy, which is a form of interference. The "non-interference" policy, coined by the first generation of Communist Party leadership, was born in the context of the 1950s, when the world was divided by two superpowers and China was weak both politically and economically.

Today, the situation has fundamentally changed; sticking to the words of the traditional motto will no doubt bring mistrust from many countries influenced by the presence of China's economic interests. However, as a country implementing a very different political system than those found in North American and European democracies, the present Chinese government is having great difficulty reconciling with the Western definition of universal values. This partially caused China's diplomatic policies, which are frequently criticized by various Western countries who accuse China of acts such as practicing neo-colonialism and cooperating with dictators and international criminals. China also realized the drawback of the lack of soft or smart power while trying to convince other countries to understand its peaceful intention and its cherishment of mutually beneficial cooperation. The establishment of hundreds of Confucius Institutes across the globe is one of the efforts to improve the situation by propagating Chinese cultural values in other nations.

One traditional Chinese value is "*yi*" (Simplified Chinese, 义; Traditional Chinese, 義), loosely translated to the English terms "righteousness" and "justice." This value is shared by all belief systems in today's China, whether it is Daoism or Confucianism. It is manifested in all layers of Chinese society, including overseas Chinese communities and even Chinese gangs. The concept is represented among business communities by the worship of Guan Gong, a prominent, historical, heroic figure during the third century CE.[55] Righteousness is an important theological concept found in Zoroastrianism, Hinduism (dharma), Judaism, Christianity, and Islam; the Semitic word for righteousness, or doing the right thing, is *tsodoq*, or *tsadiq*. The Chinese *yi* has additional layers of meaning, more than the Semitic *tsodoq/tsadiq*; for example, it emphasizes reciprocity.

Based on the concept of reciprocity and justice, Arab countries helped China in the international political arena greatly since the 1950s. Now, it is time for China to return the favor by supporting the great Arab cause, i.e., a just and fair solution to the Palestinian suffering, thus, a just and lasting peace in the region.

Needless to say, driving the existing Jews in Israel to the Mediterranean Sea is not one of the solutions. One cannot solve a problem by committing another wrongdoing. China understands that giving the Jewish people the right to stay in the region and live peacefully with the Palestinians is also important. No new atrocity should be created to bring justice to existing problems. Therefore, supporting UN resolutions 242 and 338 has been China's standard position on this issue. However, with the above background, it is not hard to understand that China has a different set of reasons behind its support for these UN resolutions. One can say that both the United States and China want to strike a balance on this issue, but while the United States tilts more to the Israeli side, China tilts more to the Arab side. Besides, the tendency of China to always have a different attitude than the United States on such issues is also at work here. Nevertheless, since the relationship with the United States is still the most important priority for China, to avoid unnecessary conflicts with the United States, China will try to respect the U.S. position on the Israel-Palestine issue, as long as this attitude is not harming China in the Middle East region.

---

55 If one pays attention in the Chinese restaurants around the world, one will notice that the small figure worshipped with two candles lit on its two sides is Guan Gong.

Due to the fact that China puts great emphasis on building a cooperative relationship with the United States, the attitude of the United States towards Israel affects China greatly. Admittedly, compared to the United States, China is still far from a superpower. China's agreement with the United States also hinges on the strong tie between Israel and the United States, as well as on the assertiveness of the United States when it comes to supporting Israel. If any of the above balances are no longer true, China's attitude, already tilted toward the Palestinians who are considered internationally as the weaker side of the two-sided conflict, will undoubtedly become more pronounced than it is now. To a certain extent, we are seeing a developing trend towards this direction already, with the financial crisis weakening the U.S. economy as well as its international political influence.

What Can China Do for Israel?

Politically, China will respect and advocate Israel's right of existence in the Middle East. This is in agreement with the United Nations Security Council Resolution 242, which all parties of the conflicts, including the Arab League, have a consensus on. Based on China's political and military philosophy to "be friendly with distant countries while being more assertive with close neighbors (*yuan jiao jin gong*)," Israel, a country with no direct conflict of interest or borders with China, is more likely to be treated as a good friend than not. However, it is the same case with all Arab countries.

Historically, China has never been a belligerent country and has rarely made expeditions abroad. There is no reason to expect otherwise for the near future. This determines the nature of China's foreign policy—peaceful and advocating dialogue and non-military measures as the only means to solving conflicts, including the Israel-Palestinian conflict. Even today's more assertive Chinese stance with Japan and other powers in the South China Sea region does not lead to serious involvement by the Chinese army. Although rhetoric by military officials, leaked either intentionally or unintentionally to the media, portrays a belligerent image for China, the central government is in full control of the army, and no military conflict is evident in the foreseeable future. Chinese philosophy advocates "subduing the enemy without fighting "(*buzhan er que ren zhi bing*), but some propaganda indicates an attitude that some military muscle is necessary.

Economically, China has acted as a major trade partner with Israel; mutual imports and exports have been growing steadily, and the trend should not wane in the foreseeable future.

Culturally, the two countries have always touted shared values and a long history of ancient civilizations. Chinese hospitality extended to the Jewish communities that migrated to China over a millennium ago was echoed with shelter being provided for tens of thousands of WWII Jewish refugees in multiple cities in China. These are not only cherished memories of the Jewish people but also are manifested by the friendly, welcome greetings modern Israeli visitors receive in China today, a country with little anti-Semitic sentiment.

What Can Israel Do for China?

As an Israeli scholar bluntly pointed out, Israel needs China more than China needs Israel.[56] Although such a statement cannot easily be justified quantitatively, if we consider the sheer size differences between the two countries, there is a certain amount of truth to it. However, if the United States stands firmly behind Israel, the equation becomes more balanced. In this regard, Israel can help China handle its relationship with its main competitor, the United States. Israel is promoting itself in Beijing as a diplomatic door to Washington by capitalizing on the influential nature of the American-Israel lobby. Rather than allow its relationship with the United States to be a burden, Israel should embrace its alliance with Washington as a way to advance the cause of Sino-Israeli relations in the twenty-first century.[57] As the link that can really influence U.S. foreign policy, especially toward the Middle East, China will always treat its relationship with Israel very seriously. On the other hand, as a typical diplomatic maneuver, China views Iran, the number one enemy of Israel,

---

56 Private communication with the scholar.
57 Simon Quint Simon, "An International Relations Detective Story: The Mysterious Case of Modern Sino-Israeli Relations, 1948–2011" (Class of 2011 thesis, Walsh School of Foreign Service, Georgetown University, 2011).

as a key partner in counterbalancing U.S. hegemony in the Middle Eastern region.[58] From this perspective, Israel serves as an effective alarm button to remind the United States of China's willingness to tip the balance if its own interest in the region is seriously threatened.

Regarding weaponry transfers, China is already refraining from irritating the United States by focusing less on the military technology transfers provided by Israel to China. Academic, cultural, and touristic exchanges have increased in weight since the establishment of a formal relationship.

Nevertheless, Israel is still considered to be among the top intelligence and security technology providers to China. Today, the westernmost Xinjiang province of China, with its mostly Uighur Muslim population, is facing both pan-Turkic and pan-Islamic Al-Qaeda-style extremism. Israeli anti-terrorist know-how and boundary penetration and human intrusion sensing technologies have already draw keen interest from Chinese high officials.[59] However, using Israeli technology to solve problems in Xinjiang is a very sensitive issue for China's international image due to the sympathy from many Muslims toward the Uighurs in Xinjiang. When considering the conflicts between Israelis and Palestinians, which also generated the need for Israel to develop a particular set of technologies, and the overall sympathy toward the Palestinians among China's Muslim friends, importing Israeli technologies to solve China's Uighur separatism, religious extremism, and terrorism problems would be at least a double-edged sword, if not a self-defeating attempt. China considers dealing with Xinjiang Muslim extremism to be an internal affairs issue. The irresponsible accusation

---

58 Christina Lin, "China's Persian Gulf Strategy: Israel and a Nuclearizing Iran 2009," *China Brief* 9.21, October 22, 2009, accessed October 1, 2011, http://www.jamestown.org/programs/chinabrief/single/?tx_ttnews%5Btt_news%5D=35633&tx_ttnews%5BbackPid%5D=459&no_cache=1. This stance of China's is confirmed by a large number of diplomats and think-tank scholars, as well as government strategic officials whom this author interviewed.

59 See in particular Jonathan Goldstein, "A Quadrilateral Relationship: Israel, China, Taiwan and the United States since 1992" and previous literature Goldstein quoted. See also Yitzhak Shichor, "Blow Up: Internal and External Challenges of Uyghur Separatism and Islamic Radicalism to Chinese Rule In Xinjiang" and "Ethno-Diplomacy: The Uyghur Hitch in Sino-Turkish Relations."

by Turkish Prime Minister Erdogan[60] that the July 2009 violent clashes between Uighur-minority Muslims, police, and Han Chinese residents of Urumqi[61] is a genocide was met with harsh criticism from China.[62]

The term "internal affairs" is used by the Chinese central government to refer to affairs related not only to Xinjiang but also to Tibet and Taiwan. In this regard, when Israel considers itself as one of the partners in the quadrilateral relationships that include China, the United States, Taiwan, and Israel, their way of thinking, albeit reflecting the reality on the ground very accurately, is already irritating to China.[63] Similar sensitivity applies to Tibet when some Israelis compare the relationship between the Chinese central government and Tibet to that of Israel and Palestine.[64] Any card the Israelis can put on the table that has Xinjiang, Tibet, or Taiwan on it might bring more trouble than benefit to their relationship with the Chinese government. Israel should be very cautious in doing so.

Back to the brighter side with more certainty, in an effort during recent years to encourage technology innovation and intellectual property protection while discouraging low-level, resource-consuming manufacturing, Chinese government and private enterprises have sought to import innovative technologies in growth industries—the very industries in which Israel excels. Israeli technology has become such an important part of China's modernization efforts that Benjamin Netanyahu once reportedly boasted, "Israeli know-how is more valuable than Arab oil."[65]

---

60 "China defends Xinjiang crackdown after Turkish criticism," accessed August 20, 2015, http://en.europenews.dk/China-defends-Xinjiang-crackdown-after-Turkish-criticism-103124.html.
61 According to the government, about two-thirds of the victims are Han Chinese.
62 Erdogan also called for the United Nations Security Council to discuss the violence and said he would welcome a visit to Turkey by Rebiya Kadeer, the exiled Uighur leader whom China accuses of organizing the initial violence by Uighurs.
63 Goldstein, in "A Quadrilateral Relationship," summarized this way of thinking among Israelis, as well as among many Western think-tank scholars, especially those in the United States and Israel.
64 Based on personal communication with Israeli scholars and lay people.
65 Barry Rubin, "China's Middle East Strategy," Middle East Review of International Affairs 3.1 (1999).

China's "Constructive Participation" Strategy

China is seeking to play a more proactive role in international affairs. In one of the recent reports advocating China's public diplomacy strategies, the authors coined the term "constructive participation" in Chinese.[66] Such a strategy, on one hand, signifies China's gradual shift away from the "non-interference" policy. On the other hand, it emphasizes the intended peaceful and constructive nature of China's role in any region of the world. During the 2014 Gaza conflict, the Chinese Foreign Minister Wang Yi traveled to the region and put out five points to help stem the undergoing conflict and encourage peaceful negotiation in the near future.[67] Although the content of Wang Yi's statement more or less overlaps previous statements by China, the assertiveness in the tone is readily discernible by any Chinese reader. The trend of a more confident and assertive China in international affairs is also observable in Israel-Palestine matters.

In regard to the Israeli-Palestinian conflict, "constructive participation" entails two types of involvement by the Chinese, not necessarily by the government only, but also by businesses and NGOs. The first type of involvement would be the act of participating instead of only making word statements on occasion, such as in the United Nations or during routine meetings with the area's leaders.

The second element of involvement would need to be constructive, i.e., contributing to the development of the region. Whether it is settlement issues or the Palestinian refugee issue, economically speaking, it is an issue of how many people the fixed amount of land can provide for.

---

66 A report was submitted by Professor Liu Kang of Duke University's Asia and Middle Eastern Studies Program and Shanghai Jiaotong University (SJTU), together with this author, as an advisory piece to the Chinese government. The theoretical framework is also discussed in a recent interview in one of China's most widely read biweekly periodicals: Chen Tongkui, "Rang zhongdong 'kanjian' zhongguo" [Make Sure that the Middle East 'Sees' China], Nafeng Chuang 450 (November 15, 2011): 78–79.

67 See, for example, "Zhongfang tichu jiejue yiba chongtu wudian heping changyi" [China Raises Five Peaceful Resolution Proposals to Solve the Palestinian-Israeli Conflict], August 4, 2014, accessed August 7, 2014, http://www.chinanews.com/gj/2014/08-04/6453655.shtml.

China's Relationship with Israel, Opportunities and Challenges

From this perspective, increasing the land's sustainability alone can contribute to finding a solution to the problem.

If we follow the traditional analysis of the sustainability of the area, there is no way to support a great number of people on such a small piece of land. But, if we look back a hundred years, no one would have believed this land could even sustain the current population size. Israel has created a miracle to support its population with technology innovations; China has done the same thing during the past several decades. For China to "constructively participate" in resolving the region's conflict, Chinese businesses may have to join forces with both the Israelis and Palestinians to think outside the box, to improve the employment situation in Palestine, and to find solutions to help the land sustain a larger population so that both the Israelis and the Palestinians, two nations that cherish the same piece of land so much, can live side by side in peace. Currently, Chinese enterprises' and investors' plethora of investments and acquisitions of Israeli agricultural-related companies works toward this goal.[68] Many other technology innovations found either investment from China, or market in China, or both. This is going on not only on the governmental level[69] but also in private sectors.[70] As a matter of fact, the venture capital community in the United States Silicon Valley and that in China, already linked closely, are working together with many Israeli technology companies to introduce the technology know-how to Chinese manufacturers and markets in both China and the United States.[71] All the effort on the non-traditional economic sectors could serve as answers to the challenges

---

68 See, for example, May 22, 2014, Tova Cohen, "Israel Welcomes Tech-hungry Chinese Investors," http://www.reuters.com/article/2014/05/22/us-china-israel-investment-idUSBREA4L0Q920140522. Accessed 7 August 2014.
69 See, for example, December 24, 2013, Sharon Udasin, "China-Israel Innovation Industrial Park to be Built in Nanxun, China," http://www.jpost.com/Enviro-Tech/China-Israel-innovation-industrial-park-to-be-built-in-Nanxun-China-336033. Accessed 7 August 2014.
70 See, for example, August 7, 2013, Inbal Orpaz, "China Seeking Technological Edge in Israel," http://www.haaretz.com/business/.premium-1.534566. Accessed 7 August 2014.
71 There are a lot of this type of activities taking place today; for neutrality purposes, no web address will be quoted here, but a simple online search will turn up many.

of supporting a vast population with a small piece of land. Eventually, the most relevant helper of the Palestinian economy might be their neighbors, the Israelis.

China is willing to work together with all countries that are willing to be part of an effort to make the Middle East a more peaceful region with vibrant economies. China hopes to make friendships with all countries in the region more constructive. As long as the sensibility of the national mentality of all countries is respected, the future direction of Sino-Israeli relationship looks bright.

Holocaust Studies and Holocaust Education in China

GLENN TIMMERMANS
Department of English, University of Macau

Holocaust studies in China, while still a comparatively new field, has impinged on Chinese academia at least since the beginning of Jewish studies, an area increasingly well established but still inadequately defined. The Holocaust looms larger in China than in other Asian countries for two main reasons: the Chinese experience of Japanese atrocity during the Second World War and China's role in giving refuge to German and Austrian Jewish refugees during the same period. Unlike most countries elsewhere in the world, China is able to hold up Shanghai's position as a place of refuge and succor when the international community turned the other way. At the same time, Chinese suffering under Japanese occupation, but particularly the Nanjing Massacre of December 1937, and human experimentation on Chinese subjects at Unit 731 in Manchuria, allows China to align itself with more widely recognized Jewish suffering in Europe in these same years.

The oft commented on similarity between Germany and Japan, both as Axis powers and guilty of extreme war crimes and crimes against humanity, has only strengthened this parallel of suffering. The legacy of both the International Military Tribunal at Nuremberg and the Tokyo War Crimes Trials (also known as the International Military Tribunal for the Far East) on international jurisprudence and definitions of war crimes and crimes against humanity serves only to enhance this connection between these two crimes committed during the war; crimes in many ways superfluous to actual military aims.

To date in China, there are still no programs specifically on Holocaust studies, something that is increasingly the norm in North American, British, and other Anglophone universities, and in many European universities too, but the Holocaust forms at least part of almost all Jewish studies programs at Chinese universities. There are four widely recognized programs in Jewish studies—Nanjing University, Shanghai Academy of Social Sciences, Henan University, and Shandong University—situated within either history or philosophy and religious studies departments. There are additionally a number of new programs, most notably at Sichuan International Studies University, Sichuan University, Northwest University, Xiamen University, Zhengzhou University, Sun Yat-sen University, Shanghai International Studies University, and their numbers continue to grow.

Given the rapid expansion of Jewish studies in China over the past decade, the field is, as of yet, still insufficiently defined, and courses on Judaism/Jewish religion, Jewish history, Jewish philosophy, and, in some cases, also Jewish literature, are taught as part and parcel of a bundle called Jewish studies. In more recent years, rather than demarcate the field more clearly, it has been further expanded by the introduction of Israel studies. All these universities and programs will teach about the Holocaust, usually as part of a larger course on modern Jewish history, philosophy or religion, or, now too, as part of area or regional studies.

Two, usually complementary, forces—one internal and the other external—motivate Holocaust studies in China. Certainly, of various fields within the social sciences and humanities in Chinese universities, Jewish studies has been more open to external or foreign influence than many others, with far less concern about ideologically harmful ideas entering the academy than is the case with national and international history, where a Marxist approach, while no longer compulsory, is still overriding. The absence of any sizeable Jewish community in China has inevitably necessitated looking abroad for training as well as primary and secondary sources, which is not the case for Buddhist, Christian, or Islamic studies, all of which are recognized as religions in China, and all of which have a tradition of scholarship from within these native faith communities. Judaism, at least as a culture rather than as a religion, has been positively perceived within China, with a significant number of Western Communist sympathizers coming to China in 1949 from Jewish backgrounds in the United Kingdom and the United States.[1] In more recent years, the opening of Jewish studies, while a field dominated by Chinese scholars, has allowed these scholars to spend time abroad, especially in the United States and Israel, and visiting academics from those and other countries are a common feature of these programs. The absence of any local Jewish community also means that in earlier years, most Hebrew teachers, whether as part of major programs or supplementary learning, inevitably came from Israel, but today there are a number of Chinese people teaching Hebrew and, indeed, translating texts from Hebrew into Chinese.

While it is difficult to pinpoint a precise beginning for Holocaust studies in China, it emerged early on as part of the Jewish studies programs, particularly at Nanjing University under the tutelage of Professor Xu Xin, and at the Shanghai Academy of Social Sciences under the direction of Professor Pan Guang. Professor Pan Guang has written extensively on the Jewish refugees in Shanghai, and this particular connection with that city has done much to give it a place in the history of the Holocaust. These two scholars are rightly seen as founders of Jewish studies in China, and to this group can also be added the work of Professor Fu Youde at Shandong University, and Professor Zhang Qianhong originally at Henan University and now at Zhengzhou University. Any discussion of Jewish and later Holocaust studies must include these four key figures and their work, as well as the younger academics they have nurtured and continue to educate.

The presence of these institutions and their inclusion of Holocaust studies necessitates asking the rather simple but important question—why is the Holocaust taught in China? Here, the internal and external—Chinese and foreign—influences should be considered;

---

1   See M. Avrum Ehrlich, ed., "Overview of Jewish Presence in Contemporary China," in *The Jewish-Chinese Nexus* (Abingdon, UK: Routledge, 2008), 3–15; M. Avrum Ehrlich, *Jews and Judaism in Modern China*, Routledge Jewish Studies Series (Abingdon, UK: Routledge, 2010), 112–116.

although neither influence can or should be seen as definitive or straightforward, they are inspired by different, as well as complementary, motivations.

In China, the subject of the Nanjing Massacre and other Japanese atrocities has only recently become a major topic of discussion in history teaching and more general consideration. The long silence on this subject is perhaps not unlike some of the apparent indifference to the Holocaust in both Israel and the United States until after the Eichmann Trial in 1961 and the Six-Day War in 1967. If at least some of that silence was motivated by Cold War expediency, so too in China, whatever silence there was, was motivated largely by political necessity, most pressingly by the need to engage economically with Japan as the latter became a global economy, and by Communist China stagnating under a totalitarian system of central planning and endless revolution. The complex history of China's own record during the Second World War, with Nationalist and Communist forces sparring with each other as much as with the Japanese occupiers, is cause also for some reticence on this subject. As China has emerged as an important economic power in its own right and now finds itself in growing tension with Japan, especially over maritime borders, it is using Japan's wartime history as one weapon in its arsenal against Japanese foreign policy. Japan, of course, has not helped an already tense situation with its own moral ambiguity over its wartime record, the place of sex slaves or so-called "comfort women," and continued official visits to the Yasukuni Shrine in Tokyo where some convicted war criminals have also been honored. Germany's acceptance of its culpability and incorporation of Holocaust education into its school curriculum is in marked contrast to Japan, and this too is noteworthy from a Chinese point of view.

The Nanjing Massacre Memorial Hall was built only in 1985, thirty-eight years after the event, and it was more recently expanded and refurbished into a major site of learning and memorialization, with obvious influences derived from the revamped (2005) Yad Vashem Museum in Jerusalem.

The more general problems and complexities of China's own use of the Nanjing Massacre and Japanese occupation, and its evolving relationship with Japan, are subjects for a detailed paper in their own right. It is sufficient to say that these atrocities do have some parallels with events during the *Shoah* in Europe, and China has therefore looked at how Europeans study that event and especially how Jewish communities, whether in Israel, the United States, or in Europe, teach about the Holocaust and remember it. The 1997 publication of Iris Chang's *The Rape of Nanking: The Forgotten Holocaust of WWII* was an important milestone in this process; she makes frequent, although often simplistic, references to Holocaust memory as opposed to the apparently forgotten atrocities in China.

At the same time, and a subject discussed elsewhere in this volume, China has a complex but largely positive relationship with Israel and, even more so, with the wider Diaspora Jewish community. It is precisely because China sees Jews, often rather stereotypically, as, on the whole, an admirable people who have survived continuous persecution and great suffering over two millennia and still maintain a strong sense of their own identity, that they do wish to know more about this small but noteworthy nation. Jewish aptitude in various fields, and especially its over representation in any list of Nobel Prize winners, is widely commented on, and any links between Jewish history, religion, persecution and response thereto is carefully studied. Jewish success in bringing the Holocaust to international attention, and requiring the world to honor the memory of the event, is something China finds noteworthy and, again, admirable. China itself has an ambiguous relationship with its own past; as it emerges as a global power, it increasingly asserts its strength and economic might as part of its foreign policy; at the same time, China casts itself as a victim, bullied and humiliated by Britain and France in the nineteenth century and Japan in the twentieth century. It no doubt sees that the Holocaust did, at least initially, gain Israel a certain degree of sympathy from parts of the international community.

The link between the Holocaust and Japanese war crimes was recently reinforced also by mounting a major exhibition, *Nazi-German Death Camp—Konzentrationslager Auschwitz*, together with the story of the Shanghai Jewish refugees, in the Museum of the War of Chinese

People's Resistance Against Japanese Aggression, in Beijing, from July to September 2013. This event was, of course, important in its own right and was the first cooperation between an official Chinese institution and the Auschwitz-Birkenau State Museum. But the link with Japanese atrocity was emphasized by its venue and by the official opening on the anniversary date (July 7) of the Lugou Bridge Incident in 1937 (also known as the Marco Polo Bridge Incident), which is widely seen as the spark which ignited the Sino-Japanese War since it was the excuse for the Japanese to launch their invasion of China.

From the external point of view, particularly for Israel and the wider Jewish community, there is a real sense of China's positive attitude toward them and a deep appreciation of the absence of anti-Semitism from China. Israel is able to deal with China, and while that relationship is not without incident, European and Islamic types of anti-Semitism are not concerns in the relationship. At the same time, Israel recognizes China's growing importance, economically but also politically, and while it can probably still rely on the United States to cast its veto at the United Nations Security Council, and on France and Britain to abstain at the very least, nurturing a stronger relationship with China, in which an understanding of Israel's vulnerability is clearly understood, must be in Israel's best interests. It is precisely because anti-Semitism has not corrupted China that there can be a real relationship of understanding of Jewish and Israeli vulnerability and recognition of how China, despite its immense size, was humiliated and exploited in the last two centuries. At this stage, China's reliance on Arab energy supplies still determines much of its realpolitik but there can be no harm in making China more aware of the Holocaust and why Israel is an essential place of refuge, offering the only secure homeland for Jews anywhere in the world.

As China continues to develop its own tertiary education system and some of its universities gain increasing international recognition, there is also the sense that in learning about the Western world and Western success over the past few centuries, history must be understood in its entirety. While there can be no doubt about Western achievement since at least the Enlightenment, there is also the undeniable fact of the Holocaust, this indelible blemish scarring the very heart of Western civilization. The Western world cannot and should not be studied without also recognizing this monstrous event, which has done so much to undermine that previously complacent sense of achievement. Western civilization runs from Athens to Apple, through Auschwitz, and one cannot celebrate only the achievement while ignoring the depravity. That central event of the modern era serves as a warning about the very fragility of culture and civilization and must be acknowledged by all.

The visit by then Chinese prime minister, Wen Jiabao, to Auschwitz on April 27, 2012, and his comment that the "tragedy of Auschwitz is the tragedy of all humanity" was noteworthy for emphasizing the universality of the *Shoah* from a Chinese point of view.

From within China itself, but more so from Western scholars engaged with China, there is also a sense in which Holocaust education might be used to raise, indirectly, pressing issues of China's own human rights record and its continuing support for North Korea. Judge Michael Kirby, in his 2014 United Nations report on North Korea, denounced its regime as having parallels with Nazi Germany and the atrocities of the Holocaust.[2]

In an article on Holocaust education in China written for UNESCO, Xu Xin has said that "Holocaust studies/education highlights human rights issues in China….questions are raised and discussed in the Holocaust courses, helping to bring out more human rights debates among the Chinese," suggesting that this link is recognized as much by, at least some, Chinese academics as by Western scholars working in the field.[3] Of course, there is, as of yet, no clear evidence that Holocaust education is in any way morally or ethically improving or that learning about Auschwitz makes students in the West, in China, or anywhere else, more sensitive to contemporary human suffering. This remains an ideal more than a proven reality.

---

2   Report of the detailed findings of the commission of inquiry on human rights in the Democratic People's Republic of Korea—A/HRC/25/CRP.1, March 2014.
3   Xu Xin, "A New Frame to Reinterpret China's Past: Holocaust Studies in China," in *Holocaust Education in a Global Context* (Paris: UNESCO, 2014), 143–152.

It is certainly the Jewish dimension of the Holocaust which is emphasized in China and very little, if any, attention is paid to other victim groups, such as Roma and Sinti, homosexuals, Jehovah's Witnesses, or the mentally and physically disabled; in this, it is not much different from Holocaust education in Israel and other Western countries. However, before the formal establishment of Holocaust studies in China in the 1990s, any mention of this subject would have been about victims of fascism. The singular persecution of the Jews has only been fully acknowledged with the normalization of Sino-Israeli relations in 1992 and with a growing willingness to establish Jewish studies as a subject in its own right.

Many Chinese school children will know something about the Holocaust, though often not much more than that it happened, and will be rather vague on the details or, indeed, its enormity. In *World History* (2008), used by all Grade 9 students in Chinese high schools, the Holocaust is covered in one chapter, which looks at the rise of Hitler in the aftermath of German economic collapse; Hitler's scapegoating of Jews as the cause of all German ills; the gradual exclusion of Jews from German society; *Kristallnacht*; the emigration of notable Jews like Einstein (easily the most famous Jew in China); and that millions were murdered. Little emphasis is given to the actual process of murder and there is no discussion of transports and death camps. Later, if students pursue history studies at university, they will learn a bit more, though still very much in the context of the Second World War. In the most widely used history textbook in Chinese universities, *World History* (2006), edited by Wu Yujin and Qi Shirong,[4] the Holocaust is covered in the following paragraph:

> The German fascists ruled the occupied territories in the cruelest and darkest way. About 20 million people were mass murdered (half of them were Soviet civilians and prisoners of war), along with which 1 million were slaughtered and tortured to death brutally in thousands of concentration camps, including the infamous Auschwitz, Buchenwald, Dachau and Sobibor.

---

4   I am grateful to Professor Zhang Qianhong, Zhengzhou University, for providing me with this information.

Hitler carried out genocidal policies against Jews. The total number of the Jews in the areas occupied by Nazi Germany was about 10 million, 6 million of whom were murdered (one in six were children). Moreover, 8 million civilians and prisoners of war (a quarter of them were women) were forced to do manual labor in Germany.

Clearly any discussion on the actual details of the Holocaust will depend largely on teachers' own interests and whatever signs of curiosity they might receive from students wanting to know more. Certainly the first paragraph is reminiscent of Soviet-type Holocaust education, where the emphasis was more on the fascist perpetrators and a generalized victimhood, and it is only in the second that the Jewish specificity of the *Shoah* is mentioned and briefly discussed, though that too is diluted by details of forced labor from occupied countries. It is only students pursuing specifically an area of Jewish studies who will learn more about the Holocaust itself.

Not all Holocaust education in China is run on a formal basis; the presence of the Jewish Refugees Museum in Shanghai prompts visitors to enquire about that story and what brought these Jews to China in the first place. Also, until very recently, many students of university age would have seen films like Steven Spielberg's *Schindler's List* (1993) and Roman Polanski's *The Pianist* (2002), and for many of them, this would be their first, and often only, introduction to this subject. But this brief introduction has sometimes been enough to inspire students to find out more and hence, in part, increase enrollment in history programs with a Jewish studies/Holocaust angle. This film-inspired interest is now on the wane as these films age and become less well known to students in their late teens and early twenties, although it is to be hoped that perhaps a future film or television series with similar credibility and impact will revive this important but little-studied effect on student imaginations.

The first, and so far only, Holocaust-related film made in China was Wang Genfa's 2010 production of *A Jewish Girl in Shanghai*, an animated tale of a young girl and her brother who find refuge in Shanghai during the war, their friendship with a young Chinese boy, and their brutalization by the occupying Japanese forces. Unfortunately, the parts of the film set in Europe, with the rise of the Nazis, are full of historical errors, and the two Jewish siblings, as well as their parents, are oddly Aryan in appearance. Nonetheless, some very fine animation, ironically strongly derived from Japanese anime, proved popular with young school children and will have had some effect on their understanding of this historical period, although probably more about the Japanese occupation than the German persecution of the Jews.

In terms of Holocaust education directed particularly at school children, the American NGO, Facing History and Ourselves, has become increasingly active in recent years, working with schools in Beijing and Shanghai in introducing this subject into the middle school history curriculum. Teachers from these schools are encouraged to attend teacher training courses in the United States or United Kingdom, and educators from Facing History also visit these schools on an annual basis. At this stage, the number of schools involved is still very small, although in all cases the schools are recognized as part of an elite group educating children of party officials and other prominent citizens. Operating in schools like these would not be possible without government approval. Facing History and Ourselves is now also actively devising units on the Nanjing Massacre for use in American high schools.

The USC Shoah Foundation is increasingly making its vast collection of Holocaust testimony available to schools and universities in China, while at the same time adding testimony from Nanjing survivors to its collection.

The Holocaust and the United Nations Outreach Programme, to which both Xu Xin and Pan Guang have contributed articles, is committed to providing Holocaust education materials in the five official languages of the United Nations, of which Chinese is one, and they, together with USHMM, now regularly produce Chinese translations of teaching units and other Holocaust education resources.[5]

---

5   See Xu Xin, "Holocaust Education in China," in *Discussion Papers Journal*, Vol. I., (New York: The Holocaust and United Nations Outreach Programme), 9–17; Pan

How effective they are in raising awareness of these resources to a Chinese audience is difficult to gauge and no system has been put in place to measure their impact.

Yad Vashem, also appreciating the growing significance of China in terms of long-term Holocaust education, is beginning to provide at least part of its website in Chinese, much of this work done by Professor Song Lihong[6] of Nanjing University, and to produce Holocaust testimonies with Chinese subtitles. This work is still in its infancy, but the major international Holocaust institutions are making resources available to Chinese educators and students, and this will only be expanded in the coming years.

In 2013, China's position as a place for serious Holocaust scholarship was recognized when the Association of Holocaust Organizations (AHO), an American-based international body bringing Holocaust scholars together, held its biennial foreign conference in Harbin in the northeast of China.[7] Harbin was a city with a sizeable population of Russian Jews, at least until the Second World War, and also was the site for Unit 731, where Japanese performed biological and chemical warfare research using human subjects. Many of the leading Chinese Holocaust scholars spoke at that event.

Even more recently, there have been moves by the Paris-based Yahad-in-Unum, an organization dedicated to improving Christian-Jewish relations and to marking the graves of Jews murdered in the former Soviet Union by the *Einsatzgruppen*, to begin excavating mass burial sites in Nanjing. This organization, under the presidency of the dynamic Catholic priest, Patrick Desbois, has become an important

---

    Guang, "Shanghai: A Haven for Holocaust Victims," in *Discussion Papers Journal*, Vol. II, (New York: The Holocaust and United Nations Outreach Programme), 63–75. Both can be found at http://www.un.org/en/holocaustremembrance/docs/docs.shtml.

6 See Song Lihong's Chinese translations, http://www.yadvashem.org/yv/en/education/languages/chinese/encyclopedia/index.asp.

7 The World Jewish Studies & Holocaust Education Conference 2013, organized by the Association of Holocaust Organizations and College of Society & History, Harbin Normal University, Harbin Modern Hotel, Harbin, China. October 9–15, 2013.

player in international Holocaust education and will almost certainly wish to extend that role in any work it might undertake in China.

While increasing numbers of international organizations are becoming active in helping to develop Holocaust studies and education in China, some vying with others to increase their impact, the level of contact between China and its special administrative region, Hong Kong, remains surprisingly low.

Very early on in the development of Holocaust studies in China, an important external role was taken up by the London Jewish Cultural Centre (LJCC), where, through the proactive initiative of Jerry Gotel, an annual summer school on Jewish and Holocaust studies has become a permanent fixture of the academic calendar. This UK-based institution, offering primarily education and cultural courses to London-based Jewry, recognized the need for advanced Holocaust education in China and took up the challenge. Having established a reputation in this field by offering teacher training in Holocaust education in Ukraine and Poland in the years immediately after the collapse of the Soviet Union, the LJCC saw China as a potential area for development and began to work closely with scholars previously mentioned—Xu Xin, Pan Guang, Fu Youde, and Zhang Qinhong. Each year the LJCC has organized a weeklong seminar on one of the campuses with a Jewish studies program, but in recent years, it has settled on Henan University in Kaifeng, partly because of its central location and also for its overall cost effectiveness.

Each summer, MA and PhD students in Jewish studies, history, literature and other social science and humanities subjects gather for a series of lectures and workshops, looking initially at questions on the origin and early history of the Jews, Jewish religion and culture, the Diaspora, and anti-Judaism as preparation for a focus on the Holocaust, which is the main, but not exclusive, emphasis of this program.

A key participant in all these seminars is Joanna Millan, child survivor of Theresienstadt, board member of the LJCC, and active Holocaust educator in the United Kingdom. Joanna Millan's lectures on her own family's fate in the *Shoah* and her story of survival is probably the first, and often only, contact many of the participants will have with a survivor, thereby personalizing the historical into a tangible reality the participants can experience for themselves.

The LJCC seminars were initially partly sponsored by the ITF (International Task Force for Holocaust Education), now known as IHRA (International Holocaust Remembrance Alliance), the Claims Conference (Conference on Jewish Material Claims Against Germany), and the *Fondation pour la Mémoire de la Shoah*, although in recent years the financial burden has been carried mostly by the LJCC with support from the Claims Conference. This financial backing has allowed the organizers to bring a number of prominent Holocaust scholars and educators to teach at the seminar, including representatives from Yad Vashem, USHMM, Wannsee House, Anne Frank Museum, *Fondation pour la Mémoire de la Shoah*, as well as leading centers for Jewish and/or Holocaust studies in the United States and the United Kingdom.

For one week every year, students and academics working in Jewish and Holocaust studies are thus able to come together to work with international scholars as well as the key figures from within Chinese academia. In recent years, a popular feature of this program has been allocating one day to lectures by emerging Chinese scholars in the field, who have this opportunity to share their research with students only beginning their graduate studies. Many of these scholars are recent PhD graduates who are beginning their careers at Chinese universities.

On average, approximately seventy post-graduate students and young scholars participate in the seminar, and their travel, accommodation, and food costs are covered by the LJCC. Clearly, this annual seminar is playing an important incubatory role in the development of Holocaust studies in China, allowing young scholars to meet each other and also to develop connections with academics from abroad, connections which often lead to visiting studentships at universities in Israel and the United States.[8]

---

8   The LJCC will cease to exist in its present form in mid 2015 and will be incorporated into the newly established JW3, a Jewish Community Centre for London. While the future financing of these China seminars has not yet been declared, their founders—Jerry Gotel, Joanna Millan, and Trudy Gold—are committed to their continuation.

Of similar importance, a more recent development has been the annual Yad Vashem Seminar for Chinese Educators, which started in 2010. This is an initiative developed by the author with Jerry Gotel from the LJCC and Ephraim Kaye, Director of International Seminars at Yad Vashem, to take thirty educators from the Chinese mainland, Hong Kong, and Macao to Israel for a two weeks intensive Holocaust education. Here, the definition of educator is broadly defined, and the organizers seek to recruit people from a variety of backgrounds—MA and PhD students, emerging and established scholars in Jewish and Holocaust education, as well as high school teachers, museum curators, journalists, journal editors, and others who can play a role in disseminating knowledge and awareness of the *Shoah* in greater China.

The Adelson Family Foundation, through Yad Vashem, sponsors this annual seminar and participants have all costs covered, including flights, accommodation, and daily board, as well as the actual seminar costs. Sheldon Adelson has been a prime developer of Macao in recent years, and his casino group, Sands Venetian, is now the largest in the world. Sheldon and Miri Adelson have been major donors to Yad Vashem and other Holocaust education projects, and this annual seminar is part of their efforts to raise Holocaust awareness, especially in China.

For the thirty participants in each seminar, this is an opportunity to learn from leading scholars, including people like Yehuda Bauer, Robert Wistrich, Alan Rosen, and Jeremy Rosen, as well as to discover areas not yet covered in Holocaust studies in China, such as music, art and literature from the *Shoah*. Participants are taken on an extended tour of the main Holocaust Museum and are exposed to what is almost certainly the most thorough and detailed Holocaust collection in the world. Of particular importance is an afternoon spent with Holocaust survivors, hearing their individual stories and having time to talk to them on a more intimate and personal level afterward. For many, this will be their only opportunity to talk to survivors of Auschwitz-Birkenau, Majdanek, other major sites of killing, and the death marches. Each seminar also includes a day and a night at Lochamei HaGhetaot, with its outstanding exhibitions and Children's Holocaust Museum, Yad Layeled, and here they have the chance to meet some of the very few survivors of the Warsaw and other ghettos.

Holocaust education in China has also received more attention at the biennial Salzburg Global Seminar (SGS) on Holocaust Education and Genocide Prevention, founded in 2010 under the patronage of Kofi Annan, where the aim has been to develop Holocaust awareness in those countries that are not members of the International Holocaust Remembrance Alliance (IHRA), i.e., countries or regions with little or no direct experience of the Holocaust, especially South America, Africa, the Middle East, and Asia, where Holocaust education is absent or still being developed. This symposium is organized by the Salzburg Global Seminar in conjunction with the USHMM, under the guidance of Edward Mortimer, Marie-Louise Ryback, and Klaus Mueller, and in addition to looking at what is happening in these different geographical areas, there is also a drive to encourage regional networks. An East Asian network bringing scholars and educators together from Japan, South Korea, and China, and possibly also Cambodia, is a project which may be developed in the very near future. Panelists from China, Korea, and Cambodia participated in the 2012 seminar and from China, Japan, Korea, and Cambodia in 2014, so a foundation for future cooperation is now being laid and IHRA has been approached to lend support for such an undertaking.

While the emphasis on this discussion on Holocaust studies and Holocaust education has been on the Chinese mainland, given that the Yad Vashem seminar seeks to cover greater China (with the exception of Taiwan) and that there is increasingly fluid movement of students between the mainland and the two special administrative regions of the People's Republic of China, Hong Kong, and Macao, some attention should be given to these two self-governing cities as well.

Despite Hong Kong having the largest resident Jewish population in Asia, generally approximated as between 3,500 and 5,000 people, a cosmopolitan mix of Americans, Australians, British, French, Israelis, South Africans, and smaller numbers from many European and South American countries, there are as of yet no established centers for, or endowed chairs in, Jewish studies at any of the seven universities.

Biblical Hebrew is taught at the Chinese University for those specializing in Christian religious studies, while modern Hebrew (Ivrit) is taught only at the Jewish primary and high school. This is surprising given the considerable endowment of the Ohel Leah Synagogue Trust, and Hong Kong might be expected to lead the field in Asia rather than lag behind even small cities in China with no Jewish communities at all with universities offering programs in Jewish and Israel studies. This has long been the case for Holocaust studies and education as well, and this has only very recently changed with the establishment of the Hong Kong Holocaust and Tolerance Centre in 2011.

Hong Kong did, however, play a pivotal role in the establishment of Holocaust studies in China, although it failed to capitalize on this important initiative afterward. In May 2000, the then chairman of the Ohel Leah Synagogue, Scott Saunders, organized Hong Kong's first Holocaust exhibition—*The Holocaust: History's Greatest Tragedy*—bringing an important part of the Sydney Jewish Museum's collection of Holocaust objects for display, as well as a panel exhibition on children's art from Yad Vashem in Israel. This exhibition was seen by over 2,000 Hong Kong school children as well as by members of the public.

In addition to a Holocaust survivor from Australia, Helen Staub, three other speakers were also invited—Szewach Weiss, Holocaust survivor, then chairman of the Yad Vashem Council, speaker of the Knesset, professor of Jewish Studies at Haifa University and later also Israeli ambassador to Poland; Professor Xu Xin, from Nanjing University; and Jerold Gotel from the LJCC. It was this meeting between Xu Xin and Jerold Gotel which led first to Gotel's participation in a symposium convened by Xu Xin in Nanjing in May 2002—*The History of the Jewish Diaspora in China*, itself a signature event of its kind in China—and his meeting Professor Zhang Qianhong. This, in turn, led to his taking up a part-time position at the Institute of Jewish Studies in Kaifeng and to the laying of plans for the LJCC summer seminars, the first being held in Nanjing in 2005.

In 2007, the Hong Kong Jewish Community organized an exhibition on Anne Frank, again aimed largely at school children, although it was only with the founding of the HKHTC in 2011 that Holocaust education has now become an ongoing project in Hong Kong schools and in the public more widely. The centre is working with the Education Bureau to find ways the Holocaust might be included in the school curriculum and is running teacher training workshops as preparation for this. The HKHTC also oversees and organizes Holocaust commemorative events both for Yom HaShoah, a more Jewish-community oriented event, and also the annual United Nations Holocaust Memorial Day, on January 27, and these have included concerts of music composed in the camps, exhibitions of artwork by children in Theresienstadt as well as by a survivor of Bergen Belsen, film premieres, and other outreach programs. United Nations Holocaust Memorial Day is not marked in any other part of China, despite its official status on the United Nations calendar.

More recently, some teaching about the Holocaust has been introduced into Hong Kong universities: in the European Studies Programme at the University of Hong Kong, Dr. Roland Vogt is teaching a course specifically on the Holocaust and at Baptist University; Dr. Martin Chung (himself a former participant in the Yad Vashem seminar) is teaching a general education course, also within European studies, which looks at the Holocaust and postwar reconciliation. The Hong Kong Polytechnic University recently ran a reading program for its 3,000 undergraduate students in which all were given copies of John Boyne's *The Boy in the Striped Pajamas* (2006); despite the very real problems with this text as an education resource, it was an opportunity to reach a significant part of the student population. These are the beginnings of growing interest in this subject in Hong Kong universities, and it is to be hoped that this interest will be further developed in the coming years. Also in the HKU European Studies Programme, a number of symposia have been held which have dealt, at least in part, with the Holocaust, and so students in tertiary education are gaining increasing exposure, although it is still, at this stage, limited in scope.

Across the Pearl River Delta in Macao, there are again no formal Jewish or Holocaust Studies programs, but the author has, since 2008, run an annual literature course within the MA in English Studies program at the University of Macau, called "Remembering and

Representing the *Shoah*: The Holocaust in Literature, Memoir and Film." For this course, the majority of students are from the Chinese mainland, and a number of these have gone on to write their MA dissertations on Holocaust subjects. Given that most of these graduates will go on to teaching positions either at high schools or universities in the Chinese mainland, this can be seen as part of a long-term Holocaust education program.

At the same time, the introduction of general education programs into universities in both Hong Kong and Macao provides opportunity for the Holocaust to be taught to a wider range of students. In Macao, a course called "The Holocaust, Genocide and Human Rights" is taught every semester and, again, at least half the classes—two hundred students per year—are from the mainland while the other half are from Macao and Hong Kong. For many of these students, this is their first exposure to this subject, and there is a high level of interest. Professor Alexandra Cook, from the University of Hong Kong's Department of Philosophy, is working toward introducing a course on the Holocaust and genocide as part of general or core education at her institution.

As an offshoot of the Hong Kong Jewish Film Festival, a number of Holocaust-related films are screened annually at high schools in Hong Kong, as well as on the University of Macau campus, to which school children are also invited. Where possible, those involved in the making of the film, whether director or, as has been the case on a number of occasions, survivors, participate in Q & A sessions afterwards.

The phenomenon of Jewish and especially Holocaust studies in China is still surprising to many Westerners, who invariably think of a local Jewish population as somehow necessary to raise awareness or arouse interest in this subject. The desire to overcome this imaginative limitation inspires much of the work of the Salzburg Global Seminar, as discussed above, and is also evident in two recent articles on Holocaust education in China, published in major international media. On January 26, 2014, for United Nations Holocaust Memorial Day, the *New York Times* published an article, "Raising Asian Awareness of the Holocaust," looking particularly at the work of the Hong Kong Holocaust and Tolerance Centre. Five months earlier, the *Economist* published an article on the global dimension of Holocaust education, with the subheading, "The study of the Holocaust is expanding worldwide—for differing reasons," and looking at the case of China, mentioned the Japanese atrocities and then the Asian situation more widely:

> Methods developed by early Holocaust centers have become guides for memorials to Asian tragedies. The Tuol Sleng Genocide Museum in Cambodia and a Chinese museum commemorating the "Rape of Nanking" by Japanese soldiers in 1937 have drawn on Yad Vashem. "Israeli people did a great job of teaching the past," says Xiaowei Fu, director of Judaic studies department at Sichuan University in Chengdu [sic]. She has tried to drum up interest in the Holocaust with an essay competition offering a cash prize.[9]

While Holocaust Studies are still developing in China, it is necessary to ask what the future holds for this field and how it can be further enhanced. One of the problems facing any discipline in China is the shear magnitude of the country, where both geographical distance and sizeable population means that scholars have to surmount a number of challenges. In terms of Holocaust studies, active participants are few, and they are working at considerable distances from each other; universities fall under different administrative units, some operating at a largely provincial level while others are subject to central control under the Ministry of Education. What this means in practical terms is that there is often little sense of how universities might complement each other in terms of research and other scholarly activity. In May 2012, the Institute of Jewish Studies at Henan University held a conference in Kaifeng, bringing scholars from all over China together for two days to address the state of the subject. Precisely because Holocaust studies are still subsumed under Jewish studies, there is now a need to establish a separate organization of Holocaust studies and Holocaust education, to which all universities and other institutions teaching this subject in greater China might belong, and where, through annual conferences and symposia there may be efforts for greater coordination and less

---

9 "Remembering the Holocaust: Bearing witness ever more," *The Economist*, August 24, 2013, 47–48.

duplication of resources in the field. A pan-China Holocaust studies organization might make use of Internet and other web resources for both teachers and students, and teaching resources developed locally or translated from other languages could also be more widely shared. One of the leading Jewish studies centers might be encouraged to establish a local academic journal devoted specifically to the Holocaust and other genocides. At a provincial level, education departments could be encouraged to include more about Holocaust education in history lessons in high schools and also in the teaching of English as a second language. The possibilities are many, but a centrally coordinated strategy from one or more universities is required if this is to happen.

An urgent task for such an organization would also be the compilation of a detailed bibliography of primary and secondary resources already translated into Chinese, of works written in Chinese, a database of all MA and PhD theses completed in various areas of Holocaust studies, and a resource index of opportunities for study abroad and other funding possibilities, so that the field can continue to be developed.

In China, there are a vast number of university and other presses, many of which are publishing both original and translated monographs and primary sources, including Holocaust memoirs, novels, key historical texts, textbooks, catalogues, and other resources, but there is no easy way to assess the current state of the field and thus no real sense of which important texts have been translated and which should take priority for future translation projects.

Indeed, the field of Holocaust translation is itself an area in need of coordinated attention, and any future organization of Holocaust studies and education in China should address this as a matter of urgency. Central to this project would be the production of an agreed glossary of Holocaust terminology, so that all working in the field can agree on exactly how certain terms might be translated, or, as is often the case with foreign words, especially proper nouns, transliterated. Some of this work has already been done by Professor Song Lihong and also by Noam Urbach of Bar-Ilan University in Israel.

At the same time, it is to be hoped that scholars might find a way to agree on a uniquely Chinese word for "Holocaust" itself, which, at present, translates as Jewish Massacre. Here there is both an element of ambiguity—is it the Jews who are doing the massacring or is it the Jews who are being massacred?—and also a certain mundaneness or reduction of the unprecedentedness of the historical phenomenon being described. Massacres, while regrettable, are hardly unprecedented, and history is unfortunately full of them; the Holocaust was a long process of discrimination, dehumanization, distortion of the rule of law, mass shootings, deprivation, and ultimately an industrialized process of killing in purpose-built death camps. In Western scholarship, the word *Shoah* is increasingly being used over the problematic term *Holocaust* to encapsulate this range of atrocity, a range both in kind—the methods of deprivation and murder—and in geographical space—from Copenhagen to Corfu; the enormity of this historical process is far too large to be encapsulated in a word like "massacre," with its suggestion only of killing and a singular instance at that. Quite how scholars might come to agree on a word like *Shoah* for use in China has yet to be established, but it will be worth trying to achieve. The phonetic and semantic limitations of the Chinese character system is well known, and neologisms are often hard to achieve, but the Chinese are certainly capable of creating and adopting new words, and a Chinese event-specific word like *Shoah* should be sought and coined.

Holocaust studies and Holocaust education have been established on a firm footing in China; the early work of the founding scholars in this field is being reinforced and developed by the next generation of scholars while they, too, are nurturing the third generation of academics and teachers. The relative absence of anti-Semitism from China has made approaching the Holocaust with an open mind that much easier, with no theories of Jewish conspiracy to distort what is largely an academic enquiry into how the greatest crime in human history could have taken place in the heart of Europe in the middle of the twentieth century.

Reflections on Chinese Jewish Studies: A Comparative Perspective

SONG LIHONG
Nanjing University

Judaism under the Aegis of neither Christianity nor Islam

At the beginning of my undergraduate course on "Jewish Culture and World Civilizations," I usually ask the students to name whatever pops up in their minds in association with Jews or Judaism. Almost without fail, they list rich, smart, persecuted, persistent, the Star of David, abstention from pork, Marx, Freud, and Einstein. Rarely, if ever, mentioned is the Bible, which seems to me telling. After all, the regnant faiths in China throughout most of its history are Confucianism, Taoism, and Buddhism. Most Chinese, of past and present, have no acquaintance with the Bible and with the common religious traditions of Judaism and the other two monotheistic faiths. This situation is in stark contrast with that in the Middle East, Europe, North Africa, and the American continents, where Jewish history is long bound up and where the Jewish people have been in intimate interaction with Christian and Islamic cultures.

Despite this historic lack of exposure to monotheism and the Bible, there is widespread interest in Jews and Judaism in today's China, on both popular and scholarly levels. As a clue to the former, the shelves of Chinese bookstores are lined with bestsellers on Jewish subjects, with such eye-catching titles as *Unveiling the Secrets of Jewish Success in World Economy*, *What's Behind Jewish Excellence?*, *The Talmudic Wisdom in Conducting Business*, and *Talmud: The Greatest Jewish Bible for Making Money*. Perhaps the only book of this kind that has achieved a somewhat cult status is *Currency Wars* [huobi zhanzheng], which is of the opinion that the ubiquitous Rothschild family controls the world economy.[1] For Jewish sensibilities, the Chinese thirst for unveiling the secrets to Jewish power and success is ominous, smacking of the spread of the conspiracy theories and anti-Semitism that have brought horrendous suffering and trauma to the Jewish people.[2] Yet to my mind, it generally does not betray a kind of Judeophobia because the religious underpinning of anti-Semitism in Europe and in Arab lands was and is irrelevant in China. Rather, it reveals some sort of Judeophilia, reflecting the eagerness and anxiety with which a nation that is focused on economic growth and technological advancement casts about for an imitable model it can employ to modernize itself in the aftermath of the Cultural Revolution and the Cold War. The Jewish secret to success is such a model, albeit an imagined one.

On a different level, Jewish studies has become broadly established in universities where it scarcely existed at all before China normalized its diplomatic relations with the State of Israel in 1992. Today, no less than ten Chinese institutions of higher learning are able to grant degrees in Jewish history and culture, Hebrew language and literature, Middle Eastern studies, or Jewish philosophy and religion. The past twenty years also bear witness to the creation of several academic centers that specialize in Jewish and Israeli studies. What's more, articles on Jewish topics are increasingly well represented in learned journals. For instance, in 2007, of all 102 articles and (book) reviews published in the bimonthly *World History* (shijie lishi), the foremost journal on world history in China, 7 pieces deal with Jewish-Israeli topics, in contrast to 18 pieces about the United States (one overlap—it's on American Jews), 9 about Japan, 7 about France, and 4 about Russia and the Soviet Union (one overlap again). The only one about Germany deals with German Jews. Considering the weakening of the humanities and the social sciences in favor of the natural sciences and

---

1   See "Currency Wars," http://en.wikipedia.org/wiki/Currency_Wars, accessed July 23, 2014.
2   Ariana Eunjung Cha, "Sold on a Stereotype," *The Washington Post*, February 7, 2007, accessed July 23, 2014, http://www.washingtonpost.com/wp-dyn/content/article/2007/02/06/AR2007020601713.html. See also James Ross in this volume.

economics in general and the non-proselytizing nature of Judaism and hence the invisibility of China's Jewish communities in particular, this development is quite phenomenal.

It is well worth asking, then, in a land that is neither Christian nor Muslim and where Judaism never developed substantial roots, what are the perceptible orientations within Jewish studies. What kinds of issues may Chinese scholars encounter when teaching and writing about Jews and Judaism? Does the unique context in which Jewish studies is emerging have a bearing upon Chinese practitioners, and in what way is Chinese Jewish studies different from that produced in other quarters of the world? In this chapter, I will try to address these questions from a comparative perspective.

An Assumption without Apologetics

The idea of Judaism and Hellenism as two major origins of Western civilization is so prevalent among the contemporary Chinese intelligentsia that any further warrant for incorporating Jewish studies courses into the university curriculum sounds superfluous. Beyond doubt, knowledge of Judaism is indispensible for our understanding of its exceptional contribution to world civilization. As a leading scholar articulated in a study on Jewish culture that is extensively used as a textbook today, Jewish culture is:

> one of the most ancient human civilizations, a culture that has exerted a tremendous and profound impact upon the progress of world civilization and especially of Western civilization.... The study of Jewish culture affords the Chinese people of the twenty-first century a salutary lesson. How to play a greater role in international affairs can be seen as both an important goal the Chinese people cherish in their "moving towards the World," and a challenge they face. To understand Jewish culture is a requisite step towards meeting both ends, because Jewish thoughts have influenced the constituents and the course of world civilization, and because the trace of Jewish culture is ubiquitous and distinctively visible in western cultures.[3]

---

3   Xu Xin, *Youtai wenhua shi* [*A History of Jewish Culture*] (Beijing: Peking University Press, 2006), 2–3 Preface.

Plainly enough, to study Jewish culture is essential for our conceptualization and reconfiguration of the world—primarily of the West—in relation to China's steady integration into international society.

This assumption, lurking in the Chinese popular imagination of Jews as well, is decidedly a far cry from that in the modern West, where the *topos* of the "Jewish contribution to civilization" is usually thought of as referring to a certain variety of Jewish apologetic rejoinder to modern anti-Semitism's denial of the full acceptance of Jews into European and American societies. As a recurrent discourse in modern Jewish history, this *topos* significantly penetrated the sense of self of many Jewish scholars, driving them, consciously or subconsciously, to prove the worthiness of Jews according to the criteria of a non-Jewish worldview, sometimes to the poignant extent of subverting the dominantly Christian master narrative of Western civilization by claiming a kind of "Jewish superiority." For example, Abraham Geiger, a pioneer of Jewish studies in the nineteenth century, wrote extensively on the historical background of Jesus in early Judaism. His main point was that Jesus was not only a Jewish religious leader but specifically a Pharisee whose goal was nothing more than that of the other Pharisees: that is, the democratization of Judaism. Nothing in Jesus' teaching was new and original. Geiger's viewpoint not only sought to counter the widespread image of Judaism as a degenerate religion, which was current in the Christian scholarship of his day, but went further, insisting that Judaism was the original, true religion from which Christianity and Islam were deviant derivatives.[4] In view of this, the "Jewish contribution to civilization," while a mode of thought that has motivated Chinese scholars, is free of its apologetic import in China. Far from marginalized, Jews in Chinese eyes stand at the very center of Western civilization.

Accompanied by the lack of this apologetic assumption is the absence of Jewish identity. The modern scientific study of Jews and

---

4 Jeremy Cohen and Richard I. Cohen, eds., *The Jewish Contribution to Civilization: Reassessing an Idea* (Oxford: The Littman Library of Jewish Civilization, 2008); Susannah Heschel, *Abraham Geiger and the Jewish Jesus* (Chicago: University of Chicago Press, 1998).

Judaism, from its beginnings in the *Wissenschaft des Judentums* to the present, is by and large Jewishly bound and fraught, as Michael Meyer has masterfully posited, with two persistent tensions: the first is that between religious and secular approaches, and the second is that between efforts directed inward toward Jewish life and directed outward toward focused goals—put differently, directed inward to serve the spiritual and cultural needs of the Jewish community and outward to serve scholarly purposes for their own sake.[5] What looms largest behind these tensions and dilemmas is the intertwined nexus between critical Jewish learning and Jewish faith. In contrast, Chinese Jewish studies, produced—at least predominantly—by and for the Chinese, could be described as Jewish studies independent of Jewish faith and without an intent to cultivate and strengthen Jewish identity; hence Chinese Jewish studies is freed of the burden of searching for its role both in the academy and in the tradition of Jewish learning, a fate that even today's non-Jewish scholars of Jews and Judaism in Germany can hardly escape.[6]

It is worth pointing out in this regard that, although the attention of Chinese scholars has been drawn to a wide spectrum of Jewish topics, ranging from Moses to Ben-Gurion, from the Dead Sea Scrolls to the Holocaust, from Philo to Levinas, from Isaac Singer to Amos Oz,[7] until

---

5   Michael A. Meyer, "Two Persistent Tensions within *Wissenschaft des Judentums*," *Modern Judaism* 24.2 (2004), 105–119; for modern Jewish studies, see also Paul Mendes-Flohr and Jehuda Reinharz, eds., *The Jew in the Modern World: A Documentary History*, 3rd ed. (New York and Oxford: Oxford University Press, 2011), 233–275; Gershom Scholem, "Reflections on Modern Jewish Studies (1944)," in *On the Possibility of Jewish Mysticism in Our Time and Other Essays*, ed. Avraham Shapira (Philadelphia: Jewish Publication Society of America, 1997), 51–71; Yosef Hayim Yerushalmi, *Zakhor: Jewish History and Jewish Memory* (New York: Schocken Books, 1989), 77103; Ismar Schorsch, *From Text to Context: The Turn to History in Modern Judaism* (Hanover and London: Brandeis University Press, 1994).
6   Meyer, "Two Persistent Tensions within *Wissenschaft des Judentums*," 115.
7   The most comprehensive bibliography until 2007 is found in Pan Guang, ed., *Youtai yanjiu zai zhongguo: sanshinian huigu: 1978–2008* [Jewish Studies in China: A Thirty Year Retrospective, 19782008] (Shanghai: Shanghai Academy of Social Sciences Press, 2008), 319–367. For recent works, see, *inter alia*, Fu Youde, et al., *Youtai zhexue shi* [A History of Jewish Philosophy] (Beijing: Renmin University Press, 2008); Qiao Guoqiang, *Meiguo youtai wenxue* [Jewish American Literature] (Beijing: Commercial Press, 2008); Zhang Shuqing, *Zhongshiji xiou de youtai funü* [Jewish Women in Medieval Western Europe] (Beijing: Renmin Press, 2009); Rao

now no single article, as far as I can tell, has dealt with any aspect of Jewish liturgy in depth. Even pieces of general description are truly few and far between. Liturgy is a living issue for Jews. The Jewish prayer book has been read and reread in every generation, in every Jewish community. The changes as reflected in the liturgy can be seen as a miniature version of the changes occurring in Judaism in general. In this sense, the prayer book "is like a garland, intertwining all the strands of Judaism and encompassing all fields of Jewish creativity in all their variegated forms."[8] The absence of Jewish liturgy from the research agenda of Chinese Jewish studies, therefore, may well be construed to mean that the Jewish experience is not comprehended in China as an entity in the totality of its spatial and temporal phenomena, and Jews and Judaism are studied not as a "living organism," but, I would venture to suggest, a "living fossil." This seems to be an unavoidable consequence of a Jewish studies not bolstered by Jewish identity and, perhaps no less important, without access to the lived Jewish experience.

My awareness of this point also touched off a new question: In what terms shall I, as an observer outside of the Jewish tradition, approach Judaism and Jewish civilization? Some elements of Judaism, such as prayer, are fundamentals of the tradition but structurally and culturally alien to the way we live now in China. How is it possible to

---

Benzhong, *Youtai lüfa de yuanyuan* [The Sources of Jewish Law] (Beijing: Intellectual Property Publishing House, 2010); Zhou Ping, *Youtai gushi suoluomen zhuan* [The Solomon Narrative in the *Jewish Antiquities*] (Beijing: Social Sciences Academic Press, 2011); Song Lihong, ed., *Cong xinai dao zhongguo* [From Sinai to China] (Beijing: Sanlian Publishing House, 2012), esp. 319–324; Zhong Zhiqing, *Biange zhong de ershi shiji xibolai wenxue* [The Hebrew Literature of the Twentieth Century in Transition] (Beijing: Chinese Academy of Social Sciences Press, 2013); Wang Shuming, *Datusha jiyi yu meiguo waijiao* [Holocaust Memory and American Foreign Policy] (Beijing: Shishi Press, 2013); Song Lihong and Meng Zhenhua, eds., *Youtaijiao de jiben gainian* [Basic Concepts of Judaism] (Nanjing: Jiangsu Renmin Press, 2013); Meng Zhenhua, *Bosi shiqi de youda shehui yu shengjing bianzuan* [The Society of Yehud and the Redaction of the Bible in the Persian Period] (Beijing: Religious Culture Press, 2013); Zhang Qianhong, *Yiselie Shi* [A History of Israel], revised ed., (Beijing: Renmin Press, 2014); Wang Yanmin, *Yiselie zhengdang zhengzhi yanjiu* [Party Politics in Israel] (Beijing: Renmin Press, 2014).

8 Adin Steinsaltz, *A Guide to Jewish Prayer* (New York: Schocken Books, 2000), 4; see also Ismar Elbogen, *Jewish Liturgy: A Comprehensive History*, trans. Raymond R. Scheindlin (Philadelphia: The Jewish Publication Society, 1993).

present these elements in my own teaching and research, so as to induce enough awareness of their intrinsic value to Judaism without, at the same time, inciting suspicion that I am trying to ferment faith commitments? How would I approach Judaism and Jewish civilization historically with all its complexity? This is a challenge.

Academic Settings

Besides this non-apologetic assumption and its problematics for developing Jewish studies in China, the academic settings and pedagogical issues also merit our attention. In a still highly sensitive and suggestive strategy paper in 2004 calling for greater Jewish engagement with China, Shalom Wald noted a phenomenon symptomatic of current Chinese Jewish scholarship:

> Reviewing the Chinese authors of Jewish and Israeli studies between 1980 and today, one finds a number of names from the 1980s and early 1990s that have since disappeared. Except for a few, there is not yet a strong and stable Jewish scholarship community with a long-term commitment.[9]

This diagnosis, apt indeed, sounds like a distant echo of a remark by Ismar Elbogen. In 1927, that great Jewish historian of *Wissenschaft des Judentums* branded the work of non-Jewish scholars of his time as necessarily inadequate because they lacked enthusiasm for their subject and also what he called an "indispensible inner feeling for the spirit of the Hebrew language."[10] The difference, though, is that Wald certainly smelled no anti-Semitic odor among the Chinese scholars. He speculated that the first reason for the dearth of continuity in Jewish studies might be the lack of long-term academic employment of Chinese specialists in this area. Second, an effect of the intifadas would make choosing Jews and Israel as research themes appear inconsonant with China's pro-Palestinian political rhetoric, and therefore the choice would no longer offer advantageous career opportunities.

---

9 Shalom Salomon Wald, *China and the Jewish People: Old Civilizations in a New Era* (Jerusalem: Jewish People Policy Planning Institute, 2004), 53–54.
10 Cited in Meyer, "Two Persistent Tensions within *Wissenschaft des Judentums*," 115.

Wald's second speculation is still basically accurate, and especially holds true for scholars whose research is closely connected with contemporary Middle East politics or may touch upon Islamic sensitivities. As Wald pointed out, this could be observed in 1993, the year that witnessed the publication of an abridged Chinese edition of *Encyclopedia Judaica*, to this day the most influential Chinese reference book on Jewish history, religion, and culture.[11] In his foreword to the Chinese edition, a famous scholar wrote that Judaism was the "mother religion" of Christianity and Islam. When the first printing was sold out and a second revised edition was planned, the ambassador of Saudi Arabia raised an official protest, followed by more effective protests from domestic Islamic associations, to the effect that Islam was a new religion that had no links whatsoever to Judaism. The initial official reaction was to prohibit this second edition. One of the editors-in-chief, Professor Xu Xin, was called up to Beijing to render an account. The authorities finally allowed the second edition but on condition that the foreword be eliminated.[12] Needless to elaborate, some areas of Jewish studies remain too sensitive to tread upon.

Wald's first speculation reflects a disciplinary framework whose nuances may need further amplification. Jewish studies at the university level in China is organized neither as an autonomous department as it is in Israel nor as an interdepartmental program as is often the case in America. As I understand it, Jewish studies in Israel seems to enjoy a disciplinary status. In the Hebrew University of Jerusalem, for example, there are independent departments of Bible, Talmud, Jewish history, and Jewish thought, all subsumed within the Institute of Jewish Studies. This is unique to Israel, for it is impossible to find under the umbrella of a school of humanities in China independent departments of Confucianism, Taoism, Chinese Buddhism, Chinese history, or Chinese thought; instead, only departments of history, philosophy, and

---

11 Xu Xin and Ling Jiyao, eds., *Youtai baike quanshu* [The Encyclopedia Judaica] (Shanghai: Shanghai Renmin Press, 1993).
12 Wald, *China and the Jewish People*, 70. Muslim opposition to possible influences on Islam is also observed in other corners of the world, see Bernard Lewis, *From Babel to Dragomans: Interpreting the Middle East* (New York: Oxford University Press, 2004); 55.

religion exist. By contrast, a "Jewish studies program" in America often consists of a single chair, around which is gathered a cadre of scholars from various disciplines.[13] Both models are presumably instrumental in fostering interdisciplinary study. In China, as an ingrained practice, the manifold areas or aspects of Jewish studies are each affiliated with quite disparate disciplines. In Chinese universities that teach Jewish studies of any kind, such courses are commonly located among four to five departments—history, oriental languages, international relations, and philosophy and/or religious studies. Jewish studies has thus developed in a fragmented way, with the concomitant problems first expressed in the dearth of interdisciplinary studies. As is well known, few scholars who work in humanities today are unaware of the degree to which disciplinary boundaries have been eroded, of the necessity of crossing traditional disciplinary boundaries, and of the constant turmoil in disciplinary identity that has resulted; these problems are not peculiar to the field of Jewish studies.

A more noteworthy issue for Chinese scholarship is how to find a common language among scholars under the label of "Jewish studies." History and religion departments offer only shorter courses of basic Hebrew. The department of oriental studies is accomplished in teaching modern Hebrew. Nevertheless, defining Judaism within the framework of the "Orient"—or the Near East—alone limits that department to an important yet relatively small segment of Jewish history. This leaves out the manifestations of Jewish experiences in the European and American diaspora, which are crucial to our understanding of today's Judaism. Those based within philosophy departments usually find it very difficult to integrate courses in Jewish history and culture into the Jewish studies curriculum, and thereby run the risk of reducing Judaism to a purely spiritual phenomenon and of disregarding the vital aspects of the Jewish people as a "living organism." Those adept at international relations

---

13 Paul Ritterband and Harold S. Wechsler, *Jewish Learning in American Universities: The First Century* (Bloomington and Indianapolis: Indiana University Press, 1994), 216–236; David N. Myers, *Re-Inventing the Jewish Past: European Jewish Intellectuals and the Zionist Return to History* (New York: Oxford University Press, 1995), 74–108.

often believe that knowledge of the background of Jewish history before the modern era is unnecessary for analyzing current Jewish international political engagement. Given their disciplinary training, it is primarily to those disciplines, rather than to their Jewish dimensions, that most Chinese Jewish studies scholars may feel their major intellectual commitment: they think of themselves first and foremost as historians, philosophers, philologists, or literary critics, then as Jewish studies scholars.

In addition, all academic centers of Jewish studies at Chinese universities are small in size, usually comprised of two to four members, while the range of Jewish studies is dauntingly broad and complex. Thus another problem arises of how to design curricula and syllabi for courses that conform to the *ad hoc* specialized fields of a few teachers while at the same time taking the students' interests into reasonable account.

Some of the practical and pedagogical challenges as adumbrated above are by no means unique for Chinese Jewish studies scholars; they have significant parallels among the scholars in other countries.[14] This intensifies the need for domestic and international cooperation. Without a network of mutual support, the small centers might face the danger of withering in isolation. Without the formation of a scholarly community in which members with diverse disciplinary training can immerse themselves in a conscious and constant quest for, to borrow Hans-Georg Gadamer's deft phrase, the "fusion of horizons" with each other, the impression that Chinese scholars are not committed long term to Jewish and Israeli studies would be destined to linger.

Since 1997, one center has organized three summer workshops on Jewish history and culture. The workshops were taught by celebrated Jewish scholars from both Israel and the United States, and were attended by more than 100 Chinese professors of Western history and

---

14 Cf. Moshe Davis, ed., *Teaching Jewish Civilization: A Global Approach to Higher Education* (New York: New York University Press, 1995); Martin Goodman, "The Nature of Jewish Studies," in *The Oxford Handbook of Jewish Studies*, ed. Martin Goodman (Oxford: Oxford University Press, 2002), 1–13.

civilization from universities and colleges across the country.¹⁵ The purpose of these workshops was to afford accurate, reliable, and unprejudiced information on Jewish history and culture in the hope that the relevant information, in turn, would be incorporated into the courses the attendees teach at their home institutions. Some participants reported in the follow-up that the course on Jewish culture they experienced for the first time was so welcome that it became a permanent part of their own curricula. A similar model, designed for graduate students across China, has been adopted by another center. A great stride was made toward the integration of resources by the creation in 2002 of a Chinese journal dedicated to Jewish studies.¹⁶ Open to "all possible research fields," this annual has proffered a seminal forum for enriching the interdisciplinary exchange of ideas. With regard to regular joint programs, the London Jewish Cultural Center and Claims Conference, in collaboration with several universities in China, have launched ten seminars on Holocaust education and Jewish history and culture to 2014. Since 2010, Yad Vashem, with support from the Adelson Family Foundation, has organized in Jerusalem annual Holocaust education seminars for Chinese educators.¹⁷ Both seminar series do not exclusively focus on the Holocaust but unravel the major problems in Jewish history and the important aspects of Israeli society as well.

Last but not least, the consequences of institutionalized academic exchange with Israel can hardly be overestimated. We should recall that the full and accelerated development of Chinese Jewish studies had not been set in motion until 1992, the year when diplomatic relations between Israel and China were finally established after twists and turns.¹⁸ Indeed, it is after 1992 that countless popular books about Jews

---

15 For the evaluation reports by the instructors, see http://www.oakton.edu/user/2/friend/sem2002__fac.html, accessed July 23, 2014.
16 Fu Youde, ed., *Youtai yanjiu* [Jewish Studies], 2002.
17 Gil Shefler, "Yad Vashem Program Aims to Teach Chinese about Shoah," *The Jerusalem Post*, October 21, 2010, accessed July 23, 2014, http://www.jpost.com/Home/Yad-Vashem-program-aims-to-teach-Chinese-about-Shoah; see also Glenn Timmermans in this volume.
18 Du Xianju, *Zhongguo he yiselie guanxi shi* [The History of Diplomatic Relations between China and Israel] (Hong Kong: Wenhua chuanxun chubanshe, 2009); see also Chen Yiyi in this volume.

were spawned and almost all academic centers for Jewish and Israel studies were created. This fact arguably shows the towering impact of the existence of the State of Israel and its accessibility, however indirect, to the Chinese people. Thanks to the exchange program launched by the governments, more and more Chinese students are able to go to Israeli universities each year, and their ongoing work on Jews, Judaism, and Israel, as well as their exposure to the breath of living Jewish experience, will surely bring formative changes in the long run.

Jewish Diaspora in China

The Institute of Jewish Studies founded in Jerusalem, the first incarnation of *Wissenschaft des Judentums* in a secular educational setting, defined its goal as "learning to know Judaism in all its forms."[19] In contrast, the topics of Jewish studies that have attracted sustained Chinese academic endeavors are highly selective. What follows will focus on three such topics as three case studies. By placing them in a comparative perspective, we shall see whether some manifestations and orientations characteristic of China crystallize.

Undisputedly, the *locus classicus* of all Chinese Jewish studies is the Jewish diaspora in China. China is the only country in the Far East in which Jews have continuously lived for more than 800 years. Although the precise beginnings of the Jewish community in China are unknown, an indigenous Jewish community existed in the city of Kaifeng in northeastern China from the twelfth century onwards. Separated by thousands of miles from the rest of the Jewish world, and largely cut off from contact with the main centers of Jewish life, the Kaifeng Jews developed a distinctive culture that was unquestionably Jewish, but it progressively absorbed Chinese elements. The greatest problem of the Kaifeng Jewish community was not so much separation from other Jews as the openness of Chinese society. Intermarriages occurred frequently, and Jews were fully accepted as merchants, government officials, and neighbors. From the mid-nineteenth century on, they were so completely assimilated

---

19 Davis, ed., *Teaching Jewish Civilization*, 18.

that few of their descendants today carry any memory of Jewish liturgy and physically are indistinguishable from other Chinese.[20]

Ever since the Jesuit missionaries discovered its existence in the beginning of seventeenth century, the Jewish community in Kaifeng has triggered surprisingly concentrated and diverse scholarly activity.[21] It is surprising because the field seems not very promising at first sight. The most important primary sources are three stelae inscriptions in Chinese that commemorate various rebuildings of the synagogue and contain quite detailed accounts of the origins, history, and beliefs of the Kaifeng Jews and an archive—thirteen Torah scrolls included—left by the community.

Chen Yuan, China's foremost authority on the history of religions, produced a groundbreaking study of Kaifeng Jewry in the 1920s. By checking names in miscellaneous, local, and mostly not easily accessible, documents and records against those inscribed on the stelae, he laid a solid philological foundation for all subsequent studies in Chinese.[22] The study was conducted in such a thorough way that any further significant progress along this line would have to be painstaking. The reason is straightforward. The authors of the classical Chinese literary texts did not distinguish Jews from the devotees of Islam and tended to lump them together. All foreigners from Central Asia and the Middle East were loosely termed "Arabs," "Persians," "Muslims," or just "people with colored eyes" [*se mu ren*]. In other words, there was no separate

---

20 For recent efforts to bring the descendants back to Judaism, see Michael Freund, "From Kaifeng to the Kotel: A Chinese Rabbi in the Making," *Asian Jewish Life* 7 (September 2011), 4–7, and see Moshe Bernstein in this volume.; Wang Yisha, *Zhongguo youtai chunqiu* [The Spring and Autumn of the Chinese Jews] (Beijing: Ocean Press, 1992) remains invaluable in its discussion of these descendants.

21 The standard bibliography is Donald Daniel Leslie, *Jews and Judaism in Traditional China: A Comprehensive Bibliography* (Sankt Augustin: Monumenta Serica Institute, 1998), which is now supplemented by Li Jingwen, Zhang Ligang, Liu Bailu, and Zhao Guanggui, eds., *Gudai Kaifeng youtairen: zhongwen wenxian jiyao yu yanjiu* [Ancient Kaifeng Jewry: A Collection of the Chinese Sources and Studies] (Beijing: Renmin Press, 2011).

22 Chen Yuan, *Kaifeng yicileye jiao kao* [A Study of the Israelite Religion in Kaifeng] (Shanghai: Commercial Press, 1923). Its English summary is found in Sidney Shapiro, ed., *Jews in Old China: Studies by Chinese Scholars* (New York: Hippocrene Books, 1984), 15–45.

official category for Jews in ancient China. For that reason, were it not for those names engraved on the stelae, it would have been impossible to identify who was Jewish in Chinese historical literature. "Who is a Jew?" is *the* question obsessing today's Jewish communities across the world, and it is also a thorny issue in the study of Kaifeng Jewry.

What makes the matter more complicated is that the stone inscriptions offer three vastly different dates for the time of the arrival of Jews to China, ranging from the second half of the eleventh century BCE to the second half of the twelfth century CE. On account of these difficulties and discrepancies, it is not astonishing to find in the myriad scholarly works of both Chinese and western authors assorted repetitiveness, wild associations, arguments from silence, and opposing hypotheses regarding the questions of when the Jews reached China, where they came from, the routes they traveled, where they settled, and how they lived.

When we compare the works by Chinese and Western scholars, a most profound difference in terms of epistemology and motivation stands out in bold relief. The modern awareness of Kaifeng Jewry has much to do with its contacts with Christian missionaries, initially Jesuits and later Protestants of various denominations. For this reason, a religious perspective dominates the scholarship in Western languages.

Kaifeng Jewry was important in two ways for Christians. On the one hand, the Torah scrolls possessed by the Kaifeng community kindled the Christian hope of finding an "original text" of the Bible. Since Justin Martyr of the second century, Christian theologians had long insisted that the verses of the Hebrew Bible prophesying the coming of Christ had been deliberately tampered with by the rabbis of the talmudic era. Surmising that the Kaifeng scriptures might have been produced before the compilation of the Talmud, they dreamed that by comparing a Torah scroll from Kaifeng with the standard Hebrew text, they would be able to find definitive evidence for the talmudists' falsification.

On the other hand, investigating Kaifeng Jewry provided an opportunity for converting as many Chinese as possible. In the eyes of Christian missionaries, the Chinese were polytheistic and idolatrous, and thus exceptionally recalcitrant to believe in Christ. Was it imperative for the Church to make concessions in regard to ritual and liturgy, thereby acclimatizing the Christian faith to the long-entrenched religious practices in China? How was it possible to translate monotheistic ideas into Chinese without offending the native sensibilities? The Jewry of Kaifeng, harmonious with Chinese society while still sticking to monotheistic belief, could conveniently serve as a frame of reference for gauging the extent to which Christianity could be acculturated. With these concerns in mind, western scholars were—and are—commonly preoccupied with the religious aspects of the Kaifeng Jews, such as their faith, their scriptures, their liturgy, and their synagogue. In any case, the knowledge about the Kaifeng Jews was valuable insofar as it could be utilized as a support for Christian polemics and proselytizing.

Mostly alien to such a religious mindset and agenda, Chinese scholars are inclined to pay close attention to Kaifeng Jews' social interaction with the host culture. Almost without exception, they are intrigued by *the* central question of why the Kaifeng Jews were eventually assimilated. More precisely, how was it that, while Jewish people all over the world are famous for their perseverance in keeping their Jewish identity and have managed to survive the severest persecution, in Kaifeng they were so thoroughly assimilated that they have ceased to exist and have vanished almost without a trace?

The reasons have frequently been ascribed to three major elements. (1) Religious tolerance. The Kaifeng Jews were allowed to live in accordance with their ancestral customs:

> No sources can prove that the Kaifeng Jews were ever subjected to persecution. Under such tolerant and peaceful circumstances, the cohesion of the Kaifeng Jewish community was gradually relaxed. We can hardly find in the world a country besides China where toleration of Jews lasted for so long. This should be one of the main reasons for the assimilation of the Kaifeng Jews.[23]

---

23 Gao Wangzhi, "The Assimilation of the Chinese Jews," in *East Gate of Kaifeng: A Jewish World Inside China*, ed. M. Patricia Needle (Minneapolis, MN: China Center, University of Minnesota, 1992), 22.

This warmth and generosity on the part of the Chinese dissolved any doubts or psychological obstacles that may have existed between the Chinese and the Jews, thus creating the conditions for natural absorption. (2) Intermarriage. (3) Equal opportunity, especially in taking part in the imperial examination for selecting governmental officials. A skilled mastery of the Confucian classics was indispensable to anyone who sought to get a good score on this examination. Yet, this was so time-consuming that it meant an abandonment of Hebrew learning. Increasing numbers of Kaifeng Jews were appointed to office, a few to quite high positions. They came under the sway of Confucian teachings, which in turn influenced the entire Jewish community. All three reasons give evidence to the irresistible charm of Chinese culture and the traditional magnanimity of the Chinese people.

Nevertheless, this master narrative of assimilation remains virtually impervious to Western scholars who seem to opt for a discourse of survival. Instead of asking why the Chinese Jews did not survive, they prefer to consider how they managed to survive so long. What the record of Kaifeng Jewry, persisting for forty or more generations, shows is that China is very slow in absorbing its minorities.[24] The question of assimilation "may be better understood as examples of creative cultural interaction than as simple submission to the norms of the majority culture."[25] Even the concept of assimilation itself seems irrelevant in describing and analyzing the gradual adaptation of customs from the Chinese environment that led not to disappearance but to retaining a

---

24 See, *inter alia*, Donald Daniel Leslie, "Integration, Assimilation, and Survival of Minorities in China: The Case of the Kaifeng Jews," in *From Kaifeng...to Shanghai: Jews in China*, ed. Roman Malek (Nettetal: Steyler Verlag, 2000), 45–76; Michael Pollak, *Mandarins, Jews and Missionaries: The Jewish Experience in the Chinese Empire* (Philadelphia: Jewish Publication Society of America, 1980); Benjamin Schwartz, "Review of Michael Pollak's *Mandarins, Jews and Missionaries*," *American Jewish History* 71.4 (1982): 546–550.

25 Andrew Plaks, "The Confucianization of the Chinese Jews: Interpretations of the Kaifeng Stelae Inscriptions," in *The Jews of China, Volume One: Historical and Comparative Perspectives*, ed. Jonathan Goldstein (Armonk, New York: M. E. Sharpe, 1999), 39.

Jewish identity for 800 years.[26] Western scholars are ingrained in their outlook of "the people of the Book" and conversant with the religious persecutions and wars of Europe. For them, the Kaifeng Jews were geographically separated from the outer world, numerically insignificant, and economically inconsequential in Chinese society. It was simply impossible for them to pose any social and political threat to the established order. Then, as the eminent French Orientalist Henri Cordier sharply remarked in a paper published as early as 1891, the official policy of China towards them was "characterized by nothing similar to tolerance or *laissez-faire*, but by sheer indifference and ignorance."[27]

To be judgmental about these intensely opposing perspectives and their many ramifications would be indiscreet. We must bear in mind that Chinese research on Kaifeng Jews did not begin until the eve of the twentieth century, when the gate of the "Central Kingdom"—the literal meaning of "China"—was blown to pieces by Western colonial powers. Leading modern Chinese scholars, not unlike Jewish pioneers of *Wissenschaft* following the demolition of ghetto barriers, were confronted by the challenges of modernity in general and of how to adjust the very best of Chinese traditional scholarship to the Western paradigm in particular.

A product of his time, Chen Yuan, to a superficial extent a Chinese counterpart to Ismar Elbogen, impresses the contemporary reader with his delight in facts and his objective, exhaustive, and rigorous style. Yet, this seemingly impersonal, positivistic scholarship was motivated by an "indispensible inner feeling" for his subject. Fervently wishing to see the center of sinology return from Paris or Tokyo back to Beijing, he used to deplore in class that "the arrival of each and every new book written by the Japanese historian was tantamount to the blast of a shell at my desk."[28] Contemporaneous with his study of the Kaifeng

---

26 Irene Eber, "K'aifeng Jews Revisited: Sinification as Affirmation of Identity," *Monumenta Serica* 41 (1993): 231–247.
27 Geng Sheng, trans., *Zhongguo de youtairen* [The Jews of China] (Zhengzhou: Elephant Press, 2005), 436. For a different evaluation, see Xu Xin in this volume.
28 See the memorial essay of Liu Naihe, his pupil and assistant, in Chen Zhichao, ed., *Liyun shuwu wenxue ji*, expanded edition (Beijing: SDX Joint Publishing Company, 2006), 190.

community, he also produced an internationally acclaimed monograph on the transformation of numerous foreign groups into Chinese in the thirteenth and fourteenth centuries, when China was under the rule of the Mongols.[29] The overtone of this book strikes a familiar theme—that the political captive took her conqueror culturally captive. About this monograph, Chen Yuan disclosed in his old age that it "was composed at a moment when the Chinese were least respectable and the claim to wholesale Westernization was put forward by some."[30] With a penetrating vision, he saw in the ancient assimilation story of foreign immigrants, Kaifeng Jewry included, a spark that might be used to kindle his compatriots' cultural self-awareness, a spur to awaken the national confidence, and a stimulus to revitalize Chinese culture when it was at its nadir.

This ethos set the tone for almost all subsequent research in this field, as an ethnic historian remarked in 1983: "Generosity, open-mindedness, recognition and reward of merit, fair and equal treatment—these are traditions we must continue to foster and develop, for in world history they are all too rare."[31] Its latest variation runs as follows: "the Kaifeng Jews had gradually weakened their Jewish identity *without any pressure from the outside world* and identified highly with Confucianism." [italics in original][32]

When the Kaifeng community gradually disappeared from the mid-nineteenth century on, more and more Jews at the same time started to move into other parts of China and settle particularly in Shanghai and Harbin, a metropolis near the Russian border. What was initially a trickle of merchants looking for economic opportunity

---

29 Written in 1923, the monograph is available in an English version: Ch'ên Yüan, *Western and Central Asians in China under the Mongols: Their Transformation into Chinese*, trans. and annotated by Ch'ien Hsing-hai and L. Carrington Goodrich (Nettetal: Steyler Verlag, 1989).
30 Chen Zhichao, ed., *Chen yuan laiwang shuxin ji* [The Correspondence of Chen Yuan], expanded edition, (Beijing: SDX Joint Publishing Company, 2010), 912.
31 Wu Zelin, "An Ethnic Historian Looks at China's Jews, 1983," in Shapiro, ed., *Jews in Old China*, 166.
32 Zhang Qianhong, "Studies on the Confucianisation of the Kaifeng Jewish Community," *Journal of Jewish Studies* 57.2 (2006): 298.

ultimately became legions of refugees seeking shelter from the dark torrents of European anti-Semitism before and during World War II.

Over the past decade, one of the most noteworthy developments of Jewish studies in China is that the Jewish Diaspora communities of the modern era, rather than Kaifeng Jewry, have attracted more and more attention, not only among scholars, especially those in Shanghai and Harbin, but also in the public media. A large number of memorials and government-subsidized conferences, photo exhibitions, and documentary films on this subject have turned up, and the momentum continues.[33]

This explosive interest, of course, directly benefits from the Open Door Policy and economic reforms adopted by Chinese leaders in 1978. With the formation of a free market economy, the old myth of the symbolic link between the Jew and money, for all its absence of religious implications, is exceedingly fashionable, as we have seen. In order to enrich local tourist resources and eagerly win over technical support and economic investment from the Jewish people, local Jewish historical sites such as synagogues and cemeteries have been marvelously renovated.[34] Accordingly, the outpouring of scholarly works in this field is marked by the emergence of a chorus of voices maintaining the image

---

33 The bibliography until 2007 is found in Pan Guang's book mentioned in footnote 7 of this chapter. For works published thereafter, see Liu Shuang, *Haerbin youtai qiaomin shi* [A History of the Jews of Harbin] (Beijing: Fangzhi Press, 2007); Wang Jian, *Shanghai youtairen shehui shenghuo shi* [A History of the Social Life of Shanghai Jews] (Shanghai: Shanghai Cishu Press, 2008); Pan Guang and Wang Jian, *Youtairen yu zhongguo* [Jews and China] (Beijing: Shishi Press, 2010); Zhang Yanhua and Wang Jian, *Kongjian, gushi, shanghai youtairen: tilanqiao de guoqu yu xianzai* [The Space, the Stories and Shanghai Jews—Hongkew Ghetto: Then and Now] (Nanjing: Yilin Press, 2011); Oren Rozenblat, ed., *Eternal Moments: Portraits of Old Shanghai—Photo Album of Sam Sanzetti* (Shanghai: Shanghai Zhongxi Book Company, Shanghai Fine Arts Publisher, 2013); Wang Zhijun and Li Wei, *Ershi shiji shangbanqi haerbin youtairen de zongjiao shenghuo yu zhengzhi shenghuo* [Harbin Jews in Early 1900's: Their Political and Religious Lives] (Beijing: Renmin Press, 2013); Qu Wei and Li Shuxiao, eds., *Haerbin youtai jianming cishu* [The Concise Harbin Jewish Dictionary] (Beijing: Social Sciences Academic Press, 2013).

34 Since 2002, former Israeli journalist Dvir Bar-Gal has led tours of Jewish Shanghai for thousands of Jewish travelers. See www.shanghai-jews.com. Bar-Gal also has been researching the four lost Jewish cemeteries of Shanghai and the 3700 Jewish graves once stood in the city. In the late 1950s these graves were moved from the inner city to the Qingpu district at the outskirts of Shanghai, where the government established an International Cemetery. That cemetery was destroyed during

of a flourishing and heartwarming haven, in stark contrast to the rest of the apathetic world.³⁵

The rise of this newfound interest is also intimately, albeit less obviously, related to international currents. For one thing, with the regional intensification of ethnic and religious conflicts have come sundry expressions of the Holocaust denial, neo-Nazism, militarism, and racism that are rampant nowadays; hence the significant relevance of this theme to those who are concerned with mutual understanding among ethnic groups, interfaith dialogue, and maintenance of world peace. It is not a coincidence that many photography exhibitions and publications came out around 2005, the year marked by a worldwide sixtieth anniversary of anti-Fascist victory.

Another reason for this focus is that the emergence and persistence of numerous diaspora communities across the world is a salient feature of post-colonial society. The ubiquitous Chinese diaspora communities, however, are not favorably treated everywhere. The sufferings of those in Southeast Asia, where the Chinese are sometimes disparaged as the Jews of the Orient, have aroused indignation in China and in Chinese cyberspace. This in turn has deepened the sympathetic understanding of the precarious situation faced by the Jewish refugees in Shanghai. It is thus not far-fetched to assume that the study of the Jewish diaspora in modern China may well also function as a disguised mechanism employed to level condemnation of the harassment and persecution of overseas Chinese.

As opposed to this rationale, Irene Eber, a noted Israeli sinologist as well as author of an extraordinary memoir recording her survival as a hidden child of the Holocaust, has defined the history as part of the Holocaust history rather than part of the history of modern China.³⁶ "Neglecting or ignoring even a portion of this [Holocaust] history," she

---

the Cultural Revolution. Bar-Gal hopes to create a memorial site in Shanghai to the Jewish people who once lived and died in the city.
35 English readers may find manifestation of this ethos in Pan Guang, "Uniqueness and Generality: the Case of Shanghai in the Annals of Jewish Diaspora," in *From Kaifeng...to Shanghai*, ed. Roman Malek, 437–445.
36 Irene Eber, *Wartime Shanghai and the Jewish Refugees from Central Europe: Survival, Co-Existence and Identity in a Multi-Ethnic City* (Berlin: De Gruyter, 2012), vii, 3.

remarked in the memoir, "puts us in danger of forgetting that, above all, this is also the history of human lives and human loss."[37]

Regarding the history of Far Eastern Jewish communities in general, Eber is of the opinion that it "underscores the importance of institutional life in the preservation and perpetuation of Jewish values and demonstrates the variety of Jewish secular culture in the assertion of Jewish identity."[38] Interestingly, the great Jewish Orientalist Bernard Lewis has a dramatically different observation on these very communities. Jews in the Diaspora, he holds, can only flourish and survive under the aegis of Christianity and Islam, two successor religions of Judaism. Jewish communities elsewhere, such as those in India and China, "appear to have played no role of any importance in the history or culture of those countries or of the Jewish people."[39]

Christianizing the Bible

Despite the hefty volumes on the Jewish Diaspora in China, my undergraduate students nowadays are increasingly curious about why Jews do not believe in Jesus. This question not only sheds some light on the Christian missionary activities in contemporary China but also registers an ignorance of the Bible's different theological implications for Judaism and Christianity and reflects the degree to which those approach Judaism through the lens of Christianity.

When we look at biblical studies in China, a problem that must be tackled head on is whether to include biblical studies at all within Jewish studies. Hebrew Bible was—and still is—not universally deemed as a Jewish heritage in China. To this day, Chinese students of the Bible rarely if ever consider themselves to be Jewish studies scholars; rather, as a rule, they think they are working within the field of Christian studies, believing the knowledge of Judaism is necessary insofar as it can either

---

37 Irene Eber, *The Choice: Poland, 1939–1945* (New York: Schocken, 2004), 205.
38 Cited in Jonathan Goldstein, "The Sorkin and Golab Theses and Their Applicability to South, Southeast, and East Asia Port Jewry," in *Port Jews: Jewish Communities in Cosmopolitan Maritime Trading Centres, 1550–1950*, ed. David Cesarani (London: Frank Cass, 2002), 191.
39 Bernard Lewis, *Notes on a Century: Reflections of a Middle East Historian* (New York: Penguin Books, 2012), 240; Bernard Lewis, *The Jews of Islam* (Princeton: Princeton University Press, 1984), ix.

illumine the academic study of the root of Christianity or enhance their understanding of their own faith commitments. Emblematic of this observation is the fact that all biblical entries of the Chinese version of *Encyclopedia Judaica* were penned by scholars from Jinling Union Theological Seminary, the most prestigious Protestant seminary in China.

Examined from a historical perspective, this phenomenon is far from parochial and unique. Even within Jewish tradition, the return to the biblical language, biblical lands, and the Bible itself is principally a child of modernity. Had Zionism not reinstated the Bible as the founding text, today's Israeli secular schools would hardly have incorporated it into their syllabi. Moreover, the modern critical study of the Hebrew Bible was pioneered by Christians. And biblical studies was not on the research agenda of Jewish scholars of *Wissenschaft* in the nineteenth century, who felt more obliged to show the creativity of Judaism in the postbiblical period, thereby dispelling the various stereotypes about Jews and Judaism rooted therein.

What is unique, and even paradoxical, in China is that Protestant biblical criticism, with its hallmark historical method, has never gained ascendancy. For Chinese theologians at the seminary, the Hebrew Bible is first and foremost a revealed text, spiritually meaningful for and functional within Christian communities. At the other end of the spectrum, most Chinese scholars at the university have long since been under the sway of Communist ideology to regard the Hebrew Bible as something unfit for objective and disinterested scholarly efforts, inasmuch as the duty of a university is by no means to cultivate religious feelings or to train priests. As a matter of fact, most of China's biblical scholars are affiliated with neither history nor foreign-language departments, but rather with a department of Chinese language and literature under the rubric of "world literature," which is equivalent to "comparative literature" in the West. Thus, there the Hebrew Bible is construed not as a collection of religious or historical texts, but rather it is seen as fertile soil that has nourished not simply all of Western literature but also a great number of modern secular writings in Chinese.[40] Quite

---

40 Marián Gálik, "The Reception of the Bible in the Peoples' Republic of China (1980–1992): Observations of a Literary Comparatist," in Marián Gálik, *Influence,*

understandably, some books on biblical narrative have been written in, or translated into, Chinese recently, whereas the Chinese versions of Julius Wellhausen or Martin Noth—not to mention Umberto Cassuto or Yehezkel Kaufmann—have not been available in China, much less any monograph on biblical archaeology.[41]

The past fifteen years have already witnessed the establishment of several religion departments in key universities in China, which will definitely diversify the approaches to the study of the Bible. Yet whether the Hebrew Bible will be consciously recognized as part of the Jewish heritage, or whether the distinctive and valuable voice of the postbiblical Jewish exegetical tradition will resonate in China, remains a moot point.[42]

It should be noted that this phenomenon of de-Judaization is closely connected to the so-called "cultural Christians." This is a significant group of Chinese scholars who have faith in Jesus Christ but who are neither baptized nor identified with any church or denomination. In order to build a foundation for Christian scholarship in the midst of tension and competition in Chinese intellectual cultural space, they have launched perhaps the most ambitious translation projects in the past three decades and have introduced a broad range of books on

---

Translation and Parallels: Selected Studies on the Bible in China (Nettetal: Steyler Verlag, 2004), 93–113; Liang Gong, "Twenty Years of Studies of Biblical Literature in the People's Republic of China (1976–1996)," in *The Bible in Modern China: The Literary and Intellectual Impact*, eds. Irene Eber, Sze-Kar Wan, Knut Walf (Nettetal: Steyler Verlag, 1999), 383–407. The normative status of the literary approach to biblical studies can be gauged from this festschrift: Lu Longguang and Wang Lixin, eds., *Shengjing wenxue yu wenhua* [Biblical Literature and Culture: Memorial Volume in Honor of Professor Zhu Weizhi on the Centenary of His Birth], (Tianjin: Nankai University Press, 2007), Professor Zhu Weizhi, the honoree, was the dean of studies of biblical literature in China.

41 The only Chinese work that systematically surveys the biblical archaeology, hence an exception to the rule, is Chen Yiyi, *Xibolaiyu shengjing* [The Hebrew Bible: An Introduction Based on Textual and Archaeological Data (till 586 B.C.E.)] (Beijing: Kunlun Press, 2006).

42 Cf. S. David Sperling's remarks on contemporary Jewish biblical studies: "Precisely because the Jewish approach is not self-evident, and training in rabbinics and Talmud is not as strong, the newer crop has worked harder to articulate the ways in which their work is distinctively Jewish." S. David Sperling, "Modern Jewish Interpretation," in *The Jewish Study Bible*, eds. Adele Berlin and Marc Zvi Brettler (Oxford: Oxford University Press, 2004), 1917.

twentieth century Christian theology to Chinese intellectuals. In their most comprehensive translation series, "Western Tradition: Classics and Commentaries" [*xifang chuantong: jingdian yu jieshi*], of which over a hundred titles have been published, the editor-in-chief Liu Xiaofeng tries to reconstruct for the Chinese a systematic genealogy of the Western intellectual tradition. In it, the "New Cambridge Bible Commentary," including thus both the Hebrew Bible and the New Testament, and many Greco-Roman writers all have their niches. More than that, these classic works' (alleged) interpreters, be they Averroes, Maimonides, Dante, Jean-Jacques Rousseau, Gotthold Lessing, Novalis, Kierkegaard, William James, Nietzsche, Rilke, Heidegger, Leo Strauss, Hans Jonas, Dietrich Bonhoeffer, or Allan Bloom, were all conflated to enjoy a place under the rubric of "Western Tradition."[43] Out of this inordinate genealogy, at least one point is not ambiguous: the editor champions a "Judeo-Christian tradition" as an ideological view of the characteristic feature of Western civilization. De-Judaization in China has resulted from this blurring of the boundary between Judaism and Christianity. Cultural Christians are committed to supplementing the historical rationalist core of Chinese culture with a transcendent spiritual dimension of which they think Chinese cultural tradition has been devoid. They never, to the best of my knowledge, think of bothering themselves to claim a *verus Israel* from Judaism. In any event, for them too, Hellenism and a seamless Judeo-Christian tradition are *the* two sources of Western civilization.

Two Tales of Yavneh

Indeed, the seamlessness of Judeo-Christian tradition is fresh with blood, and only skin-deep. Christianity claimed that God had rejected Israelites on account of their sinfulness, that Judaism had atrophied

---

43 The book series is published by Huaxia Press and East China Normal University Press. For Liu Xiaofeng and the "cultural Christians", see David Aikman, *Jesus in Beijing* (Washington, D.C.: Regnery Publishing, 2006), 249–252; Institute of Sino-Christian Studies, ed., *Wenhua jidutu: xianxiang yu lunzheng* [Cultural Christians: Phenomenon and Debate] (Hong Kong: Institute of Sino-Christian Studies, 1996). Aikman also spotted "an overwhelmingly pro-Israeli feeling among China's Christians," (Ibid., 201) but see Meng Zhenhua in this volume.

with the advent of the new Gospel, and that Christians constituted the New Israel. Partly through this lens, the Hebrew Bible, rather than the Talmud, is valued as the defining religious text for today's Judaism in China. In Chinese academic writings, the Talmud is habitually referred to as a "commentary on the Bible" (*shengjing de pingzhu*) with an apparently secondary and derivative implication. In spite of the availability of three outstanding Chinese translations of rabbinic literature,[44] the Talmud has been sweepingly understood as a business manual or a self-help book for seeking fortunes in the Chinese-speaking world. In Taiwan, there is even a Talmud Business Hotel that features a copy of a *Talmud Business Success Bible* in every room![45]

Against this backdrop, what is truly remarkable is a Chinese paper on the founding myth of rabbinic Judaism. During the Jewish revolt against the Romans in 70 CE, the Jewish leader Yohanan ben Zakkai foresaw the destruction of Jerusalem and sought to take preventive measures to avert the simultaneous destruction of Judaism. He approached the Roman general and asked if he could relocate to Yavneh, where he hoped a devastated Judaism might be healed by the formation of a new culture that would replace the Temple. The Roman general found the suggestion foolhardy and agreed without knowing that his decision would give this defeated people a chance to create a spiritual center that was destined to outlive the victorious Roman Empire.

In the 1940s, Gedalyahu Alon, the doyen of the Jewish history of the Mishnaic-Talmudic period in Israel, published a seminal paper in which he questioned the historical authenticity of this founding myth. He argued that Yavneh was a Roman internment camp for war prisoners and fugitives where Yohanan ben Zakkai was send against his will.[46] And then, about a decade ago, one of the trailblazers of Chinese

---

44 Zhang Ping, trans., *Avot: The Book of Jewish Wisdom* (Beijing: Chinese Academy of Social Sciences Press, 1996); Zhang Ping, trans., *Derech Erez Zuta: The Book of Jewish Deportment* (Beijing: Peking University Press, 2003); Zhang Ping, trans., *The Mishnah: Seder Zeraim* (Jinan: Shandong University Press, 2011).
45 The hotel's official website is http://talmud.hotel.com.tw/eng/, accessed 28 July 2014.
46 Gedalyahu Alon, "Rabban Johanan B. Zakkai's Removal to Jabneh," in Gedalyahu Alon, *Jews, Judaism and the Classical World: Studies in Jewish History in the Times of*

Jewish studies, Xu Xin, suggested that Yavneh represented a revolution because it transformed Judaism, affirming that Jewish identity was no longer anchored on race, geography, or political system, but on culture. Even more important, the revolution was led by Yohanan ben Zakkai, the very quintessence of the Jewish intellectual in his eyes:

> As intellectuals, rabbis are different from the biblical prophets who, notwithstanding their denunciation against all forms of injustice, do not believe in human progress and man's ability to make laws for history. The only demand they made for the Jewish people is to surrender to God for the final redemption. By contrast, rabbis call on the people to open the book and to seek in it the guidance of God. To open the book means to...respect both knowledge and knowledgeable persons.... In the following 2,000 years, the history and fate of the Jewish people have been grasped in the hands of Jewish intellectuals.... It is under the guidance of Jewish intellectuals that the Jewish people are able to survive the Diaspora.

Thus, Yavneh marks an unprecedented shift, not merely in Jewish history but also in human history, wherein a group of intellectuals became the national leaders.[47]

It seems to me that both interpreters of what happened in Yavneh tempered their knowledge with their contemporary concerns and social commitments; both authors imbued their interpretations with concerns about national fate and history. Alon, lauded as the "Jewish Mommsen," emigrated from Berlin to Palestine in the 1920s. When he wrote his 1940s essay, Yavneh seems to epitomize two opposite tropes; the first hinted at either the wartime concentration camp where Jews were slaughtered or the postwar internment camp where Jews were puzzled by their fate; the second alluded to Palestine under the British Mandate, where, although still impoverished, an increasing immigration harbored a hope of national resuscitation. Xu Xin, on the other hand, lived through the turmoil of the Cultural Revolution, whose dark shadow

---

the Second Temple and Talmud (Jerusalem: The Magnes Press, The Hebrew University, 1977), 269–313.

47 Xu Xin, "Lun jiabunai geming: youtai zhishifenzi zhangwo minzu lindaoquan de qidian," [On the Revolution in Yavneh: The Beginning of the Takeover of National Leadership by the Jewish Intellectual] *Xue Hai* (2005.3): 41–49, citation in 47–48.

still lingers on the title of his paper "On the Revolution in Yavneh." His words on the Jewish intellectual appear to be saturated by feelings for the innumerable Chinese intellectuals whose dignity was trampled and whose lives were deprived during the revolution.

Conclusion

Striding over the upheavals of the past century, China is now reopening itself to many foreign influences, as it did at the time when Jews settled down in Kaifeng. In a climate of economic entrepreneurship, many Chinese turn their sights westward in search of the secrets for wealth and power. Jews and Judaism were discovered and conceptualized as an integral and pivotal component of Western tradition. The knowledge about them is seen as instrumental in helping the Chinese understand themselves and their own position in the world and is seen as as valuable for China's effort to steer its way in the international scene. Accordingly, exploration of Jewish tradition has been more or less absorbed into a Chinese perspective and directed to a Chinese agenda. The preceding three case studies have, I hope, amply elucidated this orientation. It seems that they corroborate the observation made by Giovanni Battista Vico more than two centuries ago that people accept only the ideas for which their previous development has prepared their minds.[48]

Their previous development also has prepared the Chinese to discern in a parallel culture admirable ancient roots, deep-seated traditions and ongoing contemporary stature. In a land destitute of any long-held animus against Judaism or rivalry with it, Chinese Jewish studies has also developed out of a cultural curiosity, a curiosity empty of the theological implications and tensions that are ingrained in the Christian and Islamic worlds. In this regard, Chinese curiosity about Judaism and about Christianity have one thing in common: the search for a new way to anchor, to redefine, to negotiate, and to reformulate Chinese identities in a country becoming progressively diversified in its values, ideologies, and beliefs.

Apart from foreign imports, a renewed esteem for indigenous traditions is simultaneously mushrooming everywhere in China. Side

---

48 Cited in Elias J. Bickerman, *The Jews in the Greek Age* (Cambridge, MA: Harvard University Press, 1988), 305.

by side with those Jewish success books on the bestseller shelves, one also finds popular titles on Confucianism, Taoism, Zen Buddhism, and classical Chinese poetry. In addition, Confucius' ideal of "harmony without conformity" [*he er bu tong*], which seems particularly compelling in an age whose principal imperative appears to be the eclipse of universal claims, is increasingly enshrined both by the official ideology of the ruler and by the consensus among the masses.

I cannot help but think that our ancient ideal may have been similar to one held by the redactors of the Talmud. These Jewish sages, more often than not, seem to have avoided choosing an operative rule after the enumeration of diverse opposing arguments raised from the debate about a *halakhah*, even though in doing so their monotheistic mindset may have pushed them to resolve "to prove the validity of its conclusions beyond a shadow of a doubt and to preclude any alternative explanation."[49] The encounter between what Benjamin Schwartz, the late distinguished Jewish sinologist at Harvard, calls "a totalizing civilization" and "a textually based religious tradition"[50] and the consequent, largely intuitive construction of the Self by seeking out family resemblances and potential compatibilities with the Other,[51] will retain their perennial fascination.

Finally, although Chinese Jewish studies is immune from the cluster of tensions and dilemmas that lies between faith and secularity and that informs Jewish practitioners of Jewish studies, as noted by Meyer, it is still not without its own Janus-like concern. Somewhat paradoxically, it can be cast in a *reverse* direction: with popular fantasies about Jews and Judaism of that magnitude in mind, should we face inward toward satisfying academic colleagues, or should we face outward and endeavor to leaven an undistorted, meaningful and accessible knowledge of the Jewish people to a broader Chinese audience?

---

49 Adin Steinsaltz, *The Essential Talmud*, trans. Chaya Galai (New York: Basic Books, 1976), 231.
50 Benjamin Schwartz, "On Memory: Personal and Cultural," *AJS Review* 25.1 (2000–2001): 88.
51 See Fu Youde in this volume.

Index

A

Abraham, Wendy, 91
achievement of Jews, 43–46, 51–52
Adaf, Shimon, 159
Adelson, Miri, 198
Adelson, Sheldon, 198
Adelson Family Foundation, 198
Agnon, S.Y., 147
A Jewish Girl in Shanghai (Wang Genfa), 193
Ahad Ha-am, 40
Amichai, Yehuda, 146–147, 149
Anhui Literature and Art Publishing House, 148
Anne Frank Museum, 197
anti-Semitism, 44–45, 48, 172, 190, 205, 212
Appelfeld, Aharon, 147, 149
Arab Spring, 175
atheism, 121
Auschwitz-Birkenau State Museum, 190
Avraham, Shmuel, 80, 90

B

Baihuazhou Literature and Art Publishing House, 148
Bai Xiaojuan, 85, 87
Bai Ying, 87
Banaji, Amir, 159
Barak, Ehud, 172
Barzilai, Eran, 80
Bat Ayin settlement, 82
Bauer, Yehuda, 198
Beijing, Jewish presence in, 17–18
   Chabad (Lubavitch), 19–22
   Kehillat Beijing, 18–19
   Palestinian presence and PLO delegation, 19
Beijing International Book Fair (BIBF), 148
Beit Hatikvah, 81
Ben-Gurion, David, 132
Ben-Mordechai, Yitzhak, 159
Berdyczewski, M. J., 159
Bernstein, Moshe, 2
Biao, Zhou, 34–35
Bible, understanding in China
   academic studies of Chinese and international researchers, 101
   attitude of ordinary people, 104
   Bible-based films and television programs, 106–108
   Bible in Modern China, 101
   Biblical Interpretation, 100
   Chinese translations, 99–100
   Hebrew Bible/Old Testament, 99–100, 106, 115, 119, 123, 226–228
   history of, 103
   New Testament, 99, 107, 115, 119
   personal religious background and views on, 105
   reaction of audience via "bullet curtain," 108–124
   Reading Christian Scriptures in China, 102
   reading of the Bible in the Asian context, 102
   survey samples and explanations, 106–110
Bingde, Chen, 172
"black cat/white cat" theory, 166–168
blogs about Jews

discussion of Holocaust and Hitler,
	33–34
"History Forum," 33
"How to Train Children to Study
	Jewish," 32–33
on Jewish wisdom, 34
on Jews in popular culture, 36
on Medieval Europe, 34–35
"Blue Hat Hui-Hui" *(lanmao huihui)*,
	78–79
Bond, Helen, 107
books about Jews, 25
	on anti-Semitism, 28–29
	*The 101 Business Secrets in Jews
		Notebook* (Zhu Xin
		Yue), 29
	Collection of Jewish Strategies, 27
	*If You Understand the Jews, You Will
		Understand the World* and
		*If You Understand Jews,
		You Will Understand
		Japan,* 30
	intelligence of Jews, 28
	Japanese cult and anti-Semitic
		propaganda, 30–31
	*Jewish Bigwigs' Skills of Making
		Money,* 27
	on Jewish cartels and conspiracies, 30
	*Jewish Conspiracy of Destroying the
		World* (Zhang Daquan), 30
	Jewish Life of Money, 27
	Jewish Magnates of Ideas, 27
	Jewishness distinguished by noses, 27
	on Jewish rituals, 28
	*Jewish Wisdom of Family Education:
		The Cultural Code of the
		Most Intelligent and
		Wealthy Nation in the
		World,* 27
	Jews: The Secrets to their Success (Jack
		Rosen), 30
	*Jews in the Japanese Mind: The History
		and Uses of a Cultural
		Stereotype* (David
		Goodman and Masanori
		Miyazawa), 30
	*Legend of World Famous Jewish
		Celebrities,* 27
	materialization of Judaism, 28
	Philosemitism in History (Jonathan
		Karp and Adam Sutcliffe),
		31
	16 Reasons for Jews Getting Wealthy
		(Chu Ke), 26–27
	Riddle of Jews, 27
	*Secret of Jewish Success: Ten Command-
		ments of Jewish Success* (Li
		Huizhen), 27, 30
	*The Secret of Talmud: The Jewish Code
		of Wealth* (Jiao Yiyang),
		27, 30
	*Secrets of Jewish Success: The Golden
		Rule of a Miraculous
		Nation,* 27
	The Spirit of Jewish Culture (He
		Xiongfei), 28
	*Stranger from Mars: Nobel Prize and
		Jews* (Yang Jianye), 30
	success of Jews, 30
	*Uncovering the Enigma of Jewish
		Success in the World,* 27
	*Voice of Wisdom: Speeches of Jewish
		Celebrities* (Yu Xin), 30
	What's Behind Jewish Success (Tian
		Zaiwei and Sha Wen), 27
Bookworm Festival, 151
The Boy in the Striped Pajamas (John
	Boyne), 201
Brenner, Yosef Haim, 148
Brooklyn bagels, 20
Buddhism, 18, 122, 213
bullet curtain on *The Bible,* analysis,
	108–124
	anti-Jewish comments, 120
	attitude toward Jews and Israel, 116
	biblical Israelites as the Eight-Power
		Expeditionary Force,
		118–119
	comments related to Chinese context
		and their commentators,
		116
	composition of the commentators,
		112–113
	connecting with Chinese context, 115
	examples of comments, 117–120
	impact in raising human moral
		standards and promoting
		social development, 119

Index

"Jewish myth" in contemporary China, 116
knowledge of the Bible, 113–115
modern Israeli-Palestinian conflict, 120
non-religious audience, understanding of, 111–112
notes on the content and its reasons, 120–124
stories of Aqedah, 117
Burnett, Mark, 106–107

C

Cao Jie, 150
Carter, Jimmy, 139
Cassirer, Ernst, 46
Cassuto, Umberto, 228
Castel-Bloom, Orly, 149
Catholicism, 18
Central Unity Front of the Community Party of Chin, 65
Chabad (Lubavitch), 19–22
Chen, Lejen, 20
Cheng Wei, 159
Chen Yiyi, 3
Chen Yuan, 218, 222–223
Chen Zhongyi, 158
China
    changing role in the international arena, 174–178
    Chinese healthcare system, 18
    Communist rule, 57–60
    "constructive participation" strategy, 182–184
    diplomatic policies, 176
    equal rights of ethnic rights, 62
    ethnic identification, 62–63
    kosher food export, 20
    Middle East region and, 174–175
    Muslim population in, 173
    "non-interference" foreign policy, 176
    Open Door policy, 18, 67, 224
    "peaceful rise," concept of a, 176
    policies toward Jews and their religious practices, 54–57
    popularity of Christianity in, 104, 173, 226–229
    reciprocity and justice, concept of, 177
    religious freedom in, 17–19, 25
    rights of Jewish people, 177
    ties between Israel and, 36
    uniformity of Chinese, 52–53
    on U.S. position on the Israel-Palestine issue, 177–178
    vetoing of sanctions on Tehran, 176
China Social Sciences Publishing House, 148
Chindex International Inc., 18
Chinese Communist Party (CCP), 25
Chinese diaspora, 225
Chinese-Jewish culture in Kaifeng, 78–79
Chinese Judaism, 54
Chinese Mid-Autumn Festival, 72
"the chosen people," concept of, 38
Chung, Martin, 201
Cohen, Nilli, 148
Cohen, Shaye J. D., 92
communist movement, 43
Confucianism, 176, 213
Conservative Judaism, 75
contemporary Israeli literature
    Adam Resurrected (Yoram Kaniuk/Lu Hanzhen and Guo Guoliang), 149
    Adonis (Aryeh Sivan/Dai Huikun and Xiaodai), 148
    After the Holidays (Yehoshua Kanaz/Zhong Zhiqing), 148
    The Age of Wonders (Aharon Appelfeld/Yang Yang), 149
    An Anthology of Hebrew Short Stories (Xu Xin), 147
    Aunt Shlomzion the Great (Yoram Kaniuk/Shen Zhihong and Gao Sui), 148
    Black Box (Amos Oz/Zhong Zhiqing), 147–148, 151, 160
    Blue Mountain (Meir Shalev/Yu Haijiang and Zhangying), 148
    Breakdown and Bereavement (Yosef Haim Brenner), 148
    The Bride Canopy (S. Y. Agnon/Xu Xin), 147
    canonization of Amoz Oz in China, 151–156
    Collector (Birstein/Sui Lijun), 148
    Contemporary Foreign Literature, 147

creating the image of another Side of Israel via, 156–160
Death in the Rain (Ruth Almog/Zhu Meihui), 148
Dream of the Red Chamber, 159
Elsewhere Perhaps (Amos Oz/Yao Yongcai), 150, 158
To the End of the Land (David Grossman), 157
A Face in the Clouds (Yossel Birstein), 148
Fima (Amos Oz/Fan Hongsheng), 150
Frenzy (David Grossman), 151
Hebrew fiction, 147
Her Body Knows (David Grossman), 151
Institute for the Translation of Hebrew Literature and, 147–148
The Internal Grammar (David Grossman), 151
The Island on Bird Street (Amos Oz/Li Wenjun), 150
Journal of World Literature (*Shijie Wenxue*), 147, 149
To Know A Woman (Amos Oz/Fu Hao and Ke Yanbin), 150, 153
Love Life (Zeruya Shalev), 150
Lover (A. B. Yehoshua/Xiang Hongquan and Feng Xia), 149
The Lover (A. B. Yehoshua), 156
Lydia, Queen of Palestine (Amos Oz/Yang Hengda and Yang Rong), 150
The Man from the Other Side (Amos Oz/Yang Hengda and Yang Fan), 150
Married Life (David Vogel/Yang Dongxia and Yang Haihong), 148
The Mediterranean Rose: A Selection of Israeli Women Writers, 149
Mina Liza (Orly Castel-Bloom/Yang Yugong), 148
Minotaur (Benjamin Tammuz/Zheng Yalan), 148
My Michael (Amos Oz/Zhong Zhiqing), 147, 150, 152–153, 158, 160

Open Closed Open (Yehuda Amichai/Huang Fuhai), 148
A Panther in the Basement (Amos Oz/Zhong Zhiqing), 151
Perfect Peace (Amos Oz/Yao Yongqiang and Guo Hongtao), 150–152
periodicals, 149
perspective of conflicts between Israelis and Palestinians, 157–158
A Pigeon and a Boy (Meir Shalev/Mao Lu), 151
publications of, 147
The Pure Element of Time (Haim Be'er/Wang Yibao), 149
response to catastrophe of World War II, 160
Returning Lost Loves (Yehoshua Kenaz/Huang Fuhai), 149
Rhyming Life and Death (Amos Oz/Zhong Zhiqing), 150, 160
The Same Sea (Amos Oz/Hui Lan), 151–152
The Scorch Land: A Selection of Modern Israeli Stories (Gao Qiufu), 149
See Under: Love (David Grossman/Zhang Chong and Zhang Qiong), 147–148
A Simple Story (S. Y. Agnon/Xu Chongliang), 148
Someone to Run With (David Grossman), 151
Songs of Jerusalem (Yehuda Amichai/Fu Hao), 147
The Story Begins (Amos Oz/Yang Zhengtong), 151
Suddenly in the Depth of Forests (Amos Oz/Zhong Zhiqing), 151
A Tale of Love and Darkness (Amos Oz/Zhong Zhiqing), 150, 154–158, 160
"Three Days and a Child" (A. B. Yehoshua/Chen Yiyi), 147
Tiny Coat (Ruth Almog/Diaso Haifeng and Wang Mingqian), 148
translation into Chinese, 145–151

Index

A Trumpet in the Wadi (Sami Michael/
    Li Huijuan), 151
*The Western Canon: The Books and
    School of the Ages* (Harold
    Bloom), 151
Where the Jackals Howl (Amos Oz),
    150
Zigzag Child (David Grossman), 151
Cream Cheese shop, 20
Currency War book series, 172, 206

D

Dang Shengyuan, 159
Daoism, 176
David, Camp, 139
de-Judaization in China, 228–229
Deng Xiaoping, 18, 66, 167
Desbois, Patrick, 195
Deuteronomy 6:7, 41
Ding Fan, 153
distinctiveness of Jews, 37
    dietary laws, 40
    expressing different opinions, arguing,
        and debating, 43
    influence of Westernization, secular-
        ization, and non-religious
        immigrants, 48
    Kaifeng *Yicileye*, 78
    law as a principle of life, 39
    outstanding achievements and
        consequences of, 43–46,
        51–52
    rabbi, status of, 42
    reading Shema, 41–42, 51
    relationship between Judaism and the
        Jews, 41
    religious character, 39–40, 47–48
    Sabbath day, 39–40, 45
    Talmud laws and Jewish thinking, 42
    worship of monotheism, 38, 41
Downey, Roma, 106–107

E

Eber, Irene, 1, 225–226
Edward I, King, 44
Eliezer, Rabbi, 41
Emancipation, 47
Encyclopedia Judaica, 213

Enlightenment Movement, 118
evil cults, 121
Exodus
    19, 38
    20:8, 11, 39

F

Fällman, Frederik, 103–104
Falun Gong, 18
Feng Xiang, 103
Fenming, Ai, 63
Fenying, Shi, 63
Ferdinand, King, 44–45
festivals in Kaifeng, 74
    celebratory holiday feasts, 85, 87
    chronological convergence of Sukkot
        and mid-Autumn Festival,
        76–77
    convergences, incongruities, and the
        question of authenticity,
        84–91
    historical memory and contemporary
        practice, 91–97
    Orthodox Jews and, 75–76
    retreat, 77–84
    Sukkot (Festival of Booths), 72, 74–77
Fondation pour la Mémoire de la Shoah, 197
French Revolution and Jews, 47
Freund, Michael, 81, 218n20
Freundlich, Dini, 19–21
Freundlich, Rabbi Shimon, 19
Fu Hao, 159
Fu Youde, 2, 187

G

Gadamer, Hans-Georg, 215
Gaddafi, Muammar, 175
Gálik, Marián, 100, 227n40
Gamaliel, Laban, 41
Gangzheng She, 3
Gao Chao, 85, 87–89, 92–93, 97
Gao Feng, 35–36
Gao Qiufu, 148, 158
Geiger, Abraham, 47, 209
Ginsberg, Louis, 47
Gitlin, Azariah, 152
God concept, 38
Gorbachev, Mikhail, 140

Gotel, Jerry, 196, 198
Gouri, Haim, 149
Grossman, David, 146, 149, 151
Guangyuan, Jin, 81

H

Halkin, Hillel, 151
Han Dynasty, 52
Harold Bloom, 152
Hazaz, Haim, 147
Hersch, Samson Raphael, 47
He Xiongfei (Sai Ni Ya), 1, 27. 28–29
Hillel school, 41
Hinduism (dharma), 177
HKHTC, 200–201
HKU European Studies Programme, 201
Holdheim, Samuel, 47
Holocaust studies and Holocaust education in China, 185–205
  annual summer school on Jewish and Holocaust studies, 196
  Auschwitz tragedy, 191
  Chang's *The Rape of Nanking: The Forgotten Holocaust of WWII*, 189
  Eichmann Trial in 1961, 188
  general education programs, 202
  Holocaust scholarship, 195
  Holocaust translation, 204
  in Hong Kong, 200–202
  human rights issues in China, 191–192
  Jewish refugees in Shanghai, 187
  MA and PhD theses, 201–202, 204
  Nazi-German Death Camp-Konzentrationslager Auschwitz, 189
  reading program, 201
  recognized programs at Chinese universities, 186
  in school curriculum, 192–194
  seminars, 196–199
  Six-Day War in 1967, 188
Hong Kong Holocaust and Tolerance Centre, 200
Hong Kong Jewish Film Festival, 202
Hong Kong Polytechnic University, 201

I

Institute of Foreign Literature, 150, 159
Institute of Jewish Studies at Henan University, 203
Institute of Translation for Hebrew Literature, 147–148
International Holocaust Remembrance Alliance (IHRA), 199
International Military Tribunal at Nuremberg, 185
Ishay, Haviva, 159
Islam, 18, 218
Israel, Shavei, 72, 80–81
Israel as the Jewish nation state, 13
Israeli-Palestinian conflicts, 175, 178, 182
Israel's image in *People's Daily*, analysis, 129–142
  Bandung Conference, 1955, 132–133
  conclusions, 142–144
  coverage of Shimon Peres' visit to Morocco, 140
  Cultural Revolution of China and stance of Israel, 136, 139
  differentiation of "the Israeli people" from the Likud government, 140
  exclusion of Israel from the "Progressive Camp" (jinbu zhenying), 132–133
  interviews of journalists from Xinhua News Agency, 141
  Israeli Defense Force, 138
  Israel invasion of Lebanon in 1982, 139
  Israel's crackdown of the first *intifada*, 141
  Palestinian Liberation Organization (PLO), 136
  peace treaty between Egypt and Israel, 139
  relations between China and Israel, 141–142
  scientific developments, 141
  Six-Day War, 136–137
  Soviet Union influence of Israel, 129–131
  Suez Crisis in 1956, 133–136
  'UN trusteeship' conspiracy, 129
  "War of Independence" and establishment of State of Israel, 129
Israel-Taiwan relations, 169

J

Japanese occupation of China, 188–190, 194, 203

Index

Japanese racism, 30–31
"Jew" and "Jewishness" representations in modern China, 5–6
Jewish culture, 208–209
Jewish Diaspora, 46–47, 51, 75n2, 174, 189, 224
    in China, 217–226
    "marrying out," 85
Jewish identity, issue of, 73
Jewish personalities, 43
Jewish Refugees Museum, 193
Jewish studies in China, 206–232
    academic settings and pedagogical issues, 212–217
    biblical studies, 226–229
    Jewish contribution to civilization, 209
    Jewish history and culture, 214–216
    Jewish learning and Jewish faith, 210
    knowledge of Judaism and Jewish culture, 208–209
    shorter courses, 214
    spectrum of Jewish topics, 210–211
    Yavneh, tales of, 229–232
"Jewish studies program" in America, 214
Jin, Dina, 82
Jin, Shalva, 82
Jin family, 72
Joshua, Rabbi, 41
Judaism
    historical background of Jesus in, 209
    modern scientific study of Jews and, 209–210
    in today's China, 206–208
Judaism, reform movement of, 47

K

Kabbalat Shabbat services, 93
Kai, Liu, 35
Kaifeng Jewry, 54, 81–82, 217–224
    cultural revival, 83
    fundamental issues, 69–70
    immigration of young Kaifeng Jews, 81–84
    issues in China, 60–70
    Jewish identity, 61–62
    knowledge of heritage, 83
    political and social status of, 64–65, 97
    prohibitions against, 96
    protocols, 68–69
    as a separate nationality, 65–66
    statue document, 65–67, 69–71
    as "the three nos" *(san bu yuanze)*, 96
Kaifeng Jews, 2
kashrut (kosher certification) of food production, 90
Ka-Tzetnik, 149
Kaufmann, Yehezkel, 228
Kehillat Beijing, 18–19
Keret, Etgar, 149
Kirby, Michael, 191
kosher food export from China, 20
Kovner, Abba, 149
Kurman, Nirit, 159

L

Lazar, Leo, 22
Lee, Archie, 102
Legge, James, 100
Lerner, Tim, 80
Lesser, Isaac, 47
Leviticus 23:42, 74–75
Levy, David, 142
Lewis, Bernard, 226
Liang Gong, 101
Liao Huixiang, 148
Li Bo, 88
Liebrecht, Savyon, 149
Li Feng, 94
Lifshitz, Yonaton, 152
Lipson, Roberta, 18
Li, Rebecca, 82, 85
Liu Shaoqi, 66
Liu Xiaofeng, 229
Li Wei, 96
Li Xiurong, 94
London Jewish Cultural Centre (LJCC), 196–197, 200
Lubavitcher Rebbe, 21
Lugou Bridge Incident in 1937, 190
Luo Han, 148
Lu Xun, 159
Luzzatto, Samuel David, 47

M

Maimonides, Moses Ben, 40
Maoism, 13
Mao Zedong, 97, 136, 139
    "Three Worlds Theory," 166
Meng Jian, 148

Meyer, Michael, 210
Mikvah Mei Tova, 20–22
Millan, Joanna, 196
modern China, "Jew" and "Jewishness" representations in, 5–6
  construction of, 6–7
  as imperialists, 10–11
  Jew as financier, 7–8
  Jews as a nation, 10–11
  Jews as a race, 13–14
  as "New People," 8–9
  old myth and new phenomena (1949-1995), 13–17
  as a product of racial discrimination, 12–13
  in "racial war" against the "whites," 8
  stateless Jew, 9–10
  as a superior race, 11–12
Modern Hebrew Fiction (Gershon Shaked), 160
Mortimer, Edward, 199
Mosaic Law, 51
movies on Jews
  "A Jewish Girl in Shanghai," 36
  documentary about Israel, 36
Mo Yan, 150, 155, 158
Mozi's political philosophy, 52
Mrs. Shanen's Bagels, 20
Mrs. Shayna's, 20
Mueller, Klaus, 199
Museum of the War of Chinese People's Resistance Against Japanese Aggression, 189–190

N

Nanjing Massacre, 185
Nanjing Massacre Memorial, 4
Nanjing Massacre Memorial Hall, 188

O

Ohel Leah Synagogue Trust, 200
Olmert, Ehud, 43
oral law, 39
Orlev, Uri, 150
Oz, Amos, 3, 145–147

P

Pagis, Dan, 149
Palestinian Diaspora, 174

Palestinian Liberation Organization (PLO), 36
Pan Guang, 187, 194
Paulos Huang, 103
People's Literature Press, 150
People's Literature Publishing House, 149–150
Peres, Simon, 43, 140
Philip II, King, 44
philo-Semitism, 31
The Pianist (Roman Polanski), 193
Pokora, Timoteus, 66
Protestantism, 18
Protestant missionaries, portrayal of Jews, 26
Pui-lan, Kwok, 102

Q

Qichen, Qian, 142
Qin Dynasty, 52
Qiu Huadong, 158

R

Raskin, Rabbi Mendy, 19
Reform Jews, 76
Rosen, Alan, 198
Rosen, Jeremy, 198
Rosh Hashanah, 18
Ross, James, 1
Russian Jews, 26
Ryback, Marie-Louise, 199

S

Salzburg Global Seminar, 202
Schechter, Solomon, 47
Schindler's List (Steven Spielberg), 193
Schwartz, Yigal, 158–160
Semel, Nava, 149
Sephardic Jews, 26
Shabbat (Sabbath) celebrations, 73
Shamir, Moshe, 147
Shamir, Yitzhak, 141
Shammai school, 41
Shang Dynasty, 76
Shanghai Translation Press, 148
Sharon, Ariel, 140
Shi clan, 86
Shi Lei, 86–87
Silverberg, Elyse, 18, 22

Index

Sino-Christian academic biblical studies.
  see Bible, understanding in China
Sino-Israeli relations
  academic, scientific, and touristic exchanges, 169–171
  China's 1977 Open Door Policy and Jewish investments, 167
  China's respect and advocate Israel's right of existence, 178–179
  "Chinese Culture Week," 170
  criticism of terrorism activities, 166, 169
  cultural exchange, 170
  "Einstein Exhibit" incident, 172
  "Experience China in Israel" festival, 170
  formal diplomatic relationship, 165
  full diplomatic ties, 168
  Harpy controversy, 171–172
  historiography, 161–164
  imports and exports, 169–170
  Israel's help to China, 179–181
  Israel's "One-China Policy," 169
  1956 joint invasion of Egypt and, 166
  military exchanges, 166–168
  mutual sympathy, 173–174
  review of historical events, 164–168
  setbacks, 171–173
  shared national mentality, 173–174
  weaponry transfers, 180
  Zionism movement and, 174
Sino-Judaic cultural identity, 73, 78, 84–86, 90, 94, 96, 98
Sino-Judaic Institute (SJI), 72
Six Who Changed the World (Henry Enoch Kagan), 43
Song Lihong, 195, 204
stateless Jew, 9–10
State of Israel in *People's Daily*, analysis
  change of Israel's image, 129–142
  conclusions, 142–144
  literature review, 126–129
  reports on issues related to Israel, 126
  Sino-Israel relations, 126
Sukkot (Festival of Booths), 72, 74–77
Sun Yat-sen, 174
Sun Yu, 159

T

Tammuz, Benjamin, 156
Taoism, 18, 213
Timmermans, Glenn, 4
Tokyo War Crimes Trials, 185
Travel Diary to the New World (Liang), 9
Treaty of Versailles, 34
Tu Weiqun, 159

U

uniformity, 37–38
United Nations Holocaust Memorial Day, 201
United Nations Outreach Programme, 194
Unity Front of Henan Province, 67
UN resolutions 242 and 338, 177–178
Uphold Uniformity (Mozi), 52
USC Shoah Foundation, 194
USHMM, 194, 197, 199

V

Vogt, Roland, 201

W

Wald, Shalom, 212–213
Wang, Yakov, 82
Wang Meng, 102
Wang Yi, 182
Wannsee House, 197
War, Wang, 31
Wen Jiabao, 191
Wenxia, Peng (Neta), 84–85, 88, 93
Wistrich, Robert, 198
Wolfowitz, Paul, 171
World History (Wu Yujin and Qi Shirong), 192
written law, 39

X

Xiao Xian, 1
Xiaoxian, Zhang, 36
Xiao Yaozhen, 148
Xu Kun, 154, 158
Xu Xin, 2, 83, 187, 191, 194, 200, 213
Xu Zechen, 160

Y

Yad Layeled, 199
Yad Vashem Museum, 188

Yad Vashem Seminar for Chinese Educators, 198–199
Yahad-in-Unum, 195
Yan Lianke, 154, 158–159
Yaoz-Kest, Itama, 149
Yeh, Barnaby, 79–80, 84, 87
Yehoshua, A. B., 147
Yicileye School, 80–81, 86, 95, 98
Yilin Press, 150–151
Yizhar, S., 147, 156
Yom HaShoah, 201

Z

Zach, Natan, 149
Zhang Qianhong, 187, 200
Zhang Yingchun, 95
Zhejiang Literature and Art Publishing House, 151
Zhong Zhiqing, 3, 159–160
  A Study of Contemporary Israeli Authors, 160
  20th Century Hebrew Literature in Transition, 160
  translation works, 160
Zhou Dynasty, 52
Zhou Enlai, 64, 66
Zhou Xun, 1
Zoroastrianism, 177

www.ingramcontent.com/pod-product-compliance
Lightning Source LLC
Chambersburg PA
CBHW061937220426
43662CB00012B/1940